THE STORY OF THE LOVAT SCOUTS

1900–1980

SIMON JOSEPH, 16th LORD LOVAT,
KT., G.C.V.O., K.C.M.G., C.B., D.S.O.
1932

THE STORY OF THE LOVAT SCOUTS

1900–1980

by

Michael Leslie Melville

"170 HIGHLAND GHILLIES ARE BEING ORGANISED FOR SCOUTING IN SOUTH AFRICA" ~ (DAILY PAPER) ~
AFTER A
PUNCH CARTOON . JAN 1900.

Librario

First published in 1987 by
THE SAINT ANDREW PRESS
Copyright © Michael Leslie Melville, 1981
ISBN 0715204740
Reprinted 1984

This edition published in 2004 by
Librario Publishing Ltd
ISBN: 1-904440-03-7

Copies can be ordered via the Internet
www.librario.com

or from:
Brough House, Milton Brodie, Kinloss
Moray IV36 2UA
Tel /Fax No 00 44 (0)1343 850 617

Printed and bound by Digisource (GB) Limited

All rights reserved. No part of this publication may be reproduced or transmitted in any form or by any means, electronic or mechanical, including photocopy, recording, or any information storage or retrieval system, without permission in writing from the publisher. This book is sold subject to the condition that it shall not, by way of trade or otherwise, be lent, re-sold, hired out or otherwise circulated without the publisher's prior consent.

CONTENTS

List of Abbreviations	7
Author's Note and Acknowledgements	8
Foreword	
by The Right Hon. Sir Hugh Fraser, P.C., M.B.E., T.D., M.P.	10

Chapter I
Lord Lovat (1871–1933): His Early Life and Training   15

Chapter II
The Boer War and the Raising of the Lovat Scouts (1899–1900)   20

Chapter III
Boer War: The First Contingent (January 1900–August 1901)   29

Chapter IV
Boer War: The Second and Third Contingents (May 1901–August 1902)   40

Chapter V
The Edwardian Peace: Mounted Scouts (1903–1914)   46

Chapter VI
First World War: Training and Home Defence (August 1914–September 1915)   56

Chapter VII
First World War: Gallipoli (September–December 1915)   63

Chapter VIII
First World War: Egypt, the Desert and Reorganisation (December 1915–October 1916)   74

Chapter IX
First World War: Macedonia (October 1916–June 1918)   80

Chapter X
First World War: Lovat Scouts [Sharpshooters] (November 1916–November 1918) and Disbandment (April 1919)   89

Chapter XI
Between the Wars: Territorial Army Training (1922–1939)   96

Chapter XII
Second World War: Mobilisation (1st–5th September 1939)   105

Chapter XIII
Second World War: Mounted Training in the North
(September 1939–April 1940)   111

Chapter XIV
England: Mounted and Dismounted (6th April–
21st May 1940)   120

Chapter XV
The Faroe Islands (May 1940–June 1942)   129

Chapter XVI
Scotland and North Wales (June 1942–December 1943)   149

Chapter XVII
Canada (January–May 1944)   169

Chapter XVIII
Italy (July 1944–May 1945)   179

Chapter XIX
Some Memories of Italy (1944–1945)   197

Chapter XX
Austria (June–July 1945) and Greece (July 1945–
October 1946)   208

Chapter XXI
Post War (1947–1980)   215

Chapter XXII
Appendices
1   The Pipe Band, 1900–1945   225
2   Service Outside the Regiment, 1939–1945   228
3   The Comforts Fund, 1939–1946   230
4   Remembrance, 1939–1946   230
5   Colonels Commandant   231
6   The Regimental Association and Reunions   231

Chapter XXIII
Update to the First Edition, 1980 – 2002   233

ABBREVIATIONS
The following abbreviations have sometimes been used:

A.A., Anti-Aircraft
Adjt., Adjutant
Ammo. Ammunition
A.T.S., Auxiliary Transport Service
Bde., Brigade
Bn., Battalion
Brig., Brigadier
Bt., Baronet
Bty., Battery
Capt., Captain
C.I.G.S., Chief of Imperial General Staff
Cmd., Command
Cmdr., Commander
C.O., Commanding Officer
Col., Colonel
Cpl., Corporal
Coy., Company
C.S.M., Company Sergeant Major
Div., Division
Fwd., Forward
Gen., General
G.O.C., General Officer Commanding
Gnr., Gunner
H. L.l., Highland Light Infantry
Hldrs., Highianders
Hon., The Honourable
hrs., hours
H.Q., Headquarters
Ind. inf., Indian infantry
i/c, In Command
1.O., Intelligence Officer
L.A.A., Light Anti-Aircraft
Ldr., Leader,
L/Cpl., Lance Corporal
L/Sgt., Lance Sergeant

Lieut., Lieutenant
2nd Lieut., Second Lieutenant
Lt. Col., Lieutenant Colonel
Maj., Major
M.O., Medical Officer
Mtnr., Mountaineer
N.C.O., Non-Commissioned Officer
O.C., Officer Commanding
Offr., Officer
O.R.s, Other Ranks
O. & Z., Orkney and Shetland
Pln., Platoon
P.s.i., Permanent Staff instructor
Pte., Private
q.m., quartermaster
R.A., Royal Artillery
R.A.F., Royal Air Force
Recce, Reconnaissance
Regt., Regiment
Regtal., Regimental
R.H.Q., Regimental Headquarters
R.S.M., Regimental sergeant major
R.N., Royal Navy
Rev., The Reverend
R.V., Rendezvous
Sig., Signal
Sgt., Sergeant
Sqn., Squadron
Q.M.S. Quartermaster Sergeant
s.s.m., Squadron Sergeant major
2 i/c, Second in Command
T.A., Territorial Army
T.E.W.T., Tactical Exercise Without
Tp., Troops/Troop
Tpr., Trooper
Tpt., Transport
w.o., Warrant Officer

AUTHOR'S NOTE AND ACKNOWLEDGEMENTS

I wish to thank Colonel Sir Donald Cameron of Lochiel, Chairman of the Lovat Scouts' History Committee, the Right Honourable Sir Hugh Fraser, former Colonel Commandant of the Regiment and Major Sir John Brooke, President of the Regimental Association, for entrusting me with the task of writing this book and for all the help they have so kindly given me.

I am most grateful to all those who have supplied me with photographs, memoirs and other sources of information and am greatly indebted to many histories and books of reference, to the immense amount of research done by the late Dr. Allan Fraser into the Boer War and the First World War and also to the notes and diaries of many old Scouts, now dead, especially those of Colonel Duncan Baillie, Colonel the Honourable Ian Campbell, Major Kenneth McCorquodale, Major Charles Ian Fraser and my father. I thank all those whose illustrations have been used–particularly Miss Leesa Sandys-Lumsdaine for the book cover and Major Balfour-Paul for the title page, his maps and pictures. Every reasonable care has been taken to ensure accuracy over these eighty years, but if there are any errors in the text I apologise for them in advance.

In the production of this book I have deeply appreciated the unfailing help and expertise of Margaret Gibson of A.B.C. Litho Printer, Edinburgh, of Major Douglas Law (Seaforth Highlanders), Publisher to The Saint Andrew Press, and of Major Donald Callander, M.C., (Cameron Highlanders). Thanks are also due to Mary Kerr and John Leslie of The Saint Andrew Press, Deirdre Lothian (freelance editor) and Shona Robertson (design). Finally, I thank my wife and several kind friends and relations, who have helped me so much.

It has been fun to write of such an unusual Regiment as the Lovat

Scouts. There is a well-known story of a widow in Skye who remarked proudly to a visitor: "I have one son in the Lovat Scouts, one in the Merchant Navy and the other two are in the British Army". I hope that anyone who reads this book will appreciate the distinction which the widow drew.

M.I.L.M.

New Technology has allowed the Regimental Association to make arrangements for Michael Leslie Melville's splendid history of The Lovat Scouts to be reprinted and brought up to the present day.

We are grateful to Mike's son, Hamish Leslie Melville, and his family for their enthusiastic support. There has been a steady, albeit modest demand for the book. The addition of an index will, we hope, aid research. The Regimental Secretary continues to receive a steady correspondence from people interested in the Regiment. It is pleasing to note that many of them are grandchildren seeking details of their forebears who served in the Scouts.

We would particularly like to thank Lieutenant Colonel Angus Fairrie, the Honorary Curator of The Highlanders Museum at Fort George, for the support and assistance he provides the Regiment. He answers enquiries and safeguards the Regimental artifacts held there.

The reprinted book will now be held in disc form. It may be ordered individually from the publishers. We are grateful to Mark Lawson of Librario Publishing Limited in Elgin for providing help and advice to enable us to achieve this.

Lieutenant Colonel Grenville S Johnston
Regimental Secretary, Elgin. 2 Jan, 2003

FOREWORD

By The Right Hon. Sir Hugh Fraser, P.C., M B.E., T.D., M.P.

As the Scouts Boer War Memorial still dominates the wide square of Beauly in Invernesshire, so I think Major Michael Leslie Melville's story of the Lovat Scouts will become pre-eminent in the literature of Highland Regiments.

It is not only realistic and witty, quick and clear in its setting of the strategic and military contexts of campaigns within three wars, but it captures the nature of the Highlander in battle, and the very spirit and tradition of the Scouts. Within his broad sweep a skilful use of war diaries and personal anecdotes brings to life that lapidary inscription on Beauly's statue that the 'martial spirit of their ancestors still animates the Highlander of today'. As Mike shows, that was as true in both World Wars as it was in 1900, and I am sure Brigadier Sidney Robertson will vouch for it amongst those Scouts still serving with the T.A. in Orkney and Shetland.

As the member of the Lovat family who served longest with the Scouts, I am grateful, as are all my kin, to Mike for the tribute he pays to their founder, my father, Simon the 16th Lord Lovat. It is deserved. Beyond his abilities, his leadership and enthusiasm, his humour and charm, he had a vision of what the Highlander, whether English or Gaelic speaking, led by encouragement and comradeship, could do. To him the Highlands were more than a mere geographic expression, more even than a way of life, more to him than a folk memory as they are to those thousands of Highland descent scattered throughout the world. They were rather an inspiration, an indelible mark, a living thing. All that he himself epitomised. I still have a photograph of him in his middle years addressing a great clan gathering on the Isle of Mull, a gale sweeping his plaid and greying locks, hands on cromach–a giant of a man. 'Ceann-feadhna am measg a Iuchd-daimh is ceannard thairis air mile gaisgeach'–'A Chief among his own people and leader of a thousand warriors'.

He and the Scouts always had to suffer from Higher Military Authority. The Regiment, based on individual merit, allowing for every idiosyncrasy, held together by an intrinsic discipline more reminiscent of the shinty field than the parade ground, with bonds of friendship rather than of hierarchy between men and officers, never quite fitted into any Whitehall or War Office pattern or design. When in peacetime Governments ordered expenditure cuts, glassy-eyed staff officers, fiddling for savings, forgot the praises Generals Roberts or Ian Hamilton or McCreery or even Sir Winston had lavished in their times on the Scouts as they toyed with red pencils and Treasury scissors. But somehow the Regiment always got by, and at Retiefs Nek, in the rearguard action on that hell's own beach at Suvla in the Dardanelles, in Flanders trenches, and finally in the campaign amongst the Appenines against Field Marshal Kesselring that survival found national justification and regimental glory.

Indeed, in its spirit of respect for the individual's independence and undragooned discipline, the Regiment was in many ways a pathfinder for the more modern concepts of the profession of arms. In retrospect it is perhaps no wonder that both Colonel Bill Stirling, joint founder of the S.A.S. with his brother David, was the son of a Scouts Colonel and himself attended Scouts camps, or that my brother Shimi Lovat, the prototype of all Commando leadership and heroism, led a Squadron of Scouts at the outbreak of the last war.

Mike Leslie Melville in this story of the Scouts proves his ability as historian and raconteur but in his covering of these eighty years he has had the unique advantage of those family and clan ties which have so much bound the Regiment together. One of his great-uncles from

Fairburn, Charles Stirling, was a subaltern in the 1st contingent in 1900 and died in South Africa. Since then no less than seven of his uncles and two brothers-in-law were in the Scouts which his own father commanded from 1936 to 1940. Previously two of his uncles, The Earl of Leven and Colonel Ian Campbell, commanded the Regiment.

Mike himself, joined the Scouts in 1936 whilst still a sergeant in the Eton O.T.C. and, after a fine war career with them, commanded the Scouts when they were re-formed in 1947. From this book, his labour of love, comes an enduring and shining testimony to the officers and men and founder of a Regiment which has made a real and living contribution to Highland history. Eilean Aigas,

Hugh Fraser
Beauly.

TO
'THE HAWK THAT SWOOPS ON HIGH'

CHAPTER I

LORD LOVAT (1871–1933): HIS EARLY LIFE AND TRAINING

Simon Joseph, sixteenth Lord Lovat and twenty-second Chief of the Clan Fraser of Lovat, K.T., G.C.V.O., K.C.M.G., C.B., D.S.O., raised the Lovat Scouts early in the year 1900, to fight in the South African War. The very existence of this Regiment was the result of his imagination, enthusiasm and leadership. No history of the Scouts should, therefore, begin without a brief account of this great Highland Chief and man of action, and particularly of his early life and training, which were to have such a profound effect upon later events.

He was born on 25th November 1871, the third surviving child of Simon Fraser, Master of Lovat and of Alice, daughter of Thomas Weld-Blundell of Ince Blundell in Lancashire. His grandfather, Thomas, fourteenth Lord Lovat, died in 1875. His father then succeeded to the title and he himself became the Master of Lovat. He was descended from a long line of distinguished Scottish peers and warriors. Sir Francis Lindley, in his book 'Lord Lovat, 1871–1933', wrote of the Lovat ancestry:

> The Frasers, like the Gordons with whom they were often at feud, were a Norman family which settled in Tweeddale in the twelfth century. There they first made their mark in Scottish history, Sir Alexander Fraser becoming Chamberlain of Scotland and marrying Mary, sister of Robert the Bruce; whilst Sir Simon, his brother (the first Simon we hear of) was executed by Edward I for his share in the War of Succession. It is from this hero, who defeated the English invaders in three encounters in one day, for which feat he was awarded the honour of bearing on his Arms the three crowns still borne by the Lovat family, that the Frasers claim direct descent...

Moreover, the family name in Gaelic has been MacShimidh (the son of Simon) from time immemorial.

Simon Joseph, Master of Lovat, was brought up at Beaufort, the family home near Beauly, in Inverness-shire, with two sisters older than himself and two brothers and three sisters younger, in what has been described as 'the rough and tumble of true family life' and 'a mixture of Red Indian craft, English propriety and Highland valour'. Outdoor adventure and sport were his passion from an early age. It is said that despite his great ability on the hill and with gun and rifle in later life–he once shot 98 partridges in one drive at Sandringham, a British record which stood for many years–the sporting triumph of which he was proudest was when, at the age of nine, he was given a catapult by a gamekeeper and killed a partridge with a stone, an astonishing piece of beginner's luck never repeated! When he was ten, it was largely due to his presence of mind and quick action that his two younger brothers, Hugh and Alastair, were saved from drowning at Morar. He became a voracious reader from an early age and liked best books of adventure and warfare.

At the age of eleven, he went to school at the Benedictine Monastery, Fort Augustus, a small Highland school of less than 50 boys. While he was there, in 1887, his father died, and he became Lord Lovat at the age of sixteen, shouldering the early responsibility of being head of his family. When he became twenty-one he was the inheritor of estates which extended then to nearly 250,000 acres. He went for a short time to the Oratory School, Edgbaston, to prepare for his Oxford entrance exams and entered Magdalen College, Oxford in 1890 as an Army candidate.

In those days, Oxford University was an astonishing change for someone who had been brought up and educated almost entirely in the Highlands and only knew one undergraduate–a German Baron. But Lovat threw himself whole-heartedly into College and University life and, because of his enthusiasm for so many different activities, his charm, his sense of fun and his natural good manners which instinctively prevented him from ever hurting the feelings of others, he soon made an enormous number of friends. In the North, he had excelled at shinty and had been allowed, from the age of ten, to play with grown-up men in the annual New Year's matches. Often, when older, he played for the Lovat team; and the revival of shinty through the Camanachd Association was later achieved largely through his efforts. At Oxford he played both Rugby football, at which he twice broke his nose, and cricket, at which his unorthodox fast bowling was known to his friends as 'the Highland Fling', for his College. He was blessed with a powerful physique and an exceptionally good eye, and many thought that if he had learnt these games earlier in life he would easily have gained a double 'Blue'. Though not a regular oarsman, he rowed in several races. He managed to keep one or two horses near Oxford and took up fox-hunting with the Bicester and the Warwickshire Hounds. It was a sport of which he became passionately fond and it was recorded that 'his natural eye for country and his determination carried him ahead of many finer horsemen and his frequent falls served only to increase his enthusiasm'.

Despite all his sporting and social activities and his other commitments, which included his coming of age at Beaufort in 1892 and his service as a Lieutenant in the Militia (Queen's Own Cameron Highlanders), he also worked hard enough to get his degree and was commissioned into The First Life Guards in 1894.

Lord Lovat's three years as a regular officer in the Life Guards, though the ceremonial nature of their duties in London and Windsor would not ultimately have satisfied his zest for adventure nor given him enough time to run his own estates, left a marked influence on his subsequent career. He was a keen soldier and, during these three years, he learned the groundwork of that profession and developed his remarkable eye for detail. He also met many influential people and, Lindley tells us, 'made more friends even than he did at Oxford'. Cavalry training greatly improved his riding and his knowledge of horses and their management. He adored hunting and also became an enthusiastic and successful rider in point-to-points and steeplechases. Once, with his brilliant mare, Halma, he nearly won the most coveted of all point-to-points, open to the whole Army, over a four-mile natural course in the cream of the Quorn country. After a thrilling race, which he described vividly in a letter to his sister, he jumped into the last field with a lead of five lengths but was just beaten in the long, up-hill finish, one length and half a length by Captain Hoare and Lord Shaftesbury. He had a number of bad falls and, eventually, in the Regimental Race at Hawthorn Hill in 1897 (shortly before he was due to leave the Army), he was badly concussed and ordered a complete rest.

By a strange turn of fate, Lord Lovat decided to go to South Africa. He was there for several months and at one time contemplated buying a farm for his brother, Alastair. He learned much about South Africa and its troubled politics, all of which was to stand him in good stead within two years.

Next, in the late autumn of 1898, he set out with his celebrated and adventurous uncle, Herbert Weld-Blundell, accompanied by a well-known naturalist and a doctor/geologist, on an expedition to Northern Somaliland and Abyssinia. Their objects were to explore and map new country, to collect ornithological and other specimens and to interview, at Lake Haik beyond Shoa, the famous Lion of Judah, Emperor Menelek. They achieved all their objects, had some astonishing adventures, some elephant shooting, and long, arduous treks through uncharted country to the Blue Nile, a route of well over 300 miles. Their zoological success was outstanding in that they brought home 303 different species of birds, of which 16 were new (two were named after Lord Lovat) and 25 species of small mammals (one hitherto unknown to science), as well as many game animals. All the specimens were given to the British Museum, where a private exhibition was held.

In those days, long before the advent of modern equipment and technology, such expeditions called for exceptional endurance and sheer toughness. Lovat's constant energy, his quickness and skill with rifle and telescope and his complete indifference to ordinary comforts amazed even his companions, and he took risks with his health which may well have laid the seeds of sickness later. But it was a most successful venture and an experience of infinite value to him.

Such was the background and early training of Simon Joseph, Lord Lovat. By the time he got home in 1899, aged 28, the long quarrel with the Transvaal Government was coming to a head. When he next visited Africa it was to be under very different circumstances and nearly 3,000 miles south of the scene of his Abyssinian adventures.

CHAPTER II

THE BOER WAR AND THE RAISING OF THE LOVAT SCOUTS (1899–1900)

The Lovat Scouts were not raised until three months after the outbreak of the Boer War but it is relevant to consider briefly, even at the risk of over-simplification, the causes of the war and its disastrous opening phase.

The Boers (which means 'Farmers' in Dutch) came to South Africa as long ago as 1652, when the Dutch East India Company founded a settlement on the Southern Cape. It soon became the thriving community of Cape Colony. It changed hands between the Dutch and the British several times until, finally, Britain paid £6,000,000 for it in 1815, largely to ensure her route to India. The Boers hated British rule and resented our Emancipation Act of 1834, which deprived them of their black slaves. In the next few years about 10,000 of them made the 'great trek' north to create their own farming and ranching country of the Orange Free State. From there, some trekked east-wards over the Drakensberg Mountains into Natal and others pushed on northwards to found the Transvaal Republic between the Vaal and the Limpopo Rivers. When Britain successfully 'annexed' Natal in 1843 many Boers fled westwards. In 1852 and 1854, Britain officially recognised the two Boer Republics of the Orange Free State and Transvaal, but did not give them complete independence. The Boers were never happy with this arrangement and there was constant friction, including a three-month war in 1881, known as the 'First Boer War', which ended in the somewhat vague Treaty of Pretoria.

When gold was discovered near Johannesburg, sudden wealth came to the Transvaal but with it a great influx of foreigners ('Uitlanders'). Determined to keep control of their own country, the Boers taxed them heavily but did not give them full rights of citizenship. In 1895, the Uitlanders appealed to Britain for help and, when this was refused, contemplated an armed rising. The great Cecil Rhodes, then Prime Minister of British Cape Colony, offered to support the Uitlanders by sending a small party of mounted police under Dr. Jameson, who would ride into the Transvaal once the revolt broke out. Although the Uitlanders called off their proposed rebellion, Dr. Jameson unfortunately continued with his 'raid', which proved a fiasco. He was ambushed, lost 30 men and soon found himself with the rest of his party in Pretoria Jail. This unhappy incident served only to infuriate the Boers and to increase both their mistrust of Britain and their determination to gain total independence for their two Republics, Transvaal and Orange Free State.

In March 1899, the Uitlanders again asked Britain to intercede for them. A meeting between President Kruger of the Transvaal and the British High Commissioner, Sir Alfred Milner, ended in failure. Tension mounted and on 8th October President Kruger and President Stein of the Orange Free State issued an ultimatum to Britain It included demands that she should give up all control over the two Republics, withdraw troops from the Transvaal border and remove all reinforcements from South Africa. If the conditions were not accepted by 5 p.m. on 11th October, both Republics would regard it as a declaration of war. No one imagined that these terms would be agreed to, but few British people thought that the resultant war would last long or be a serious problem to the greatest Empire in the world. The Times humorously reported that on 11th October 'at about tea time' war had broken out. The joke proved to be out of place. The South African War was to become Britain's greatest conflict since the time of Napoleon. It lasted nearly three years, cost £222,000,000 and involved roughly 450,000 Imperial troops, of whom 22,000 died, nearly three-quarters of them from disease.

The Boer armies amounted at most to 88,000 irregular soldiers. They boasted no uniform save their dark, home-spun working clothes and slouch hats, often provided their own horses and weapons, and, above all, were acclimatised to the country in which they were fighting. They were organised in locally-raised 'Commandos', sub divided into 'Precincts', and 'Corporalships'. It is worth quoting a masterly description of the Boer, written by Conan Doyle, who was a military surgeon in that war:

> Take a community of Dutchmen of the type who defended themselves for 50 years against all the power of Spain when Spain was the greatest power in the world. Intermix with them a strain of those inflexible French Huguenots who gave up home and fortune and left their country forever... The product must obviously be one of the most rugged, virile, unconquerable races ever seen upon earth. Take this formidable people and train them for seven generations in constant warfare against savage men and ferocious beasts, in circumstances which no weakling could survive, place them so that they acquire exceptional skill with weapons and in horsemanship, give them a country which is eminently suited to the tactics of the huntsmen, the marksman and the rider. Then finally put a fine temper upon their military qualities by a dour, fatalistic, Old Testament religion and an ardent and consuming patriotism. Combine all these qualities and all these impulses in one individual, and you have the modern Boer—the most formidable antagonist who ever crossed the path of Imperial Britain...

At the outbreak of war, Britain had only 13,000 troops in Natal and Northern Cape Colony. The Boers immediately advanced south, and the British forces, after several minor but disastrous actions, retreated and were besieged in three towns—Ladysmith in Natal, and Kimberley and Mafeking in the north of Cape Colony.

Meanwhile, Sir Redvers Buller V.C., the newly-appointed C.-in-C., South Africa, divided his 47,000 British troops at Cape Town into three separate columns. They advanced north and, during what became known as 'Black Week', 10th to 17th December 1899, suffered three heavy defeats in succession. On the right, Buller, advancing towards Ladysmith, engaged the enemy at Colenso, where he lost ten guns and had over a thousand casualties, while the Boers' losses were said to be only six killed and twenty-one wounded. In the centre, at Stormberg, General Gatacre lost 135 men and had 600 taken prisoner. On the left Lord Methuen, making for Kimberley, suffered grievous losses at Magersfontein, where the Highland Brigade led a night attack. While still in close formation, they came under murderous fire at point blank range and hundreds, including their leader General Wauchope, were mown down. Despite great courage and heroism, the British attack was repulsed with over 1,000 casualties, some 700 of them from the Highland Brigade. Magersfontein became an accursed name in the Highlands: anger and a passionate wish for revenge were certainly sentiments that swelled the great response Lord Lovat was to have when he called for volunteers.

Britain as a nation was gradually rising in wrath. In two months, she had suffered 3,000 casualties and a series of humiliating defeats. As usual, some blamed the politicians; others, rightly or wrongly, criticised the Generals. Certainly the Boers seemed delighted with British generalship, for one captured Boer even reported that it was a capital offence for any of them to shoot a British General. Something had to be done urgently. Considerable reinforcements were sent out and Field Marshal Lord Roberts took over from General Buller as C.-in-C. with Kitchener as his Chief of Staff.

Other changes were needed too – changes in outlook, method and tactics. The British regular army, although magnificently disciplined and courageously led, was no match for this elusive enemy with his superior use of speed and surprise and his far greater ability in field-craft, reconnaissance and marksmanship.

No one knew this better than Lord Lovat. He admired the skill and fighting qualities of the Boers, but he had complete faith in the Highland countrymen amongst whom he had been brought up. He believed that with their natural ability at spying, stalking and shooting, they could be trained and led to help in defeating the Boers at their own game. He felt certain that he could raise such a body of men and, with all his determination and charm, his gifts of leadership and his personal influence with important people, he set about making his vision a reality the very day after Magersfontein.

He approached the War Office on 12th December 1899. After a fortnight's delay, he received permission to raise one or, if possible, two Companies, 'primarily for scouting purposes', to be attached to the Black Watch. After a meeting in Inverness with some Highland proprietors and the Officers of the 1st Volunteer Bn. Cameron Highlanders, it was decided to raise two Companies, one of mounted infantry and the other on foot. To give effect to the idea 'primarily for scouting', of the 236 men in the two Companies, up to eighty were to be chosen with stalking ability as a first qualification. The remainder were to be selected with special regard to marksmanship, stamina, military service and riding, and were to include the necessary number of trained signallers, shoeing smiths and craftsmen. Of the ten officers to be chosen, five were to have had previous military experience abroad and the others to have had some training with the Volunteers.

It was almost miraculous that Lord Lovat got his unorthodox proposals accepted so quickly. The War Office was won over, but there was criticism to face from nearer home. For example, the Marquis of Breadalbane wrote scathingly to The Scotsman that although stalkers could use a glass (telescope) better than most men, they were generally inexperienced shots; that ghillies, keepers and shepherds had usually had no experience with either a glass or a rifle; that the stalker's garron was 'a sort of small carthorse', and that, as a rule, Highlanders could not ride. He ended, 'I greatly fear that His Lordship's corps will not come up to the expectations of those who support it!'

The critics were soon to be proved wrong, as were any who doubted Lord Lovat's ability to raise volunteers. Recruiting centres were set up at Inverness, Kingussie, Fort William, Dingwall, Lairg, Perth and Oban. Within a few weeks, by the end of January 1900, over 1,500 men had applied for enlistment. Only one in six of these first volunteers for the Lovat Scouts could be accepted in filling the 236 places available. Typical

25

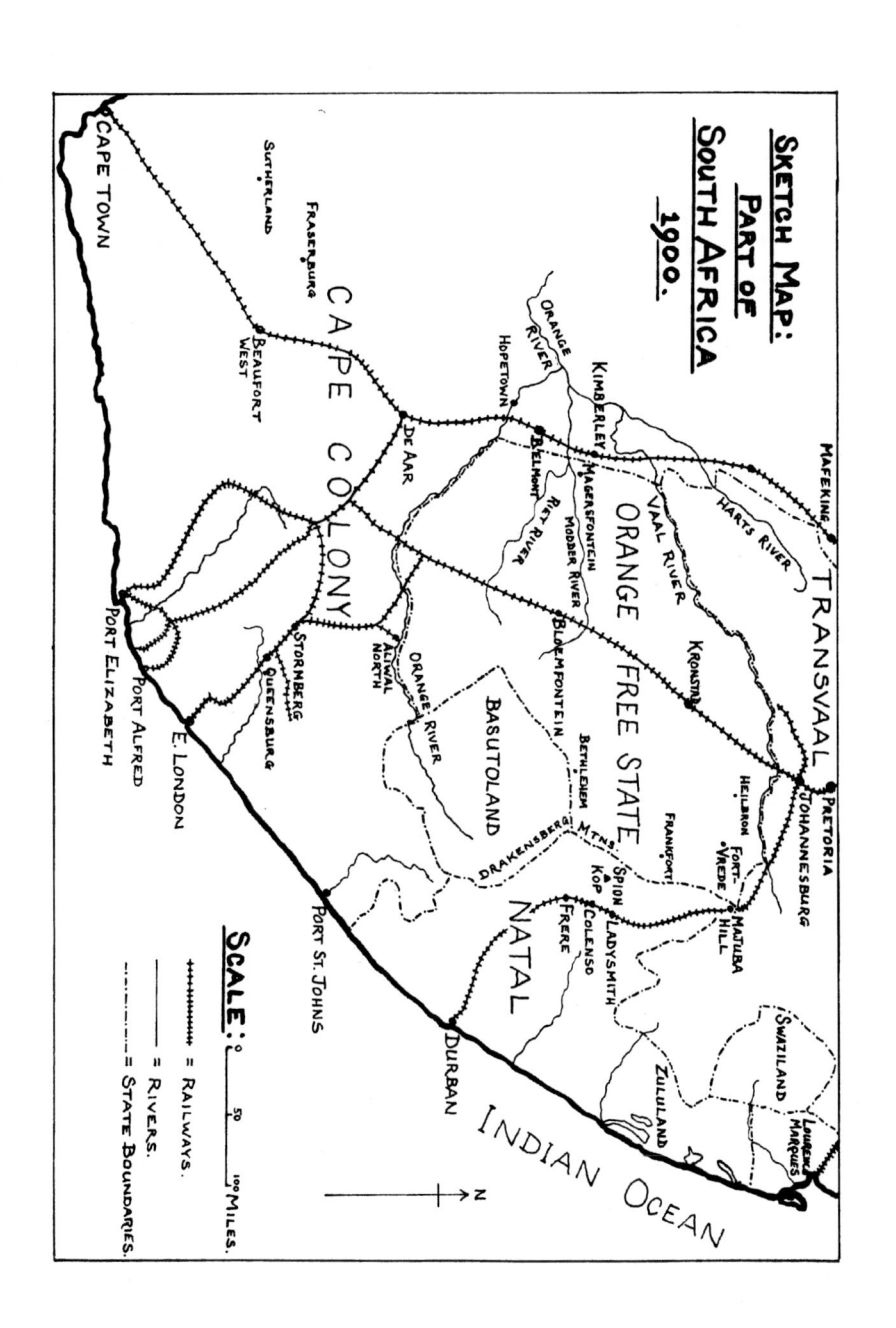

of the excitement and determination to join was a telegram received on the very first day of Lord Lovat's appeal from Rory Chishoim, head stalker at Glendoe. It read simply, 'ARRIVE BEAU FORT TOMORROW WITH HORSE'.

The Nominal Roll of these original volunteers reads like a list of the Highland Clans and was to be typical of the Lovat Scouts for the next fifty years. There were 19 Macdonalds, 9 Frasers, 9 Macleans, 8 Grants, 6 Mackays, 6 Maclennans, 6 Rosses, 5 Mackintoshes, 5 Mackenzies, 4 Camerons, 4 Mathesons, 4 Robertsons, 4 Morrisons, as well as two or three from each of the Clans Chishoim, Davidson, Forbes, Gordon, Henderson, Macleod, Murray, McPherson, Macrae, Stewart, Sutherland and Urquhart. There were some Border and South of Scotland names too, perhaps descendants of those who came north with the Cheviot sheep; and there were six chosen from foreign parts – from Suffolk, London, New Zealand, Bangalore and Australia. The 236 chosen were, as Lindley wrote, 'as pretty a lot of fellows as ever assembled at Castle Dounie in the old Clan days'.

Among the senior N.C.O.s there was great talent and experience. The Colour Sergeant of the 1st (Mounted) Coy. was Corporal of Horse Anderson, chosen by Lord Lovat as Riding Master from his old Regiment, 1st Life Guards. Sergeant Major James MacNeill (of whom Lord Lovat had written to all Highland proprietors, 'Any technical difficulties will be looked into by Sergeant-Major MacNeill, 13 Lombard St., Inverness') was Colour Sergeant of the 2nd (Foot) Coy. There were also Sergeants Binnie, Leitch and Scott, all from the 1st Camerons; and an Inverness gunsmith and crack shot, Sergeant D. Gray, was the first Armourer Sergeant.

Lord Lovat could have commanded the Scouts, but having never seen active service, he considered that someone with more experience should be in charge. On Lord Lovat's application, the War Office appointed as the Scouts' first Commanding Officer Major Hon. Andrew Murray, 1st Cameron Highianders, then in command of the Inverness Depot. He was thirty-six, a younger brother of Lord Mansfield and an officer of great ability and courage who had served with distinction in the Sudan. Lord Lovat, as a Captain, commanded the 1st (Mounted) Coy., Captain V. Stewart of Ensay (1st Argylls) commanded the Foot Coy., and the Adjutant was Captain A.W. ('Willie') Macdonald (1st Camerons). The Lieutenants in this first contingent of the Scouts were: I. Brodie of Brodie (Scots Guards), E.G. Ellice of Invergarry (Grenadier Guards), K.L. ('Kenny') Macdonald of Skeabost, Skye, and Sir A. Campbell-Orde, Bt., of Kilmory, North Uist. The 2nd Lieutenants were E. FraserTytler of Aldourie, Ewen Grant, yr. of Glenmoriston, Rowland Hunt, MFH (Northamptonshire Regt.). W.T. Fraser-Tytler, also from Aldourie, and Charles Stirling from Fairburn.

There were many difficulties to overcome in raising the Scouts. There was a possibility at one moment that the force would have to be dressed in 'Lovat mixture' tweed, as there was such a shortage of khaki cloth, but eventually the latter was obtained through private contractors. All wore khaki tunics with leather buttons and while the Mounted Coy. had breeches, brown boots and puttees, the Foot Coy, wore khaki knickerbockers with stockings, spats and stalking shoes. Most of the tailoring and cobbling was done locally, much of it at less than cost price. Slouch hats turned up at one side were worn,– topees were a later issue in South Africa – and each had at the side a patch of Red Fraser tartan, sewn on by the ladies of the Lovat family and their friends, which added a romantic touch to this already dashing headgear.

Luckily there was no shortage of .303 Lee-Metford rifles, but 'glasses' (telescopes) were not an army issue. Officers and some of the O.R.s provided their own, many were given by deer forest proprietors and Lord Lovat combed the country to buy the remainder out of a special fund of £4,000 which had been raised for the Scouts. It also helped to buy other equipment and some of the ponies, which had to be 'over five years old and between fourteen and fifteen hands high'. Highland proprietors were most generous in giving ponies. The Duke of Portland, for example, provided twelve and Lord Tweedmouth thirty-five. The latter gave immense help and support to the raising of the Scouts and Lord Lovat wrote later, 'But for Tweedmouth's help... no Yeomanry or Scouts would have left the Highlands in the early part of the war'.

Among many other gifts to the Scouts were thirty cases of whisky from Fraser of Glenburgie Distillery. The Adjutant wisely lodged them in bond at Cape Town. They were deeply appreciated by the 1st Contingent on its return from South Africa the following year.

CHAPTER III

BOER WAR: THE FIRST CONTINGENT (January 1900–August 1901)

By mid-January 1900, the Scouts were mobilised at Beaufort. Training began in bitterly cold weather with snow lying deep till well into February.

The men were billeted in the home farm and the officers in the castle, while the park served as a parade ground and training field. Lord Lovat's brother, Hon. Hugh Fraser (Scots Guards), was in charge of the musketry, assisted by Godfrey Macdonald of Sleat. Lord Lovat and Corporal of Horse Anderson ran the equitation and 'some strange experiences were witnessed'. But there were no serious casualties and soon field training for their role as scouts was going at a great pace. Lindley described part of it thus:

> A good many of the sham fights and manoeuvres centred round a mound in the park, which did duty as a "kopie". Galloping up and dismounting at the bottom, the men rushed to the top and got out their telescopes, leaving a couple of troopers to struggle with the loose ponies. Very soon more ambitious manoeuvres were allowed and at one of these Corporal Angus Chisholm's powers of observation turned the scale. Going along a road, he called his officer's attention to a mark in the snow made by a rising pheasant which would, he said, unless alarmed, have merely hopped on to the low wall. The enemy must be in the little wood. The off icer surrounded it and captured them.

Lindley mentioned this typical incident because a year later the same Cpl. Chisholm was to act similarly in real warfare. The Scouts had had a sharp fight with some Boers and due to lack of cover had lost sixty horses.

Shortly afterwards, Captain Kenny Macdonald was sent out with a recce patrol to spy and report whether some telegraph wires had been cut. It looked like being a slow job as they first had to 'make good' several small hills on their left. After taking the first hill and having a spy, Angus Chisholm noticed there were vultures on all the other hills, 'and commented that they would not be there if the Boers were about'. So, leaving an outpost on the first hill, they galloped to their objective, spied, saw that the wires were intact for three or four miles and reported back to camp very quickly.

After concentrated training for seven weeks at Beaufort and an inspection by O.C. 42 District, who said that he had 'never inspected a finer body of men', the First Contingent of Lovat Scouts departed with a great 'send off' from Beauly Station on 9th March 1900. They received a special message from Queen Victoria and many useful gifts from local well-wishers. Each Scout was given a scarlet envelope containing 'The Hillsman's Hymn', to be sung to The Old Hundredth, as well as a pocket compass, suitably inscribed and presented by Lady Lovat.

The two companies left Beauly by separate trains and did not meet again until 17th April at Cape Town.

The 1st Coy, commanded by Lord Lovat, had bad luck. They went by train to Glasgow docks and embarked on the 'America' for Southampton. They had a very rough voyage and some of the ponies contracted 'pink eye', a highly infectious form of horse influenza, from which four died before reaching Southampton. The others all had to be handed over for isolation. Newly-imported Argentinian horses were provided instead and, embarking with these on the 'Glengyle' on 25th March, the 1st Coy. reached Cape Town on 17th April.

Meanwhile the 2nd Coy., commanded by Captain V. Stewart, were more fortunate. They were originally a foot company, but it was decided during their training that to do their job properly in South Africa they too would have to be mounted. The day before they left Beauly, the local paper stated, 'It is authoritatively announced that on arrival at Cape Town, the infantry section will receive horses and so become metamorphosed into mounted infantry'. Corporal of Horse Anderson, the Riding Master, travelled with them and 2nd Lieut. W. Fraser-Tytler had already been sent ahead to Cape Town to acquire suitable horses, which he did most efficiently. From Beauly they went by train to Southampton, embarked on the 'Tintagel Castle' and arrived at Cape Town on 31st March. They camped nearby at Maitland where mounted training started immediately and was well advanced when the 1st Coy. joined them there on 17th April.

The whole aspect of the campaign since 'Black Week' and the further disaster of Spion Kop, had meanwhile changed. Both Ladysmith and Kimberley had been relieved, although Mafeking was still besieged. Roberts had beaten the Boers at Paardeberg, capturing their giant General Cronje, victor of Magersfontein, and 4,000 men. Roberts had then occupied Bloemfontein, capital of the Orange Free State, and was pausing there, about to go on to Pretoria, capital of the Transvaal, when the Scouts arrived in South Africa. His army's rapid advance northwards had left many pockets of resistance, which caused trouble with communications. There was much sickness in the British Army from typhoid and dysentery.

The 2nd Coy, of the Scouts was the first to be ready for battle. Under command of Major Murray and Captain Stewart, they left Cape Town in railway cattle trucks for Bloemfontein on 2nd May, the day after Lord Roberts' Army had left Bloemfontein for Pretoria. A Private of the 2nd Coy. wrote triumphantly home:

> ...I don't know how No. 1 (that is the old mounted) Company is to go, for pink-eye has again broken out among their horses. They are unlucky dogs right enough. We all say here that there must be a Jonah amongst them. Poor things, we used to be looked down on by the mounted boys at Beaufort, but they are green with envy now, and a lot of them have volunteered to get along with us, but it's no use.

Hardy as they were, the 2nd Coy. suffered much with only one blanket per man on the three day journey to Bloemfontein. The intense night cold even froze their water bottles solid. Some became very ill with dysentery, including Captain Stewart, who had to be invalided home and was succeeded as Company Commander by Lieutenant Brodie of Brodie.

From Bloemfontein they hastened north for a week, riding and marching by turns, with their supplies on mule waggons. They caught up with the Army at Kronstad, where they were inspected by Lord Roberts and attached to General Hamilton's Mounted Infantry Division. They took part in the operations which led to the capture of Johannesburg and Pretoria. One Scout, Roderick Maclean, son of an Inverness Baillie, wrote an exciting letter to his mother:

> ...31st MAY, saw a couple of snakes about 5ft long; also any amount of whirlwinds
>
> ...1st JUNE, marched into a suburb of Johannesburg... The reception we got from the native population was great. For miles in front of their tin houses, niggers were lumping and flinging, dancing all sorts of war dances and howling
>
> ...5th JUNE, took part in the grand procession of troops through Pretoria. It is an exceedingly nice little town, with a square worthy of any city. We just passed through and camped three miles eastwards... 8th JUNE rode through an orange grove where there were scrumptious oranges and we made short work with them
>
> ...11th JUNE, was in the hottest spot I was ever in my life and when the day ended was thankful I was still alive. We left camp early in the morning and, after some walking, came right into the middle of a hot shell fire. The ugly things came squealing right overhead and burst as they landed, raising up clouds of dust and stones a few feet from me... We had to gallop across this place as fast as we could till we got behind a kopie. Then, after resting a while, we advanced up the hill,

dismounted, left our horses under cover and up on the top of the hill lay down on our faces as flat as flukes, and were there firing away at them, with bullets whistling past our ears and shells landing amongst us for three and a half hours. How they did not hit more of us passes my comprehension. Only one of us, Sgt. Sirn, got hit, through both thighs, and he had to be there for two hours, unattended, till we chased the Boers away...

The action described by Maclean was part of the battle of Diamond Hill. Mr. Winston Churchill, war correspondent to the Morning Post, was near the Scouts. He described them in his report as 'The Gillies' (sic) writing:

From where I lay, on the left of The Gillies' firing line, I could see the bullets knocking up dust all round the retreating horsemen, while figures clinging to saddles or supported by their own comrades and riderless horses showed that some at least of the bullets had struck better things than earth. So soon as they reached fresh cover, the Dutchmen immediately re-opened fire, and two of The Gillies were wounded about this time...

Mr. Churchill's 'Gillies' then moved with the Division eastwards to Heidelburg and thence, with General Buller's Army, towards the Basutoland Border. The Highland Bde. commanded by that famous Highland soldier, General Sir Hector Macdonald, was coming south eastwards from Heilbron to link up with them, and on 3rd July the two forces met at Frankfort. With the Highland Bde. was the 1st Coy, of the Lovat Scouts and so, at last, after two months, the Regiment was united again and remained so for the rest of the Campaign. The 2nd Coy. had been first in action and had done well, but the 1st Coy. had meanwhile had some great adventures, which may now be described.

* * * * * * * *

It had been mid-May before the 1st Coy. was ready to leave Cape Town. They had had sickness among their horses and many men had been ill with fever or dysentery. Sergeant Morrison died of it, and Lord Lovat was not fit to go north with them. Captain Willie Macdonald took over command of the Company, 120 strong. They went by train to Bloemfontein and thence rode on with various mounted units to Kronstad.

They were supposed to be going on to Pretoria to join Lord Robert's main Army. They discovered, however, that another force under General Paget had just left for Heilbron, where the Highland Bde. was virtually surrounded by Boers. Captain Willie Macdonald, entirely on his own initiative, decided that they would follow after Paget by themselves, to join the Highland Bde., which had been the Scouts' original intention. They set off at once, not knowing that Paget had suddenly changed direction to rescue a force of 500 British Yeomanry who had been surrounded by the Boer General de Wet. Paget, alas, arrived too late; the Yeomanry, hopelessly outnumbered, had already surrendered. But meanwhile the Scouts were pushing on for Heilbron as hard as they could go, still thinking that Paget was ahead of them. They were frequently attacked, but on the last evening of their ride, with Boers closing in behind them and Lieut. Fraser-Tytler's section fighting a rearguard action, they were greeted by an outlying picket of the Seaforths.

They had joined the Highland Bde. and they received an enthusiastic welcome from General Sir Hector Macdonald. As there were about 7,000 Boers in the area surrounding Heilbron and the Scouts were the only force that got through at that time, it was a good and lucky performance. It more than justified Captain Willie Macdonald's bold decision and started them on their war service with flying colours.

General Macdonald used them in their proper role, as scouts. Their frequent recce patrols and spying brought him important and accurate news of the Boers surrounding Heilbron. He was delighted with them from the start. Once, when General Macdonald wanted a message taken through the encircling Boers for delivery to General Methuen, one Scout, John MacPherson from Ardgay, was chosen for the task. He got through, delivered the message and then returned with much useful information about the Boers' positions. He well deserved his mention in despatches and the compliments of General Macdonald.

They did some stalking too. In a letter home, Lieut. E. Fraser-Tytler described an occasion when he and Lieut. Ellice spied while:

> Cpl. Macdonald and Dugald Macdonald stalked a Boer sentry over bare ground, till within 500 yds, and had the light not suddenly failed, they would have got right in and killed him. They did just as one would with a close stalk after deer. That is, one crawled forward a few yards, while the other kept his telescope on the sentry, and so they crawled closer and closer, stopping whenever the sentry looked their way. Dugald says it is better sport than deer stalking, and he wanted to stalk the sentry before dawn, but was not allowed to. Our telescopes are simply invaluable... The field glasses the other officers have are of little use, and also I see that hardly any of them understands spying. They couldn't understand how Ellice and I could follow every movement of our men at that distance...

Three days later, Methuen's column fought its way through to Heilbron thereby relieving the Highland Bde. The Scouts' 1st Coy. was then sent to escort a convoy to Vredefort. They had a brief encounter with Boers but got through and there, at Vredefort, to their great delight, was Lord Lovat himself, who took over command of his 1st Coy. once more. He was lucky to be there. After his recovery he had travelled north and, but for missing a train at Bloemfontein, would have been with a convoy of Highland Bde. re-inforcements, who were surrounded and captured by de Wet.

While at Vredefort, a Scout O.P. on a nearby hill spied waggons and a large body of men halted in a secluded valley over five miles away. The Scouts telegraphed the news to Methuen's H.Q., but no action was taken.

Subsequent information confirmed that the Scouts had discovered de Wet's hiding place where he was resting his horses, with 800 prisoners. With 5,000 British troops in the vicinity, it was later considered possible that if Methuen had acted quickly on the Scouts' information, he could have shortened the war by nearly a year.

From Vredefort, the 1st Coy, went with the Highland Bde. in pursuit of de Wet's force which was making for the Roodebergen mountains. On their way, at Frankfort they were, as already described, at last re-united with their comrades of the 2nd Coy.

* * * * * * * *

When General Hunter's army, of which the Highland Bde. was part, reached the foothills of the Roodebergen mountains, Hunter's main need was information as to the whereabouts of the Boers. Of the Lovat Scouts, he wrote in his despatches::

> I paused at Bethlehem to regulate supplies and gain news. The mountain range to my front concealed forces whose numbers and whereabouts were a mystery. It possessed ins and outs, shepherd tracks, even occasional cart roads, none marked on maps. To get news, Lovat Scouts were used. The idea was General Macdonald's, instigated by Lord Lovat. In ones, twos and threes these men crept, climbed and spied, were absent for days at a time, but always came safely back with the truth discovered. Major Hon. Andrew Murray, who commanded them, Captain Lord Lovat who raised them, and each officer and man in the corps is a picked man and a specialist. AS SCOUTS, SPIES, GUIDES, ON FOOT OR ON PONY, AS INDIVIDUAL MARKSMEN OR AS A COLLECTIVE BODY IN THE FIGHTING LINE, THEY ARE A SPLENDID BAND OF SCOTSMEN, WHICH IS THE HIGHEST COMPLIMENT I CAN PAY THEM.

By a brilliant manoeuvre de Wet escaped north from the mountains, but another Boer General called Prinsloo was still there with about 5,000 men. A Scout patrol under Captain Willie Macdonald reported that a pass named Retief's Nek was strongly held by the Boers and that there were about 300 of them on Vaal Krantz, a high ridge and the key to the position. An attack on it next day by three Battalions failed. From information brought back by Captain Ewen Grant's patrol, Major Murray and Lord Lovat volunteered to capture Vaal Krantz with 100 Scouts, but General Macdonald refused to risk the 'eyes' of his force on such a venture. Instead, he agreed that three picked Scouts should reconnoitre the ridge that night. The men chosen were Sgt. Dewar from Beaufort, Cpl. Dugald Macdonald from Roy Bridge and John Macdonald from Fort William. They had to pass through the lines of the H.L.I. on the way and Colonel Kelham, H.L.I., was instructed to act immediately on any information the three Scouts brought back.

It was a bitterly cold, wet night as they climbed to the snow-clad summit. To their surprise, it was completely deserted and they saw the flicker of Boer camp fires on the plain below. They guessed that the Boers had left the summit for the night, thinking that there could be no attack in such filthy weather, but that they would return before daylight. The three Scouts raced back to inform Colonel Kelham. He sent one Company immediately to the summit with the Scouts as guides. They got there just in time to meet the Boers returning and drove them back with heavy losses. The capture of Vaal Krantz forced the Boers to evacuate the whole Retief's Nek position. The three Scouts who had done so well were mentioned in despatches.

It must be admitted, however, that the Scouts were not always popular heroes with the regular army. Before the Vaal Krantz engagement a small party of them with their signaller were posted on a very steep hill to spy and report enemy movements. Almost immediately the Scout signaller began flag-waving furiously, but nothing could be made of his messages: they were not in the code book. Some suggested that he was signalling in Gaelic; others that he had gone mad. Major George Mackintosh of the

Seaforths, in despair, climbed the steep hill himself to find out what was wrong. To his breathless and rather angry inquiry, came the reply, "Och, I was just practising".

After much hard fighting in the Roodenbergen mountains, General Prinsloo and 4,000 Boers were captured. The rest escaped but were relentlessly pursued. All through the winter of 1900/1901, the Scouts were actively engaged with the Highland Bde. and their services were repeatedly acknowledged by General Macdonald as being 'beyond all praise'. A letter home from a Private described Lord Lovat as being 'the finest Scout of them all, telescope in hand and always leading'. Forty Scouts, who had obtained posts in the newly formed Transvaal Constabulary, were given a farewell dinner in Pretoria by Lord Lovat.

In late November 1900, Kitchener had succeeded Roberts as C.-in-C. Stern measures were taken to pacify the country. These included lines of block-houses connected by barbed wire, against which Commandos were rounded up by mounted troops, and a 'scorched earth' policy. It was distasteful work for British troops, especially the herding of displaced Boer families into large, guarded compounds, known by the ill-fated name of 'concentration camps'.

The Scouts had enlisted for one year and, as the war showed no sign of ending by April 1901, Lord Lovat came home to raise a Second Contingent. He was invested by the King with the D.S.O. and at the age of twenty-nine made his first speech in the House of Lords. It was on the shortcomings of Army organisation in South Africa.

Fresh from the war with his bronzed face and long beard, he soon won the sympathy of his audience, as he dwelt on the lack of reliable maps, on Regiments depleted of their best officers,.., on the Remounts Dept., which had once supplied him with 132 horses and 218 shoes amongst them, and on the Supply Dept. which paid extravagant wages for labour and absurd prices for supplies... *(Lindley)*

Having organised the raising of a Second Contingent at Beaufort (there were over 1,000 applicants for 250 places) and chosen new officers, Lord Lovat returned to the Scouts in South Africa.

On 12th July 1901, the Second Contingent arrived at Aliwal North on the Orange River to take over from the war-weary First Contingent. The latter were out on a job with the Connaught Rangers, but turned up two days later. To these new boys of the Second Contingent, the old campaigners, in their battle-worn uniforms and soiled equipment, were barely recognisable. One of the newcomers wrote home, 'They were as like a circus procession as ever you saw'.

A few of the 'circus procession' gallantly stayed on to strengthen the Second Contingent, but the main body of 160 went home on the 'St. Andrew' under command of Captain Willie Macdonald. An immense crowd greeted their train in Inverness, where they were given a civic reception and luncheon. In a unique ceremony, each officer, N.C.O. and man was awarded the Freedom of the Burgh. At Beauly they received a great welcome too. They marched to Beaufort, where there were bonfires, fireworks and plenty to drink that night. Next morning, 14th August 1901, they went back to their homes, deservedly honoured for what they had achieved.

It was proof of their skill, as well as their good fortune, that – apart from the wounded and those who died from sickness – only four Lovat Scouts of the First Contingent were killed in action. A far greater sacrifice was to be demanded of the Second Contingent.

CHAPTER IV

BOER WAR: THE SECOND AND THIRD CONTINGENTS
(May 1901–August 1902)

The Second Contingent of the Scouts were Yeomanry and private soldiers therefore became Troopers, otherwise they resembled the First Contingent. They were organised in two Companies, 'The 99th and 100th Coys, Imperial Yeomanry (Lovat Scouts). The Regiment was still commanded by Lt. Colonel Hon. A. Murray with the Hon. E.O. Murray of Elibank as Adjutant. The 99th Coy. was commanded by Major Lord Lovat, his officers being Captain Mackintosh of Kyllachy, Lieut. Hon. Alastair Fraser and Lieut. C. Lamb. Captain the Master of Sempill commanded the 100th Coy, and his officers were, Captain Hon. F. Gathorne-Hardy, Lieut. C.W. Chalmers and Lieut. C. Burn Murdoch. Captain Brodie of Brodie, recovered from his wound, joined them later. During their training at Beaufort, which one observer described as 'perilously short', the Cameron Highlanders provided Instructors and the Scots Greys the Riding Masters. Ponies for training were hired locally.

They sailed from London on the 'Englishman', landed at Port Elizabeth and went by train to join the Highland Bde. at Aliwal North. Their main job was to be that of active patrolling to prevent Boer Commandos from entering Cape Colony. Six shepherds in the Scouts brought their sheep-dogs with them, an experiment for rounding up Boer flocks and herds on the veldt. The dogs proved useful, 'but always ran away when shot at'!

Lord Lovat was somewhat worried about the inexperience of the Second Contingent to start with and wrote, 'Our advance guards are hardly the things of joy and safety that our old men made'. In another letter he wrote:

> The great difficulty of the new hands was in recognising their horses after they had off-saddled and been turned out. There

were conversations such as: 'He's my horse'; No, it's my y'en'; 'Gosh man, but it's awfu' like me ane'; 'Gie's a look'; 'I had a bit string on mine'.

On starting the other day hurriedly, I spotted a sportsman without his gun. "Where's your rifle?" "Dash it, I clean forgot her!"...

Within a few days of his arrival, Tpr. John Macdonald, Inverness, wrote home:

> At night Donald Mackenzie and I slept out, and it was that awful cold we could not sleep, so we got up about four and lit a fire. We saw a man corning on horseback as hard as he could gallop. He asked for Colonel Murray, and we showed him the tent. I said to Donald there's something up, and ten minutes later came the order to get the old Scouts' horses and 150 rounds, as the Connaughts were attacked as soon as the other Scouts left them. It was a pretty tall gallop for us–thirty miles and not being on a horse since we left Beaufort... The Boer outposts spotted us and when we arrived there was not a Boer to be seen... We got in the Connaughts' dead and wounded. Six dead, twenty-one wounded and a few missing. There was one poor chap I saw with his hands straight up. He was shot above the eye and through the leg and all his clothing was taken off. We took in two wounded Boers but they both died.. The names of all that live in any house here has to be posted up on the door and if there is anyone more in the house than on the card, you have to take them with you. The road all along here is strewn with dead horses and cattle. So that was the first of our work on the veldt.

In mid-August, the Scouts moved fifteen miles to Lemonfontein, from where they patrolled the Orange River and watched the fords to prevent

Boers entering Cape Colony. Lord Lovat mentioned in a letter that they had had some sport at Lemonfontein, "our best bags as yet being four buck and six partridges, one lost in an ant bear hole. We are making a golf course and have challenged the Connaughts at polo".

It is not known whether the Scouts and the Connaught Rangers ever played polo and if so who won, but it is recorded that the Master of Sempill had a long walk at this time, He and an orderly were chosen to ride a day's journey to take a Proclamation from Lord Kitchener to Myburg, leader of a small Commando, offering him terms if he would surrender. Myburg refused to do so, seized the two Scout horses and told Sempill and his companion to walk back. This was avenged the following year when the Scouts virtually wiped out the remains of Myburg's Commando.

On the night of 19th/20th September 1901, the Scouts suffered their only major disaster of the campaign at a place called Guadeberg. The two Companies were operating about five miles apart, each with a fifteen pounder gun and its team attached. Colonel Murray had moved with one Company to Guadeberg in the foothills, and Lord Lovat with the other Company was camping four miles northwest at Eland's Kloof. On a patrol together on the afternoon of 19th, they spied 170 Boers riding westwards and guessed it was Kruitzinger's Commando going into laager for the night. They decided on their plan of action for the next day, parted and each returned to camp. They never met again.

Kruitzinger's Commando doubled back and rode by early moonlight to a small farm in the Guadeberg foothills. At midnight, when it was pitch dark, a foot party under command of a Boer officer called Wessels crept up on the east side of Colonel Murray's camp and, although one of the Scout outposts heard a noise and sent a man back to report, the Boers were already in the camp. They poured two volleys into the officers' bivouacs and then turned and raked the men's bivouacs and two sections of the horse lines with heavy fire, There was chaos and confusion in the dark with rifle fire, the screams of dying men, and horses, shouting and horses galloping. But the Scouts fought back with never a thought of surrender. Colonel Murray rallied the survivors for a bayonet charge and was shot dead while doing so. Cpl. D. Macdonald and Tpr. J. Cameron got the machine gun into action, but were both wounded, one fatally, Captain Sempill, though wounded, mustered thirty-five men with Captain Gathorne-Hardy, Lieut. Chalmers and Sgt. Barret on the west side of the camp and firing continued for about forty minutes. They then made their way under cover of darkness to Lord Lovat's camp.

The Boers remained in the camp for about an hour, collecting all the food, clothing and ammunition they could get. They then departed, taking the fifteen pounder gun and their own wounded. They left two of their own dead and the Scouts' wounded, to whom they had 'behaved with courtesy'.

Lord Lovat had heard the firing, stood his Company to arms and tried to communicate by flash lamp. At dawn he trained his fifteen pounder in the enemy's direction and fired but probably with no result. At daybreak he sent a heliograph message to Thorneycroft's Mounted Infantry, who pursued the Commando, inflicted casualties, recaptured the gun and took twenty prisoners.

The Connaughts and the Scouts pooled doctors and mule transport to deal with the wounded. There had been fifty-four casualties, of whom eighteen were killed and thirty-six wounded. The dead were buried near Eland's Kloof and the site was appropriately marked. The body of Colonel Andrew Murray was later exhumed and brought back to Scotland for burial. He had been a courageous and fine first Commanding Officer of the Scouts, Lord Lovat took over command of the Regiment and Captain Brodie of Brodie became Adjutant in place of Captain Hon. E.O. Murray, who had been killed in the first burst of fire. The survivors of the 100th Coy, went to Aliwal North to refit, and the 99th Coy, continued their duties as before.

The tragic news of Guadeberg soon reached Inverness and there was an immediate demand from old Scouts and others to take the places of those killed and wounded. Provost MacBean telegraphed to the War Office that many were willing to join 'but only on the distinct understanding that it was to take the place of Scouts who had fallen, as they would not join any other Corps'. The War Office replied that H.M. Government accepted with great satisfaction this patriotic offer, and Captain Willie Macdonald was authorised to raise a Company.

From 400 applicants, 125 were chosen and they formed the Third Contingent. Several of the original Scouts, including Lieut. C. Stirling and Sgt. John Dewar, rejoined. They were billeted and trained this time at the Cameron Barracks, Inverness, and the equitation took place in Macrae and Dick's Riding School and the Victoria Park.

The Company was commanded by Captain James Brander-Dunbar, later the well known Laird of Pitgaveny, who had already fought with distinction in the Sudan and South Africa. The other officers, mainly from Highland Regiments were Captains H. Galloway and E.B. Mackenzie, Lieutenants Donald W. Cameron, younger of Lochiel, A. Pelham Burn, R. Thurston, C.N. Macdonald and A.C. Clarke.

They were raised in October 1901, and left for Cape Town on the 'Manchester Merchant' on 1st December, arriving there on Christmas Eve. They went by train to Aliwal North, where they were provided with good horses and underwent a week's rigorous field training before joining their comrades of the Second Contingent. By 11th January they had already been under fire and in action at Mooihoek. Captain Brodie of Brodie was awarded the D.S.O. for his gallantry there. He also became renowned for his cryptic orders as Adjutant. It is said that once, when thoroughly dissatisfied with the men's rations, he sent a famous message to Army H.Q., reading simply, SEND MORE BREAD, BRODIE. Much bread arrived by return.

The work of the Scouts continued to be the harrying and rounding up of the surviving Boer Commandos, notably those of Fouche and Myburg. There was much hard riding with some fighting and a few casualties. Early in 1902 an officer in the Highland Bde. wrote home:

> The Lovat Scouts are now very strong in the field, over 300 and doing excellent service... Their officers are far above the average irregular officer out here and the men, Highlanders, have much better go for the country than town-bred men...

The war was gradually drawing to its close. Most of the civilian population longed for an end to the suffering and devastation of their country but a few indomitable Commandos with brilliant guerilla leaders like Smuts, de Wet and de la Ray, fought on. As late as 7th March 1902 there was a British disaster at Tweebosch with 200 casualties and Lord Methuen and 600 men captured. Finally after a month of negotiations, the Boer War ended with the Treaty of Vereeniging, signed on 31st May 1902, the terms of which included the Boers acknowledging King Edward VII as their lawful sovereign and Britain contributing £3,000,000 towards the restoration and restocking of farms destroyed.

In August 1902 the Scouts came home. They sailed on the 'Tintagel Castle' from Cape Town to Southampton. Once again Inverness gave them a real Highland welcome and a civic luncheon. They went on to Beaufort where they had one last night together of bonfires and celebrations. The next day they were disbanded.

As they went back to their homes throughout the Highlands, they may have thought that the legend of the Lovat Scouts was now over. In reality it had only just begun. For Lord Lovat and they had lit a bright star in the North which was to lead and guide many of their sons and grandsons both in peace and war and which still, to this day, beckons to men of the Northern Isles.

CHAPTER V

THE EDWARDIAN PEACE : MOUNTED SCOUTS (1903–1914)

On his return from South Africa, Lord Lovat was awarded the military C.B. for his achievements in the campaign. There was a civic function in his honour in Inverness and the Lovat tenantry and feuars of The Aird and Fort Augustus raised £500 with which they wished to present Lord Lovat with his portrait. He suggested, instead, that it should be spent on a Memorial to the Scouts and, in particular, to those who fell in the Boer War. It was completed in 1905 and unveiled by Mackintosh of Mackintosh, Lord Lieutenant of Inverness-shire. Of simple design and nearly fifty feet high, it stands in the centre of Beauly and is suitably inscribed.

So much for the Boer War and the memory of those who died in it. But what of the future? Lord Lovat was determined that something of the Scouts should be kept in being. He had shown that Highland countrymen and particularly deer stalkers could, with a minimum of additional military training, excel at observation and reconnaissance in warfare, and he felt that they must now be organised so that their special skill could always be readily available. His success in this aim was described thus by Lindley:

> He first tried to persuade the War Office to keep a perrnanent nucleus of stalkers on regular pay. They would have forrned an invaluable cadre round which to build a force, but the novelty was too much for the authorities. They agreed, however, to authorising him to raise two Regiments of Yeomanry, each 500 strong, to be called 1st and 2nd Lovat Scouts. Recruiting men from Caithness, Sutherland, Ross and Cromarty, Inverness-shire, Nairnshire and the Outer Hebrides, he raised two Regiments in 1903, when he was transferred back to the

OFFICERS OF THE FIRST CONTINGENT, 1900
Standing (L to R) –
E. Fraser Tytler, Hon. H.J. Fraser, K. Macdonald, Ewen Grant, Capt Stewart, Rowland Hunt, Sir Arthur Campbell-Orde, Brodie of Brodie, Capt Ellice
Seated –
Major Hon. A. Murray, Lord Lovat. Capt A.W Macdonald
Absent –
W Fraser Tytler and C. Stirling

Fort William Members of the First Contingent, 1900.

*A Section of the Second Contingent
South Africa, 1901.*

*Machine Gun Section
South Africa, 1902*

48

Yeomanry and promoted to Lt. Colonel to command the force. Although called Yeomanry, the new force was really more like the Mounted Infantry used so extensively in South Africa.

By June 1903, recruiting had been completed and the 1st and 2nd Lovat Scouts were already in camp at Beaufort for their first annual training. Lord Lovat was in command of a thousand mounted Highlanders.

The astonishing speed with which they were recruited may be attributed to the great prestige the original Scouts had gained in South Africa, to the personal popularity and fame of Lord Lovat himself throughout the Highlands, and to the very favourable terms of voluntary service which he secured for his men. An extra capitation grant was allowed because so many of the Scouts lived in outlying districts. Besides payment for drills and camp, £5 hire was given for each pony passed as suitable and also a mileage allowance from the men's homes to camp. As a rule, men who could bring a pony to camp were chosen, and care had to be taken not to interfere with existing Volunteer units.

The Uist and Skye Squadrons crossed to Kyle of Lochalsh and rode on from there. The mainlanders, too, came by road, riding from distant glens and villages, from Caithness and the far northwest of Sutherland, from Ross-shire, Nairnshire, Lochaber and all other parts of Inverness-shire. It was a long trek for some of them; a man from Scourie or Kinlochbervie, for example, had ridden over ninety miles before he got to Beaufort. Recruiting had outstripped the tailors and some Scouts had to come in civilian clothes. Some even wore their Sunday best for this occasion – dark suits and bowler hats!

The organisation was unusual: Lord Lovat commanded the whole force, while his two Seconds-in-Command (Major Willie Macdonald and Major Augustus C. Baillie from Dochfour) each commanded a Regiment. There were two Adjutants: Captain Hon. Hugh Fraser and Major Hon. Ralph Campbell from Cawdor, who was succeeded in 1905 by Captain Ewen Brodie of Lethen, but only one Quartermaster, Captain H. Pocock.

There were eight Squadrons A to D in the 1st Regt. and E to H in the 2nd Regt. The Squadron Leaders were Major Willie Macdonald, who as well as commanding the 1st Regt. dealt with Lochaber; Major Sir A. Campbell-Orde, Bt. with Uist; Major Kenny Macdonald with Skye; Major E. Fraser-Tytler with The Aird; Major A. Stirling of Keir with Wester Ross; Major Barclay with Sutherland; Captain Munro-Ferguson with Easter Ross, and Major Brodie of Brodie with East Inverness-shire and Nairnshire. Many of the N.C.O.s were veterans of South Africa and there was a regular Permanent Staff Instructor Sergeant (P.S.1.) for each Squadron area. Supreme on parade was the majestic figure of R.S.M. Anderson, originally of the 1st Life Guards.

The most obvious change in the Scouts lay in their uniform. They now wore Lovat Scout bonnets of dark blue with blue and white dicing and two black ribbons at the back. The silver badge on it was the crest of the Erasers of Lovat – a Royal stag, with the motto 'Je Suis Prest' (I am ready). An exception was made for the Coronation Parade of George V in 1911, when the contingent of twenty-four wore the original Boer War hats with blue hackles. Apart from their bonnets, the Scouts wore Yeomanry uniform; khaki tunic and bandolier, breeches, khaki puttees, rolled downwards in the cavalry style, black boots and spurs. There were Regimental brass buttons now with the crest on them and the words, 'Lovat Scouts, I.Y.' (Imperial Yeomanry). The pipers, of which there were four for each of the eight Squadrons, wore for the first time kilts of Hunting Fraser tartan.

The officers wore Scout bonnets (but occasionally Boer War hats on exercises) and cavalry uniform with black riding boots or ankle boots with dark blue puttees. Their shirts and collars were soon to be of a standard pattern of blue and white, worn with a black tie. This odd feature of their uniform was worn – except in war-time, when they reverted to khaki shirts and ties – until 1939. For reasons of economy, there was no fixed cut or design of khaki tunic for officers, and a certain diversity was permitted. Similarly, although it was usual for officers to wear a dark blue stripe down the outside of their khaki slacks and breeches, this was not compulsory during the following forty years and it was also left to individual taste as to whether the slacks should be turned up or down at the bottom. Within reasonable limits there was thus always a slight variety in officers' dress. Later, some officers wore blue patrol jackets and Hunting Fraser tartan trews for Mess Nights, but this was also optional.

Training was carried out in equitation and horse-mastership, foot and mounted drill, musketry, signalling and scouting and towards the end of camp there were manoeuvres. A special Squadron was formed for training purposes of experts in the use of the telescope under Major Ewen Grant, and they worked in groups of four. Major Stewart of Ensay was in charge of a Machine-gun Section.

During the first camp there were two general inspections. One was by General Baden-Powell, the hero of Mafeking, who was now Inspector General of Cavalry. He expressed his satisfaction and said that the mounted drill was better than he expected, although the ponies were 'somewhat rugged and irregular in size'. The second inspection was by General Sir Archibald Hunter, who had known the Scouts in South Africa. It was recorded that during the march past 'one Tpr.'s horse got out of hand, careered along the park, and eventually threw the young fellow'. His nasty knock on the head was 'promptly attended to by Surgeon Lieut. Leach'. General Hunter then addressed the entire parade as follows:

> It must be clear to you, as it is to me, that in raising the Lovat Scouts, Lord Lovat has done what very few men in Scotland could do. By the use of his name and high position in Scotland, Lord Lovat has raised a corps which in the King's armed forces has got no parallel. There is not, throughout the length and breadth of the British Empire, a corps composed of men such as you are. I do not mean to say for a moment that there are not other very fine and magnificent corps of loyal, brave and patriotic men who serve the King; but there is no corps, unique in its character like the Lovat Scouts, drawn as it

is from men employed in such employment as farming, shepherding and as ghillies in the North of Scotland. Lord Lovat, in bringing a corps like this together, has done a very loyal, patriotic and valuable act, and he deserves the thanks of the whole Empire, and he also deserves the thanks of every man in the Lovat Scouts.

On the last Saturday of camp a Sports Day was held, which was to become an annual event in the North. There were races, mounted contests of all kinds, 'heavy' events, piping, an inter-Sqn. tug-of-war (won by The Aird Sqn.) and refreshments for all. There were many guests and a lengthy report in the local press commented that 'Mr. Fletcher of Rosehaugh arrived in a motor car' (a rare event in 1903) and that, 'It must be inspiring to the Gaels present to hear so much Gaelic spoken along the line'.

In 1904 they camped at Fearn in Easter Ross, in 1905 at Tain, in 1906 at Brodie and each year after that in a different place in the Highlands. Each year, too, the training became more advanced and the manoeuvres more ambitious. Several times, a school of instruction for Scout and Scottish Horse officers was held at Beaufort to advance their military knowledge. Lord Lovat was also keen to improve the type of pony brought to camp and he arranged for the purchase of four good stallions to serve approved mares belonging to Scouts. They were of different breeds – Highland garron, thoroughbred, Basuto and Welsh pony.

During these years, a number of exercises were carried out against the Scottish Horse, who were the neighbouring Yeomanry in Perthshire. They had a unique history in that when first raised by the Marquis of Tullibardine (later the 8th Duke of Atholl, K.T., P.C., G.C.V.O., C.B., D.S.O.) they were recruited from Scotsmen already in South Africa. A second Regiment was then raised of Scotsmen from home and Australians of Scottish descent. Both served with great distinction in the Boer War and, in 1903, were re-formed as two Regiments of Yeomanry, commanded by the Marquis of Tullibardine. Their bonnets were similar to those of the Scouts but with red and white dicing and red 'tourie'. They were to have a magnificent record in two World Wars, often fighting shoulder to shoulder with their old friends and rivals, the Scouts. But at this time they were 'the enemy' and the mock battles that took place became almost like a final chapter in the annals of inter-clan warfare. Blows were sometimes not averted and it was said that some of the Uistmen, who then had little English, thought that the main object of joining the Scouts – apart from the pay and allowances – was to get a chance of attacking these strangers from south of the Drumochter Pass!

Typical of the stories about these clashes, which lost nothing in the telling, was one often recalled by an old stalker. His Troop had been sent on ahead to ambush a Scottish Horse Squadron. They were behind a high ridge, overlooking a narrow glen, and spied the 'enemy' coming. The Scout officer called for three volunteers. They would each get £5, and he would be responsible for their ponies, if they would charge with him at the Scottish Horse straight down the very steep hillside. Everyone volunteered. He chose three of them and, when he gave the signal at the crucial moment, they set off, shouting in Gaelic, galloping and slithering down the steep face as hard as they could go. Their astonishing descent ended with one Scout in hospital, one Scout pony having to be destroyed and the officer being liable for much more than he had bargained for. After describing the pandemonium he watched in the glen below, the old stalker would say, 'It was suicide right enough; but that's war!'

In June 1907, a large-scale exercise took place. Lord Lovat commanded the Northerners (Blue Force), consisting of the two Regts. of Scouts, The Royal Scots Greys, The Fife and Forfar Yeomanry and a Section of R.A. The Southerners (Red Force), commanded by Tullibardine, comprised the two Regts. of Scottish Horse, The 18th Hussars and another Section of R.A.

Starting on a line from Brodie in the east to Spean Bridge in the west, Blue Force advanced southwards through the Grampians in a movement which culminated in a dramatic night attack on Tullibardine's Red Force camp at Loch Ordie. Lord Lovat left 200 men and the guns to protect his baggage at Pitlochry. A local guide, who was afterwards, perhaps rightly, regarded as a spy and had to leave the district, led the Scouts by night across the hills to the head of the glen that leads to Loch Ordie. Scouts were sent out to locate the enemy camp and by 3 a.m. had found it. The attack went in just before daylight and was wholly successful.

The exercise was watched by General Rimington and Major General Douglas Haig with several foreign military attaches. Today, old Scouts and Scottish Horsemen, who were not even born at that time, still enjoy an argument about what happened before and during the Battle of Loch Ordie. The official report states:

> The attack was carried out with great spirit... The men, were full of dash, but after covering some fifty miles they had nearly reached the limit of their powers of endurance... The march of the main body of Brodie's detachment of Lovat Scouts was very remarkable, they having covered a distance of at least fifty miles, of which some forty were on horseback and the remainder on foot, within a period of twenty-four hours.

The following year, Lord Lovat was appointed to command the Highland Mounted Bde. consisting of the 1st and 2nd Lovat Scouts, the Fife and Forfar Yeomanry and the Inverness Royal Horse Artillery: He was given the rank of full Colonel and also became A.D.C. to the King. He managed to get first class regular officers for his Staff, including his old friend, Major Frederick Allhusen, as Bde. Major. Majors Willie Macdonald and Augustus Baillie were both promoted to Lt. Colonel and commanded the 1st and 2nd Regts. respectively.

In 1912, Lord Lovat's four year command of the Bde. ended and he retired, aged forty-one, handing over to Brigadier General Tyndale-Biscoe, a regular cavalry officer. Soon the Scouts' Commanding Officers were succeeded by two other excellent Boer War officers, Lt. Colonel E. Fraser-Tytler and Lt. Colonel Archie Stirling of Keir.

By the summer of 1914, the world was of course on the brink of the greatest conflict ever known, between the Central Powers (Germany, Austria, Turkey and Bulgaria) on the one hand and the Allies on the other. The latter were to include The British Empire, France, Belgium, Russia, Japan and Serbia and later the United States, Italy, Rumania, Portugal, and China. Some thirty million men were to be under arms, ten million lives to be lost and millions of people maimed. But when, in the early days of August 1914, the Scouts mobilised as part of the Territorial Army, such a holocaust was almost inconceivable. King George V certainly expressed the feelings of his people when he wrote in his diary on 4th August, 'It is a terrible catastrophe, but it is not our fault.. Please God it may soon be over'.

CHAPTER VI

FIRST WORLD WAR: TRAINING AND HOME DEFENCE
(August 1914 – September 1915)

Both Regiments of the Lovat Scouts, with a total strength of about 1200 men, started mobilising on 4th August 1914. They were to be billeted in farms near Beaufort with the officers in Beaufort Castle and the Lovat Arms Hotel, Beauly.

The 1st Regt. with three of its Sqns. coming from the islands, took longer to mobilise than the 2nd, but by the night of 17th/18th August they were all on their way by train to Huntingdon, which was the 'Battle Station' of the Highland Mounted Bde. That night is morable for the famous rumour of 'Russian Troops with snow on their boots'. The story was that Russians had landed in the north of Scotland and were passing through England on their way to surprise and drive back the German armies. Some say that the Scouts were the innocent cause of this wishful thinking. Charitable English ladies, serving tea by night at York Station, saw strange, wild-looking men conversing in a foreign language, and in the horse trucks they saw hundreds of rough, shaggy ponies. 'Where do you come from?', asked an astonished lady. 'Ross-shire', replied one of the warriors. That was enough: the Russian steam-roller was on its way.

For three months, the Highland Mounted Bde. consisting of two Regiments of Scouts, the Fife and Forfar Yeomanry, the Inverness Royal Horse Artillery, a Field Ambulance and an A.S.C. detachment, trained very hard in the area of Huntingdon. Billets were bad, but the surrounding country was ideal for military exercises. To the delight of all, Lord Lovat returned as their Brigadier General and his great ability in teaching tactics and organising realistic schemes inspired them all. It was a wet autumn with much mud in the horse-lines and there was an epidemic of 'strangles' among the ponies, from which several died.

There was recreation as well as hard work. Some played football, others shinty; bathing in the River Ouse was popular at first, and some enjoyed running with a local pack of beagles. An N.C.O., describing his Squadron Leader, Major Duncan Baillie, out beagling, wrote, 'He can keep going forever, and he runs just like a dog...' A few Scouts were asked to shoot pheasants locally. The best invitation came to the elder of two Wood brothers, nephews of a former Adjutant, who had joined the Skye Squadron as troopers. His Troop Sergeant, formerly his father's keeper on Raasay, loaded for him and they both enjoyed the day tremendously. He and his brother later got commissions and both had distinguished war careers.

Sometimes, as part of their mounted training, a Troop at a time went out hunting with the Cambridgeshire Foxhounds. They surprised the other followers by always taking with them their ponies' midday feeds in nosebags. Of one such occasion, Colonel Hon. Ian M. Campbell (from Cawdor) wrote in his memoirs:

> One of the men, McDonald, stalker to John Stirling at Monar, came out with his glass, although mounted. He said there were far too many dogs out – he had always done well enough after foxes with a few terriers and a gun. We had a short dart across one or two fields, hounds running into a cub just on the far side of a large "bullfinch". John Munro, who was known as the Lion Tamer because he had once entered the lion's den in a travelling circus at Brora, had a mare that would jump anything, in spite of the way he rode her. He crashed through the "bullfinch" and landed in the middle of the pack, shouting. "I'm first! Give me the tail" Grossman, the M.F.H., said he would give him anything if he would only take his mare out of the middle of the pack. The Lion Tamer came back to billets in triumph with the brush stuck in his bonnet.

Yeomanries now had to be put on a 'war footing' of three Squadrons instead of four. This was much resented in all Regiments recruited territorially and particularly in the Scouts; but B Sqn. (Uist) and F Sqn.

(Sutherland and Caithness) had to suffer the fate of being distributed among the other three Squadrons in their respective Regiments. By this time Lord Lovat had organised the raising of two second line Regiments of Lovat Scouts, called the 2nd/1st and 2nd/2nd, commanded to begin with by Lt. Colonel Willie Macdonald and Lt. Colonel Augustus Baillie. They were formed from N.C.O.s and men too old or unfit for active service and also from recruits, first from the Highlands and then from the whole of Scotland, with a few from overseas, including Canada. They provided replacements for the first line Regiments and were stationed at Lowestoft and Beccles. They were amalgamated in 1916 under command of Lt. Colonel E. Fraser-Tytler.

At the end of October 1914, the Highland Mounted Brigade was inspected by King George V at Huntingdon. Major K. McCorquodale wrote 'The whole Brigade was drawn up on the Port Holme in column of Squadrons by Regiments. Afterwards, the Brigade rode past the King by Squadrons, and the King came out and watched a field day and talked with several officers and N.C.O.s'.

Suddenly on 15th November, the Brigade was ordered to go by train next day to Grimsby, to help in defending the East Coast against a threat of invasion. From Grimsby, they rode south for two days and took up guard duties on a sixteen-mile stretch of coast between Sutton-on-Sea and Skegness. It was cold, monotonous and depressing work, especially for units which felt they were now well trained in their role and ready to fight. 'We all thought and talked of nothing but war, wondering when we should be considered fit to go out' (Colonel Campbell). Once, in the early morning mist of 16th December, German battle cruisers came in near the coast and shelled the towns of Hartlepool, Scarborough and Whitby for an hour, causing many civilian casualties, and then escaped unscathed. Otherwise there were few excitements, and there was interminable work erecting miles of wire entanglements on the shore, often washed away by high tides and on-shore gales.

At last on 15th April, the Highland Mounted Brigade was relieved by the Second Brigade of the Scottish Horse, and rode southwards for three days in spring sunshine to take over billets in the area of Hunstanton on the Wash. They were succeeding an English Yeomanry Brigade which had just gone on active service to Egypt, and they hoped that it would soon be their turn to follow. The Scouts were billeted in Hunstanton, Houghton, Harplay and Great Massingham. Vigorous training continued, but it was not till 21st August that orders came to sail at an early date for the Mediterranean. Colonel Campbell wrote:

> We got the order late at night, but I at once went round to tell the troops, who all cheered like mad. We decided we were for Gallipoli... The next fortnight was rather hectic, our establishment being altered considerably. We were issued with six Vickers guns per Regt. instead of two. We handed all our horses over to the Second Line and drew new rifles, sun helmets, drill clothing, fresh saddlery and transport harness. We also drew cavalry swords, the first and only issue we ever had.

It was a sad blow to many Scouts to lose their own ponies, which had done so well, but at least they went to the Second Line Scout Regts. 100 mares were sent back for the good of the breed, to be sold in the Highlands and some of their progeny may well have become Scout ponies later.

During their year in England, the Scouts had made many friends and had gained the respect of local people. Lord Lovat received the following letter from the inhabitants of Hunstanton on 28th August 1915:

> My Lord,
> We learn with regret of the departure of Your Lordship and your Lovat Scouts. Words fail us when we tr̄ to express our respect and admiration for them, and the pleasure it has been to have them in our midst. We hope and pray Your Lordship and the troops may be spared to return to your homes and the

Country for whose freedom you are nobly going out to fight. Had there been time, but we know that there is not, it would have given the residents great pleasure to see the Scouts march through the town headed by the pipers.

Hoping Your Lordship may be able to convey to the troops our appreciation of their Visit and our earnest wishes for their welfare,

We remain,
The Inhabitants of Hunstanton.

H SQUADRON AT HOUGHTON HALL, NORFOLK, 1915

Sqn. Ldr. Major D. Baillie; 2 i/c Captain J.P. Grant; Tp. Ldrs: W. Macrae, Hon. D. Leslie Melville and A. Kennedy.

THE SERGEANT' MESS, NAIRN CAMP, 1934

(Back Row) – Sgts. J. MacKenzie, W. Mackenzie, H. MacLean, J. MacKay, A. MacDonald, A.J. Macdonald, M. MacDougall, J. MacRae, I.D. MacLeod.
(2nd Row) – S.S.M. J. Kippen, Sgts. F. MacKenzie, J. Findlayson, G. Reid, J. Ross, T. Martin, S.S.M. Loam, Sgts. Barnett, A. Wilson, MacRury, J. MacDonald, S.S.M. Dunlop.
(3rd Row) – Sgts. K. MacLeod, T. Fraser, M. Johnston, J. Cumming, J. MacEachan, D. MacKay, W. Sutherland, D. Murray, J. Matheson, R. Calvert.
(Front Row) – P/M A. MacAulay, S.S.M. Hunt, S.Q.M.S. Macmillan, S.Q.M.S. F. MacCook, S.S.M. J. MacKenzie, S.S.M. J. MacKay, R.S.M. E. Jones, Lt. Col. The Earl of Leven and Melville, K.T., Capt. and Adjutamnt P.C.H. Grant,R.Q.M.S. MacLennan, S.S.M. A. Morrison, S.Q.M.S. S. Griffin, Sgt. A. Lindsay.

CHAPTER VII

FIRST WORLD WAR: GALLIPOLI
(September – December 1915)

On 8th September 1915, the Highland Mounted Brigade, commanded by Brigadier General Lord Lovat and including the 1st and 2nd Lovat Scouts, embarked on the 'Andania' at Devonport, bound for the Mediterranean.

At Malta they lay alongside a hospital ship with fifty Scottish Horse casualties from Suvla Bay. By semaphore, the Scottish Horse asked for pipe music. As the 'Andania' slipped out of harbour at dusk, her crew perpetually on the look-out for U-boats, the Scouts' Pipe Band started to play; but not for long. The English Captain demanded complete silence and 'threatened to put them all in irons' (Colonel Campbell). During three days coaling at Alexandria, they went ashore for a route march. They also handed over all their cavalry kit, and were issued instead with infantry packs and web equipment. On 20th September, they sailed to the Greek Island of Lemnos where, although Greece was still officially neutral, Mudros Harbour was the base for the Allied forces fighting at Gallipoli.

The great strategic plans for the Balkans, so strongly advocated by Churchill, required first that the Allies should force the narrow passage of the Dardanelles. Both sides of it, the mainland on the east and the long, narrow peninsula of Gallipoli on the west, belonged to Turkey. Control of the Dardanelles would then enable a British fleet to be sent through the Sea of Marmara to command Constantinople (Istanbul) and so drive Turkey out of the war. An extension of this plan was for the fleet next to go through the Bosporus into the Black Sea, linking up with our Russian allies.

The British and French fleets began bombarding the western forts of the Dardanelles on 19th February 1915, but there was strong retaliation. A more determined effort to force the passage a month later resulted in considerable Allied losses, including the sinking of three battleships. It was decided that land forces would have to be used as well.

British, French and Anzac (Australian and New Zealand) forces, under General Sir Ian Hamilton made their historic landings on 25th April; the British 29th Div. at Cape Helles, the western tip of the peninsula, and the Anzacs at a small bay on the northern shore, known ever since as 'Anzac Cove'. Gallipoli is rugged country with steep cliffs rising from the shore and the Allies were pinned down by unexpectedly strong and stubborn Turkish forces on the higher ground. There was bitter fighting with very heavy casualties on both sides and little progress. An even stronger effort was made to capture the Gallipoli peninsula on 6th August with a three pronged attack from Cape Helles, Anzac Cove and a new landing at Suvla Bay. This renewed attack developed into a great and bloody battle, which soon turned into stalemate and trench warfare of an appalling kind, with rampant disease and terrible casualties.

Such was the battlefield which the Highland Mounted Brigade, equipped as dismounted Yeomanry, approached during the night of 26th/27th September aboard S.S. 'Sarnia' and S.S. 'Abassieh'. 400 yards out from Suvla Bay, they trans-shipped everything into 'beetles', special landing lighters, and came ashore. In the dark they took over some reserve trenches near the Salt Lake. They were part of the 2nd Mounted Division (dismounted) with the Scottish Horse Brigade and several Brigades of English Yeomanry.

At dawn, they could see the dominant positions, which the Turks held above them, a huge semi-circle overlooking the whole of the Allied trenches, except for a small area under the cliffs of Anzac Cove. They spent twelve days in the Salt Lake reserve trenches with every available man on night fatigue duties, unloading and carrying ammunition and stores, drawing water and rations, and digging trenches. They toiled throughout the hours of darkness with a half-hour break at midnight. Major McCorquodale wrote:

> Anyone on the shore fatigues at Gallipoli will never forget

them... It was difficult to sleep during the day because of the heat, the sun and the flies. They crawled all over you and must have spread disease everywhere, as the sanitary arrangements were very bad. There were open latrines, rubbish dumps all over the place and, between the lines, a large number of unburied corpses. After about two days, men began to go sick, mosty with stomach trouble, dysentery and heat stroke. Water was scarce and bad and had to be boiled and rationed. The Scouts also had several casualties, including the 1st Regt's M.O., badly wounded in the head. The best thing in life was a bathe in the sea, which we were able to get every day or so although having a shell drop near you, when naked, makes you feel more vulnerable than ever)!

On 6th October, the Scouts moved up into the front line trenches, where they were to be for the next month. At some points, the Turkish lines were only about 200 yards away. There were frequent engagements with the enemy during night patrols, much sniping and occasional night attacks to straighten the line. The Scouts killed and captured a number of Turks and had a few battle casualties themselves, but sickness – particularly dysentery – took a much heavier toll. Lord Lovat himself became dangerously ill and was evacuated to Malta, as were a great many other Scouts, including both Lt. Colonel Willie Macdonald, C.O. of the 1st Regt. and his Second-in-command Major Ewen Grant. Lt. Colonel Archie Stirling took over the Brigade and was promoted to Brigadier-General; Major A.J. McNeill succeeded him as C.O. of the 2nd Scouts, and Major Kenny Macdonald commanded the 1st Regt.

The most outstanding night attack occurred when E Sqn. commanded by Major I.M. Campbell, and the Du Pres Sqn. of the Fife and Forfar Yeomanry captured a very important strong point. It was a barricade built and held by the Turks across a steep dried up watercourse (or 'dere' – pronounced 'derry'), called the Azmac Dere barricade. It had to be taken before the British line could be advanced. The ground was very carefully reconnoitred by night patrols, during one of which Lieut. Forsyth Grant, 'an exceptionally fine officer', was killed. The attack, brilliantly planned by Major Allhusen, was a complete success. Fourteen Turks were killed and the remainder fled. They counter-attacked but were driven off, one Scout being killed and three wounded. By dawn, Major Campbell's men had turned the barricade round and dug adequate new trenches. The position was re-named 'the Highland barricade'.

There was a great deal of sniping on both sides and the Scouts soon achieved mastery over their Turkish opponents. They became very keen on it and Colonel Campbell records that when the 2nd Regt. was moved slightly to its left and had to give up a particularly good sniping position, Cpl. Carver, one of the best snipers, 'complained that we had given up all the best of the ground as though it were the best beat on a deer forest'. There was one renowned Turkish sniper operating in that area and nicknamed 'Percy', who had shot dead several troopers of the Scottish Horse and of the Fife and Forfar Yeomanry. Some Scout snipers were detailed to find and deal with 'Percy'. They soon located him: he was stalked and killed by L/Cpl. Angus Mackay from Strathnaver.

Early in November, they were relieved by a Welsh Infantry Brigade and returned to the Salt Lake reserve trenches and the back-breaking work of shore fatigues. There had been further casualties – particularly from snipers and broom-stick bombs – but 'dysentery, para-typhoid and now jaundice of a very nasty kind were widespread especially among the younger officers and men... The number of troops went down daily and very few who went to hospital returned to duty' (Major McCorquodale).

The Gallipoli campaign had became a costly and hopeless stalemate with huge Allied losses. The question for the higher command was whether to attempt another large-scale attack – Sir Ian Hamilton estimated that 100,000 new troops would be required – or to abandon the enterprise altogether. Rumours were rife. Kitchener himself had been out there, and General Sir Charles Monro had taken over supreme command. Finally, on 25th November 1915, officers were informed that the peninsula was to be evacuated. It was explained that the evacuation

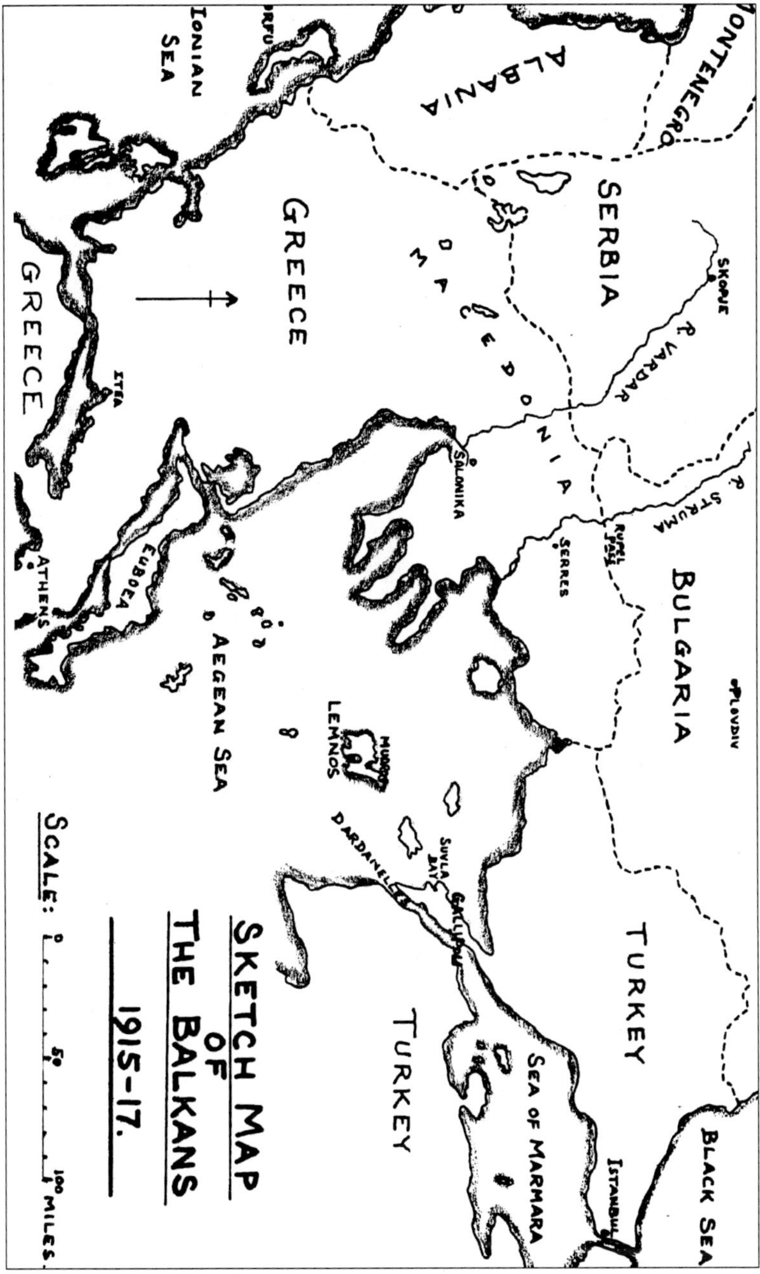
SKETCH MAP OF THE BALKANS 1915-17.
SCALE: 0 50 100 MILES.
ONTENEGRO
ALBANIA
SERBIA
MACEDONIA
GREECE
GREECE
BULGARIA
TURKEY
TURKEY
IONIAN SEA
RFU
ITEA
ATHENS
EUBOEA
AEGEAN SEA
LEMNOS
MUDROS
DARDANELLES
SUVLA BAY
GALLIPOLI
SEA OF MARMARA
ISTANBUL
BLACK SEA
SKOPJE
R. VARDAR
SALONIKA
R. STRUMA
RUPEL PASS
SERRES
PLOVDIV

might prove as difficult and as costly as the original landings. Sir Charles Monro, although in favour of total evacuation, estimated that casualties would probably be 30 to 40% of the Army. Luckily, he was proved wrong.

One of the greatest tributes ever paid to the Lovat Scouts is that they were chosen to cover the retreat from Suvla Bay. That they did it successfully is something of which they and the Highlands may always be proud; but during the next three weeks, before 20th December, circumstances were to change and they were to suffer almost indescribable hardships.

On the morning of 26th November, the Highland Mounted Brigade received orders to take over the front line from an Infantry Brigade on the night of 27th. That very afternoon, 26th, the weather broke with a heavy thunderstorm and torrential rain at 5 p.m. There was a second and worse storm between 7.30 p.m. and 9.15 p.m., and by 8.30 p.m. all the reserve trenches had become completely flooded. The trouble began with flood water pouring down the Azmac Dere and piling up against the barricades built by both Turks and British. The barricades burst and a river, carrying dead Turks, their dead pack ponies and every kind of filth and debris, rushed down into the British trenches below. Colonel Campbell wrote:

> Just below the barricade, the communication trench which we had worked on crossed the Dere. We, knowing something about mountain streams and their spates, had, when digging this part, not crossed the Dere, but some other enthusiast had completed the bit we had omitted and the trench crossed the Dere about three or four feet below the bottom of the stream. The natural result was that the water swept down the trench, instead of going down to the sea, and in a very few minutes all the trenches in the back areas were full of water. Bde. H.Q. were said to have been four ft. deep in water five minutes after the first drop arrived. A battery of guns near Bde. H.O. were buried in mud and water.

The Scouts sheltered as best they could in sandhills near the sea. Much kit was lost: everyone and everything were soaked. The next day, 27th November was one of almost continuous and heavy rain. The Scouts' relief of the front line that night had to be made 'over the top', as all the communication trenches were flooded, and it took over two hours through deep mud. Flooding had been severe in the front line trenches too, parapets had collapsed and the units relieved by the Scouts had found conditions almost unendurable.

Then the snow came, and soon after it, there were eighteen degrees of frost. Rations were in desperately short supply and the water was unfit to drink. Soaked clothing froze into hard boards. Colonel Campbell wrote of these hardships:

> The worst of it was that one could do so little for the men, but they were splendid, remaining cheerful in spite of very real discomfort. In spite of the snow which fell all day on the 28th, we got a lot of sniping, the men taking full advantage of the many targets presented. The Turks must have been in an even worse plight than we were, They were to be seen, all over the place, walking about, trying to keep warm and, in the early morning, there were a lot sitting, like scaups on a rock, along the top of their parapet. We accounted for about thirty by midday. One of the men told me it was better fun than hind shooting.
>
> It was really a very trying time for a bit, and I never was as proud of the Squadron, who took everything with a smile. We were mostly more or less frost-bitten; I removed my boots about three days after the flood for the first time, and it was a fortnight or so before I could put them on again; so I went about in the canvas shoes which I fortunately had put into my pack. My fingers were bad too, and peeled for about half their length: they were still sore and swollen when we left.

Casualties from exposure and jaundice were fearful. Some units lost half their strength in two days, and one Army Corps alone had to evacuate 6,700 men. Only the hardiest and fittest survived. The two Regiments of Scouts continued to hold the front line for the Brigade, all three Squadrons of each Regiment being required for the job because of their reduced strength. The Fife and Forfar Yeomanry, who had suffered even more severely, went into reserve. Lieut. K. McCorquodale, who at that time was the only officer left in 6 Squadron, except his Squadron Leader, Malor Brodie of Brodie, wrote later:

> The Scouts stood up to the conditions better than many other Regts.. and although a number of our men went to hospital with frost-bite, none were drowned in the trenches or died of exposure, as happened in several Pegts... A certain number of casualties occurred from snipers and artillery fire, including Capt. Hon. Alastair Fraser and Lieut. J. Dewar, both wounded, the latter seriously. Two men, mess orderlies, carrying tea to the front line, missed their way and walked into the Turkish trenches. They were taken prisoner and were the only Lovat Scouts captured in the whole war.

The evacuation of Gallipoli was brilliantly and successfully handled over a period of three weeks. It was greatly helped by the fact that the sea remained calm at night with fine, cold weather. The general plan was to withdraw troops and stores gradually at night so that the Turks would not realise that our forces were dwindling. There were intervals of complete 'cease-fire' during darkness, in the hope that when the final silence came the enemy would have no immediate suspicions. Many mechanical devices were used to imitate the sound of sporadic rifle fire. Prominent in such inventions was Lieut. Joe Pease (later Lord Gainford) of the Lovat Scouts. He had been a mine manager before the war and his knowledge of and enthusiasm for explosives, although sometimes a grave danger to his comrades and, on one famous occasion, to himself, were of great value.

He had used explosives effectively on night patrols and now invented a way of attaching the fuses of detonators to the wicks of candles so that they kept exploding at irregular intervals, like occasional rifle fire. Another stratagem was to arrange damaged rifles so that they were fired off automatically when sufficient water fell from one tin into another, the second one being connected to the trigger. Such devices and dummy figures on the firesteps were successfully employed by the Scouts and the Ghurkas, who were on their right, in the last week and, particularly, on the last night of the evacuation.

The Highland Mounted Briaade was the rearguard at Suvla Bay and the Lovat Scouts were to provide the rear party to cover the final withdrawal. By 11th December, the Scouts remaining on Gallipoli had been reduced by stages to 188 men. On 18th December came the final order to evacuate Suvla Bay and Anzac Cove on the night of l9th/2Oth December, provided the weather remained calm. Major Hon. l.M. Campbell was detailed to command the Scouts' rear party with two officers and seventy other ranks, half of them from each Regiment. Naturally, the fittest and best were chosen. The two officers selected were Lieut. J. Pattersen and Lieut. J. Ross, the latter having only recently received his commission on promotion from Sgt. Major of G Squadron.

Last-ditch defences had been constructed at the hill called Lalla Baba, where the rear party were to make their final stand, should the Turks attack. Just after dusk on 19th December, the rest of the Regiment withdrew and Major Campbell and his small but formidable force took over the whole of the front line, formerly held by the Brigade. On his right, and also under his command, was a rear party of fifty Ghurkas. It was considered easier to embark them with the Scouts at 'C' Beach of Suvla, rather than at Anzac Cove further west. Colonel Campbell wrote:

> The trenches seemed strangely deserted. At the head of each communication trench there was an N.C.O. and a double sentry group. Eyeryone else was moying about during the periods when we tried to keep up the usual part of many. For

the rest of the time we had sentries looking out and small patrols going up and down the trenches. After 10 p.m. we had silence, except for one final burst of activity iust before the M.G.s left... One was rather on edge, although I did not realise it until I was safely on the boat going to Imbros, when I suddenly felt dead tired. Once during this wait, a couple of rats fell, fighting, into the dug-out and I almost jumped out of my skin!!... At 1 a.m. I saw the two M.G.s off, reporting their departure to Division. The various wheezes were started about now, and they were working well as we passed out of earshot of the trenches. The Ghurkas had made up some good dummy figures on the firestep...

At 1.30 a.m. on 20th December 1915, the rear party moved silently back from the front line, Troop by Troop. They met at a rendezvous in the Dere and, with a small rearguard, made for the beaches. By 3.10 a.m. everyone was aboard ship: Major Campbell was the last soldier to leave the shore of Suvla Bay. As they sailed away, the Scouts' final sight of Gallipoli was that of the blazing dumps on the beaches.

The Lovat Scouts had been there, mainly in the front line trenches, for nearly three months. They had missed the early battles, which had cost so many lives; but they had fought well, had distinguished themselves in patrolling and sniping, had been chosen to provide the vitally important rear party and, above all, had shown their exceptional toughness and resolution in the face of many hardships. Major F.H. Allhusen, Major Hon. l.M. Campbell and Major Kenny Macdonald received the D.S.O. and Major Brodie of Brodie (who had won the D.S.O. in South Africa) was awarded an M.C.

Gallipoli, with its half million total of Allied and Turkish casualties, has been described as a holocaust second only to the carnage of the Somme. Yet, strangely, British soldiers never really hated the Turks. As early as October, Lord Lovat wrote in a letter home, 'They fight wonderfully fairly, allowing parties out to fetch in the wounded and never shoot at hospital ships'. In the cruel and disgusting game of war, the Turks were at least considered honourable opponents. In ten months time, they and the Scouts were to meet again.

CHAPTER VIII

FIRST WORLD WAR: EGYPT, THE DESERT AND REORGANISATION (December 1915 – October 1916)

From the grim shores of Gallipoli the Highland Mountain Brigade sailed to the small Greek Island of Imbros and thence to Mudros Harbour in Lemnos. There they trans-shipped to the 'Scotian', and, after a well-deserved Christmas party on board, arrived at Alexandria on 28th December. The Scouts camped with the Fife and Forfar Yeomanry at Sidi Bisch nearby.

A week later, in early January 1916, the Brigade moved to Mena House Camp, Cairo, for a period of recuperation, re-equipment and weapon-training. The Scouts, now at less than half their original strength were reinforced hv the arrival of officers and men who had recovered from wounds and sickness and also by a draft from the Second Line Regiments. They had a few weeks in comparatively good billets, enjoyed seeing Cairo, the Pyramids and the Sphinx and a route march to the Cairo Zoo was popular with everyone, especially John Munro the Lion Tamer!

Egypt, though nominally a Turkish province, had been under British 'protection' from the beginning of the war and was vital to the Allies for their control of the Suez Canal. The Turks in Syria, led by a German General, had made an unsuccessful attack on the Canal early in 1915. Almost all our troops surviving Gallipoli had come to Egypt and, together with the five divisions already there, formed a strong British force. Cairo itself enjoyed a social and military life of almost pre-war character, but there lay, beneath that veneer, all the mystery of the Middle East, and Cairo was said to be a hot-bed of German and Turkish espionage. Lord Lovat's sister, the Hon. Mrs. Stirling of Keir, brought several Scout officers' wives out to nurse in the Cairo Military Hospital. One of them, who had both a husband and a brother in the Scouts, got a job in the Secret Service but it did not last long. When asked by a General what her job was, she innocently replied, 'I work for M.I.5' and was sacked next day as a security risk!

Now that the Regiment was no longer in the front line, there were some official enquiries about various stores unaccounted for or acquired at Gallipoli. One of these so enraged Major Kenny Macdonald, D.S.O., who had been commanding the 1st Regt., that he said he would put the whole matter in the hands of his solicitor in Portree if he heard one more word about it. This awful threat effectively silenced the authorities.

Major Kenny, one of the original Scout Officers in the Boer War, embodied so much of what was best and most unorthodox in the Regiment's tradition, that a few of the many stories about him should be recorded. A relative of Flora Macdonald and Laird of Skeabost and Tote, he was a hardy Highlander of infinite charm, humour and courage. He loved Skye passionately, and bred race-horses there with which to win the Derby, for he claimed that Skye's pastures were the best in the world and its stock the hardiest. Certain apparent failings in his batman were always excused on the grounds that the man was 'the best bee-keeper in Skye'. Major Kenny was never at a loss. When one pony in his Squadron proved to be mad and dangerous, he had it shot dead; he then had its leg broken with an axe, reversing the order of events for the official enquiry. When his Squadron was medically examined early in the war and several men, whom he regarded as totally unsuitable for active service, were passed 'FIT' on their medical cards, he inserted the letters 'UN' in front of it and thus ensured that they never went abroad. In the tough, latter days of Gallipolli, he commanded the 1st Regiment magnificently without a Second-in-command, Adjutant, Quartermaster or Medical Officer. He did all these jobs as well as his own and, surviving everything cheerfully, took Sick Parade each morning. He often prescribed a 'No 9', the dreaded army aperient pill, and when the supply ran out he issued a 'No 4' and a 'No 5', or any two pills whose numbers added to nine. Sick parades dwindled! With loyalty and enthusiasm, he reverted to being Second-in-command in Egypt, and fought with distinction in Macedonia. He was by then the oldest of the officers and at last, in February 1917, he retired to Home Service after a legendary career in the Regiment of which he was so proud. For seventeen years he had practised what he first proclaimed in South Africa, 'It is all right to take soldiering seriously in peace, but you should never do so in war!'

The Brigade's rest at Cairo did not last long. On 11th February 1916, orders were received to entrain the next morning for the task of reconnoitring and guarding certain isolated oases in the desert, west of the Nile delta. There was a threat that the Senussi, a camel-riding Bedouin tribe, paid by the Germans and led by a Turkish Colonel called Ja'far, were about to start a guerilla campaign raiding villages in the cultivated Nile valley. Before making such raids, it was probable that they would first concentrate at one of the oases. The Dorset Yeomanry did much to nip this campaign in the bud with a brilliant charge at Agagiya in late February 1916, in which the leader, Ja'far himself, was wounded and captured. But the threat remained and so the Scouts, as part of the Brigade, were stationed for over six months at various places in the desert – Oasis Junction, a few miles north of Luxor; Dakhla, some sixty miles further west; Miniah; Sohag, and Assiut. The Brigade was at various times strengthened by the Southwest Yeomanry Brigade, a Squadron of Egyptian Cavalry, the Hong Kong Mountain Battery and a Squadron of the Australian Camel Corps. A few Scouts learned to ride camels and on one occasion an officer and his Sergeant were lost with their camels for nearly twenty-four hours in a sand storm. Only once did the Scouts see a genuine Senussi tribesman and, unfortunately, he had already been captured by the Australian Camel Corps.

Major McCorquodale wrote of the Scouts' time in the desert as follows:

> It was a very unpleasant summer for everyone. The heat became intense and sand storms were frequent; guard and fatigue duties were very heavy, rations poor, and all forms of recreation extremely difficult to organise. From June to September it was impossible to do anything during the middle of the day because of the heat, which for weeks on end was over 100 degrees and went up to 120 – 122 degrees in the

shade for about a fortnight in August. Parades and working parties took place in the early morning. It had been decided to extend the railway beyond the Kharga terminus into the desert towards Dakhla Oasis – and a great deal of heavy work was done on this. The railway had extended by nearly 20 kilometers by September... The nights were quite cold after the heat of the day and several cases of pneumonia occurred. Three men died of it in Kharga and were buried at Merkez el Sherika, and Sgt. D.G. Mackintosh died in Cairo.

The Scouts were still organised as two Yeomanry Regiments, but there seemed no chance of their becoming mounted again nor, for the time being of their getting into action. Ten officers were granted transfers, mainly to go to the western front. Some joined the Royal Flying Corps, others the Brigade of Guards, two became A.D.C.s to Generals, and Major Campbell D.S.O. was given command of a Battalion of the Argylls. Some of these officers were on board the 'Arabia' when it was torpedoed by a U-boat in the Mediterranean, the survivors being rescued and brought to Malta, from where they continued their journey.

In mid-September, orders came for both Regiments of Lovat Scouts to leave the Highland Mounted Brigade and move to Cairo to be formed into one infantry Battalion. The Scouts were to become the '10th (Lovat Scouts) Bn. Q.O. Cameron Highlanders'. The Scottish Horse were similarly to be made into the '13th (Scottish Horse) Bn. of the Black Watch'. Despite these changes in name and role, the Scouts retained their identity, continued to wear their Scout bonnets and badges with shoulder patches of Hunting Fraser tartan, and were always knows as 'The Lovat Scouts' to the end of the war. They were sad to be parted from their great friends, the Fife and Forfar Yeomanry.

As the two Scout Regiments were not numerous enough to form a complete Infantry Bn. one of their new Companies (D Coy.) was provided by the 3rd Scottish Horse, consisting of seven officers and about 200 O.R.s. They were excellent soldiers and became an integrated and popular part of the Lovat Scouts, commanded by Captain G.F. Henderson with Captain Sir J.A.C. Campbell as Second-in-command. As Lt. Colonel Willie Macdonald was on leave when the Battalion was formed, it was commanded by Lt. Colonel Duncan Baillie with Major Kenny Macdonald as Second-in-command and Captain A.H. Campbell as Adjutant. The Companies were commanded as follows: A Coy., Major Hon. A. Fraser; B Coy., Major J.P. Grant; C Coy., Captain G.L. Craik; and D Coy., Captain G.F. Henderson.

After being reorganised, re-equipped and taught to march and drill as Infantry, the Scouts left Cairo by train on 16th October 1916 for Alexandria, where they embarked on the 'Minnewaska'. Their destination was Salonika, the Allied base for the Macedonian campaign against the Turks and the Bulgars, in which the Scouts were to take part for the next year and eight months.

MACEDONIAN CARICATURES

1. Lt. Col. D. Baillie, D.S.O.
2. Maj. Hon. A. Fraser, D.S.O.
3. Maj. J.P. Grant, M.C.
4. Capt. W. Mackintosh, M.C.
5. Capt. A. Fraser Lee, M.C. (M.O.)
6. Lt. Hon. J. Pease

CHAPTER IX

FIRST WORLD WAR : MACEDONIA
(October 1916 – June 1918)

The Lovat Scouts landed at Salonika on 20th October 1916. They marched for six consecutive days north-eastwards through several torrential storms along the busy, muddy road which was the supply route to the Struma front. They carried full infantry packs, and the Battalion transport for the rest of their time in Macedonia was a column of pack mules, with Scout muleteers under command of Lieut. G. Munro, a Boer War veteran.

The Allied armies fighting the Turks and the Bulgars under the supreme command of a Frenchman, General Sarrail, were of many nationalities. There were French and French colonials – black Senegalese from North Africa and yellow Annamites from the Far East – as well as Russians, Italians and two Divisions of Greek troops, raised by the deposed premier, Venizelos, when the Greek King went over to the German side after Gallipoli. There were also Serbs, heroic survivors of the army which had been overwhelmed by the Central Powers' invasion of Serbia and, finally, there were British troops, arriving in increasing numbers under command of General G.F. Milne.

The front in October 1916 stretched for some 200 miles from Albania on the left and thence in a south-easterly direction via Lake Doiran and along the Struma valley to the Gulf of Rendina, an inlet of the Aegean Sea. The main defences of the Struma valley were the responsibility of the British. Progress had been slow, partly because of difficulties over supplies and communications but perhaps mainly because of the unhealthy malarial climate. The campaign had become almost as static as that of the Western front; nevertheless, it was on the Struma that the enemy first cracked in the autumn of 1918 before victory was achieved in the West.

The Struma River rises in the Bulgarian mountains to the north and flows down through a huge, fertile valley into Lake Tahinos and thence into the Aegean Sea. In much of the valley the river banks are higher than the surrounding country, so that while no tributaries run into the river there, many streams flow from it, losing themselves in the marshes, winter home of innumerable wildfowl. The country in which the Scouts were to fight consisted of marsh with shallow-rooted reeds, thick scrub, sometimes impenetrable, and fertile land formerly growing crops of fruit, grain and tobacco but now deserted. Virtually all the civilians had fled, leaving some of their dogs and pigs to go wild.

At the end of their six-day march, the Scouts joined 82 Inf. Bde. in which the other three Battalions were the 2nd Gloucesters, the 2nd Duke of Cornwall's Light Infantry (both regular Battalions) and the 10th Hampshires. They were in the 27th Division, commanded by General Ravenshaw, which formed part of the 16th Army Corps. At first they were supplying up to 600 men daily for road and bridge repairs, but on 7th November, 'Lieut. J.A. Cameron, than whom there was no finer Scout, led a mounted patrol across the Struma river under direct orders of Brigade' (Major McCorquodale).

They moved up into the line near Nigrita on 10th November and immediately every telescope was trained on the Struma valley, some twelve miles wide, which lay ahead of them. 'The light in Greece for long-distance spying is very good and, with the best men in the world to use a telescope, we were able to see all sorts of things behind the enemy lines which no other unit could possibly do' (Major McCorquodale). They noticed that the soldiers moving in and out of Serres, the enemy H.Q. on the east side of the valley, were marching in threes, a practice of the Turks but not of the Bulgars. This information was of great interest to Intelligence, as it showed that the Turks, who were the better fighters, had taken over from the Bulgars. It was confirmed a few days later when a Scout patrol found a notice on a tree in no-man's land reading 'You now have to fight the victors of Gallipoli, not the Bulgars!'

After a week of patrolling and spying from Nigrita, the Scouts were moved across the Struma to take up positions around Kakaraska, while the 2nd D.C.L.I. made a frontal attack on a strongly-held enemy position called Tumbitsa Farm. The attack failed and the D.C.L.I. had about eighty casualties. Tumbitsa and Virhanli, another enemy strong point, were considered of great strategic importance. Behind them lay tracks leading to the railway, which was in enemy hands.

On the night of 17th/18th November, a force under command of Lieutenant Colonel Baillie and consisting of two Companies of the Scouts, a Greek Battalion and some Royal Engineers were given the task of making a pontoon bridge across the Virhanli river and then of capturing Virhanli. The waggons, carrying the heavy pontoon boats, soon capsized in the rutted, muddy track, whereupon the Scouts man-handled them one and a half miles to the river, only to find that it was too wide to be bridged and too deep to be forded. They managed to drag the boats back before dawn and the attack was called off.

During the rest of November they sent out frequent patrols in the directions of Virhanli and Tumbitsa, all of which confirmed the strength of both enemy positions. But, in early December, orders were received for another daylight frontal attack to be made on Tumbitsa. Such attacks, without any elements of surprise or originality, were usually preceded by an intense artillery barrage, during which the defenders went to ground and then, when it stopped, popped up and met the assaulting infantry with withering fire. This had been the story of the D.C. L.I.'s costly attack on Tumbitsa and now on 5th December, it was to be the Scouts' turn. A special difficulty was that the Virhanli river had to be bridged by the Royal Engineers under fire before the attack could go in. Major K. McCorquodale, who won a very well-deserved M.C. in this engagement, wrote the following account of the attack and its failure:

> At about 10.30 a.m. our guns opened a heavy bombardment on Tumbitsa and the trenches around it. Many of their shells were duds or failed to burst owing to soft ground, nor did the aiming seem very accurate. The R.E.s built a bridge across the river with great speed and efficiency, although from what happened afterwards the enemy probably allowed them to do

so, expecting to get better targets later. The R.E.s and the Scouts' fatigue party with them had about five casualties.

At 11.20a.m. the guns stopped and C Coy. started to advance, No 12 Pln. (Lieut. K. McCorquodale) leading. As soon as the men began going over the bridge, the enemy opened very heavy machine gun fire onto the bridge, causing at once a number of casualties. Lieut. McCorquodale stopped the men coming over the bridge and ordered them to wade through the river, which came up to well above their waists. The remainder of No 12 Pln. and half of No 11 Pln. (Lieut. P.G.D. Muir) got across and took cover behind the far river bank. Casualties now began to occur among the men attempting to cross the river and it was impossible to move from behind the river banks. No 12 Pln. had three of its Section Ldrs. Sgt. A. Fraser, LlSgt. H. Mackay and Cpl. O. Morrison hit, the last dying of wounds, and Sgt. Gondie of No 11 Pln. was also killed. Many men were hit as well and the attack entirely held up. Captain Craik, C Coy. Commander, managed to get across the river, but was wounded in the shoulder. The rest of the Company were held up on the original side of the river.

The enemy now began to shell the river banks and the woods beyond, in which the supporting Companies of the Scouts were sheltering. The shelling was very heavy, continuing far two to three hours and making movements almost impossible. Lieut. McCorquodale crossed the river back to R.H.Q. to report the position and was sent back with orders for the party across the river to withdraw. Lieut. Muir, organising the forward troops, was killed. He had done a fine job and the Regiment had lost a fine officer. The remnants of 11 and 12 Plns, withdrew across the river and managed to bring back all the wounded and equipment. Cpl. W.B. Wilson took charge of 11 Pln. after his officer and Sergeant became casualties. L/CpI. N. MacMullen of 12 Pln. in charge of the Lewis gun team, did a fine job, giving covering fire.

The Gloucesters attacked in the afternoon, but were driven hack with some fifty casualties into the wood, which was under heavy Turkish fire all day and where there were further casualties. After dark, the Scouts were relieved by the D.C.L.I.. who, with the Gloucesters, held the wood all next day before withdrawing.

The Scouts had 118 casualties. 28 were killed and 90 wounded, including Captain Craik, Lieut. A. Miller and Lieut. K. Murray. the latter being rescued and carried to cover by Sgt. D. Reid (Glenferness). The Gloucesters' M.O. was killed early the first day and all the wounded of both Regiments were dealt with magnificently by the Scouts' M.O., Captain A. Fraser Lee, often under fire. The total casualties in the Brigade were about 450 and no ground was gained at all. The Turks' positions at Tumbitsa were never taken until the whole line gave way in 1918.

Lieut. McCorquodale and Captain Fraser Lee were both awarded the M.C. and Corporals Wilson and McMullen the M.M. Privates P. MacGregor and D.H. Duncan were awarded the Greek Medal for bravery under fire, while acting as telephone operators to the Greek Battalion. The citation said that they behaved avec toute ardeur et grand sang froid en zone bombarde. They were the first British soldiers to win this award. Those killed at Tumbitsa and in other actions were buried in war graves nearby, which were visited by a later generation of Scouts in Macedonia 1945/46.

For the next five months, the Scouts held part of the line east of the Struma between Homodos and Jeminah. There was heavy rain, some snow and much mud during December and January. They sent out frequent recce and occasional fighting patrols, killed and captured a few Turks and had some casualties themselves. One successful long-distance patrol was carried out by Captain Alan Gilmour with seven picked men from each Squadron, riding mules. The Scouts regularly manned two night outposts near Ada, which were held during the day by a Troop of mounted Yeomanry. Horses were occasionally used for less military purposes too, for at about this time Lt. Colonel G. Railston, D.S.O., commanding the Scottish Horse, brought some foxhounds out to Macedonia and was later portrayed by Lionel Edwards hunting them in very rough country amidst shellfire!

By January 1917, Lt. Colonel Willie Macdonald, D.S.O., one of the original and greatest of Lovat Scouts, had been invalided home and was succeeded by Lt. Colonel Duncan Baillie, who then commanded the Scouts continuously until 1919. Major Hon. Alastair Fraser became Second-in-command. The Scouts' skill at spying and observation had greatly impressed the Higher Command: Major J.P. Grant, M.C., was ordered to set up a School of Observation for 16 Corps with a training team of 'glassmen' to instruct officers from all Regiments, and Lieut. Calder with six Scouts manned the Corps O.P. at Ahinos.

At the end of May 1917, the whole Corps was moved back west of the Struma onto higher ground, the object being to avoid the malarial valley during the mosquito season, but still to hold the line of the river with small outposts and bridgeheads. The Scouts, near Nigoslav, had ample space, found neglected fruit orchards, erected a shower bath and a threshing mill, and dug a garden where they planted 3000 cabbages. But they did not escape malaria. The move had been rather too late and also they were constantly sending patrols down to contact the enemy. There were sometimes sick parades of up to seventy a day, almost all with malaria and, during the summer, only about twenty men in the Battalion escaped infection. Many suffered from recurrences of it after the war.

Opposite the Scouts, the Bulgars had taken over from the Turks. They were sending strong patrols into the valley at dawn and withdrawing before dusk when the mosquitoes came out. At irregular intervals during the summer, Major Hon. Alastair Fraser led six fighting patrols, usually two Companies strong to ambush Bulgar patrols as they came down to the valley at dawn. These actions were all highly successful and about fifty Bulgars were killed or captured, apart from the wounded who were not picked up. The Regiment was constantly being congratulated by the Brigade and Divisional

Commanders and Major Fraser was awarded the D.S.O. On one of these ambushes they captured a set of Bulgar bagpipes, which were so dirty and disgusting that not one Scout would attempt to play them.

In October, when the mosquito season was over, 16 Corps moved forward again into the valley and on 24th the Scouts took part with 82 Bde. in a most successful raid on the enemy. It was perhaps the Scouts' greatest achievement in Macedonia, and known as the Salmah affair.

There were three Bulgar-held villages behind the enemy wire – from left to right, Salmah, Kispeki and Ada. The Brigade plan was to attack by night with two separate columns. One, led by the Scouts and followed by a half Battalion of Hampshires, was to get behind Salmah before dawn, and then destroy or capture all the enemy there. Meanwhile the Gloucesters and the rest of the Hampshires were to do likewise on the right at Ada. After that both columns were to descend upon the enemy in the centre village, Kispeki, before withdrawing. The Scouts were led by two officers, Lieutenants J.A. Cameron and W.G. Paterson, who had carefully reconnoitred the cross-country route and, after cutting the Bulgar wire, passed silently between two enemy posts without incident. By 5.30 a.m. they were safely behind Salmah. At 6.10 a.m. the zero hour, A and D Coys. of the Scouts attacked Salmah with complete surprise and success. Having captured it, A and D Coys. went on to attack Kispeki, their comrades taking over Salmah and forming a rearguard. Unfortunately, the second column (Gloucesters and Hampshires) had got into difficulties beyond Ada, lost their way and never reached Kispeki, so that a number of Bulgars escaped. The withdrawal took place successfully with C Coy. as rearguard, but the enemy had started shelling the villages before it began and there were casualties. Major McCorquodale wrote:

> The bag was good – 2 officers and 109 other prisoners, of which 106 were captured by the Scouts. About 70 dead Bulgars were left. 2 M.G.s and about 100 rifles were taken. Our casualties were 9 killed (4 by one shell) and 29 wounded, including Lieut. F. Thomson. Captain Alan Gilmour died of

wounds later. No officer was more popular or had done more for the Scouts both during the war and in Sutherland before it... The Gloucesters and Hampshires had about 50 casualties.

Immediate awards – the only ones given in the Brigade – were made to the following Scouts: D.S.O. to Lt. Colonel Baillie and Major Fraser-Tytler; M.C. to Lieutenants J.A. Cameron and W.G. Paterson; D.C.M. to L/Cpl. H. Campbell; M.M. to Sergeants W. Sutherland and B.C. Spry, and to Privates J.A. Gillies and A. Williamson.

The following message was received from the Officer Commanding 82 Bde.:

> My dear Baillie – I want to express to you my very high appreciation of the splendid work carried outlast night by your Battalion. In my opinion it was an exceptionally fine piece of work which reflects the greatest credit on you, your officers and all ranks. I have always been proud to have Lovat Scouts under my command and I am still prouder after last night's performance.
> Yours sincerely, C.M. Maynard.

In early January 1918, the Scouts moved with 82 Bde. to a part of the line between Lake Tahinos and the sea, which they held for the next five months. Of this period, Lt. Colonel Baillie wrote:

> We relieved the 2nd K.S.L.I. at "K.B.",a hill believed to be the site of Amphipolis, mentioned in the Bible. The K.S.L.l., mostly recruited from miners, had excavated excellent underground shelters and firing posts, which were of great assistance as "K.B." was overlooked by the enemy. The distance between our front lines and the Turks was small, and our night patrols were able to get quite close to enemy observers and had occasional encounters with enemy patrols.

Meanwhile, as will be seen in the next chapter, another branch of the Scouts, called 'Lovat Scouts (Sharpshooters)', had been formed and, with their natural skill at spying and sniping coupled with special training in map-reading and signalling, had provided extremely useful Observer Groups on the Western front. Sir Douglas Haig wanted the Scout Bn. in Macedonia to be brought to France to augment these Groups. It seems that General Milne was reluctant to let them go, but, after some delay, orders were finally received for the Battalion to move to France. On 21st June they started on their long journey from the Struma valley. They went by lorry and train to Itea on the Greek coast, crossed on the French transport, 'Amazone' to Taranto in southern Italy and, after a week's journey on a troop train, reached Serqueux in France. Another train took them to Etaples on the Pas de Calais coast and they camped at Merlimont.

By 23rd July 1918, 16 Lovat Scout officers and 438 O.R.s, many of them veterans of both Gallipoli and Macedonia, were at Merlimont, training in observation, advanced map-reading and signalling, before going to the Western front to join the Observer Groups of the Lovat Scouts (Sharpshooters).

CHAPTER X

FIRST WORLD WAR: LOVAT SCOUTS (SHARPSHOOTERS)
(November 1916 – November 1918)
AND DISBANDMENT (April 1919)

The Lovat Scouts (Sharpshooters) were formed by Lord Lovat in the autumn of 1916. They made a great name for themselves with their skilled Observer Groups on the Western front from then until the end of the war, and ultimately they included the whole Regiment.

Lord Lovat had been evacuated from Gallipoli in 1915. He was desperately ill, first in hospital in Malta and then in London, but finally recovered at Beaufort. He was forbidden to return to his Brigade in the Middle East, as another attack of dysentery might well have killed him. Instead, he was given command as a Major General of the Second Cyclists' Division with four Brigades in East Anglia for Home Defence.

He was, however, still convinced, as he had been since he first raised the Scouts in 1900, that a Highlander experienced in stalking and in using a telescope, the genuine 'glassman', was the finest material for sniping and observation in war and would be invaluable on the Western front. His views were readily accepted by the Higher Command, especially by Sir Douglas Haig, and when Major Ewen Grant, D.S.O., of Glenmoriston, was invalided home early in 1916, Lord Lovat enabled him and Lt. Colonel Willie Macdonald, D.S.O., to begin training, as snipers, some picked men from the 3rd Reserve Regt. of Scouts. Soon afterwards, on a visit to France, he realised that observation was of far greater importance than sniping and the training was changed accordingly. By October 1916 a force called 'Lovat Scouts (Sharpshooters)' had been formed. It was organised in Groups, each of one officer and 21 O.R.s, and all ranks were trained in every branch of observation both for Intelligence and for Artillery, first at St. Andrews and then at Beauly. By November 1916, the first few Groups were in France and Lord Lovat was there in charge of them with the rank of Colonel (Territorial Forces).

Recruits of ability and intelligence were obtained from both the Reserve Regiments and also from among Scouts who had been invalided home from the Middle East. Other Highland Regiments were combed for experienced ghillies and stalkers, who were permitted to transfer to this special force. Lord Lovat was also allowed to enlist suitable volunteers over military age and the following advertisement appeared in all Scottish papers:

>WANTED – 100 Stalkers and Glassmen
>Between the ages of 41 and 45,
>For stalking – Bosches!
>
>Apply Colonel Macdonald of Blarour, Spean Bridge

Some of the Scouts who came out to France were indeed as ripe in years as they were in stalking experience. They included, for example, 2nd Lieut. C.B. Macpherson of Balavil, 'a true expert with the telescope and map, who came out at the age of 62 with his splendidly trained Group of Lovat Scouts' *(Major H. Prichard)*.

Their Chief Instructor throughout was Major (later Lt. Colonel) Ewen Grant, D.S.O. His lectures, which were printed, were not only on spying and observation, but also on advanced map-reading, the use of the compass, protractor and alidade and on all calculations needed for pinpointing objects observed to an accurate map reference, so that other troops, particularly the Artillery, could exploit the information obtained. Signalling and reporting were also important parts of the training.

In February 1917, Lord Lovat again fell ill, but he made a quick recovery and was soon afterwards given a vitally important job as Director of Forestry in France with the object of making the British Army out there self-supporting in timber. It called for all his powers of leadership, tact and organising ability. With his old friend, Colonel Fred Allhusen as his Chief of Staff, he made a great success of it and at one time had an 'army' of nearly 30,000 men under his command. He got on well with the

French and was awarded both the French Legion of Honour and the Order of Agricultural Merit.

In May 1917, shortly after Lord Lovat's appointment to his new job, Lt. Colonel Donald Cameron of Lochiel took over command of the Lovat Scouts (Sharpshooters). An expert at spying and stalking, he originally served with the Scouts as a Lieutenant in South Africa. At the beginning of the Great War he personally raised three Battalions of Cameron Highlanders and commanded the 5th Battalion which was almost wiped out at the Battle of Loos. His eldest son, the present Lochiel, was to command the Scouts in Italy in the Second World War.

Major H. Hesketh Prichard, D.S.O., M.C. was the pioneer of Sniping and Observation in the British Army of the First World War. He founded the Army School of Observation and Scouting (S.O.S.), at which he trained men and officers from many units and many countries. In his book, 'Sniping in France', he claimed that the Lovat Scouts were the best material of all, and a few extracts from that book may give some idea of his reason for this belief:

> ...Although the first Battalion of Lovat Scouts went to Gallipoli and later to Salonika, only coming to their true work in France in 1918, since 1916 this splendid Regiment was represented in France by the Lovat Scouts Sharpshooters, of whom nine Groups, each about twenty strong and each under an officer, were attached to a certain Army Corps. Every man of these Groups was a picked stalker and glassman, and they were used largely for long-range observation... Keener men never lived, nor more dependable. I remember once a Zeppelin was reported as falling in the enemy back areas some six or seven thousand yards behind the German line. This report was made by divisional observers, but it was promptly denied by the Lovat Scouts, who stated gravely that there was a difference between a Zeppelin and a half deflated balloon!
>
> ..At this time their raison d'etre was not always apparent to

the units to which they were attached and some of them were put on to observe for enemy aeroplanes, in which their skill was rather thrown away. But this was largely put right by Lochiel, whose work was invaluable.

...But for long distance work and the higher art of observation, the Germans had nothing to touch our Lovat Scouts.

...The 1st Corps had a splendid system under which the Lovat Scouts attached to it worked. It possessed a grand Group under Lieut. Whamond, M.C., whose equal at his work I never saw in France. The system was this: Scouts from the Group were available on application to the Corps Intelligence Office. Thus, if a Battalion had been ordered to raid the enemy trenches, the Commanding Officer of that Battalion could indent for some Lovat Scouts to go and make a reconnaissance of the enemy wire for him. Or if a Divisional Commander thought the enemy activities increasing, he could obtain some special pairs of Scouts to watch the part of the line he considered threatened. The Groups, in fact, were at the service of all units in the Corps, and the result was that when they were applied for, their assistance was fully valued, and they always went to a definite job... In the Vimy Ridge battle did not Lieut. Whamond and Sgt. Fraser observe, and did not the guns they warned break up, a mighty counter-attack before ever it was launched?

...The final arrangement in the B.E.F., which never took effect, allotted Groups of Lovat Scouts to each Division. At each Army there was to be a Major in charge on the H.Q. Staff, and a Captain at Corps, but, as I have said, this system had hardly begun to operate when the war ended.

...It sounds a bold statement to make, but the Lovat Scouts never let one down. If they reported a thing, the thing was as they reported it. Certainly the men who follow the red deer of

Scotland proved themselves once again in this war to possess qualities which, let us hope, will never pass from the British race.

Major Hesketh Prichard relates a story, which he says was often told in the 1st Corps, of a gigantic Corporal in the Scouts who stood six feet five inches in height and was certainly one of the strongest men in the British Army. On a dark night, he was talking in Gaelic to his companion (for the Scouts worked in pairs) when his conversation was overheard by a Section of men of a new formation. Thinking that they were listening to German, the N.C.O. in charge of the Section demanded instant surrender. Instead, the whole Section was overpowered, disarmed and marched to H.Q. as prisoners!

The following are two extracts from an article in Blackwood's Magazine which appeared after the war:

> During the great German offensive of March 1918, Lovat Scouts manned several of their observation posts until the advancing enemy were only a few hundred yards away. Telephone wires were cut during the first half hour of the preliminary bombardment, and at times the intensity of the enemy barrage made it impossible for runners to carry back their reports. Carrier pigeons were used successfully so long as the supply lasted. When the last pigeon had been dispatched from one observation post a Lovat Scout Corporal stood in the open and, by semaphore signalling, transmitted his messages to a patrol which was supplied with pigeons. Those who watched him calmly spelling out his report in that inferno of bursting shells cannot to this day understand how he survived to wear his well-earned D.C.M.
>
> During operations in September 1918, it became urgently necessary to locate an enemy strong-point which was holding up the British advance. Owing to the slope of the ground, direct observation was impossible except from a ridge some

fifty yards in front of the furthest point reached by the infantry. A patrol of four Lovat Scouts was twice driven back by trench-mortar fire, but on a third attempt gained the ridge, located and reported the position of the strong-point, directed the artillery fire which destroyed it, and continued to observe from that ridge during the rest of the day. Every man in the petrol was awarded the M.M.

Although the Scouts had fought exceptionally well both as Dismounted Yeomanry at Gallipoli and as Infantry alongside regular Battalions in Macedonia, they had always shown, in both campaigns, their unique ability and success at spying, observation and patrolling. When these natural talents were developed by expert training, as they were for the Observer Groups in France, there can be little doubt that the Scouts were then being used in the most effective role possible. Of the men who formed the original first ten Groups of the Lovat Scouts (Sharpshooters), one out of every five was awarded a military decoration.

When the war ended, the Scouts remained in France, at Merlimont for several dreary months as demobilisation gradually took place. Lord Lovat visited them on 18th November 1918. With Colonel Duncan Baillie he initiated a system of interviewing each Scout to find out his intentions and wishes in civilian life, and to find jobs for those who had no prospects. By February 1919, demobilisation was almost over and, finally, on 17th April 1919, the unit was disbanded. Lt. Colonel Duncan Baillie, D.S.O., Lieut. J. Ross and nine O.R.s 'proceeded to Beauly in charge of Regimental Records'.

The names of 481 Lovat Scouts who lost their lives in the First World War are recorded in the Roll of Honour at The Scottish National War Memorial, Edinburgh Castle. Their supreme sacrifice has been well remembered in the Highlands. And what can be better said of all those who died for their country in that devastating conflict than the immortal words written by Lawrence Binyon?

They shall grow not old, as we that are left grow old;
Age shall not weary them, nor the years condemn.
At the going down of the sun and in the morning
We will remember them.

CHAPTER XI

BETWEEN THE WARS: TERRITORIAL ARMY TRAINING (1922 – 1939)

The Lovat Scouts were re-formed in 1922 as one Regiment with a strength of about 400. There were three Squadrons, each consisting of four Troops. A Sqn. was recruited from Inverness-shire, B Sqn. from the Islands (North and South Uist, Benbecula and Skye) and C Sqn. from Sutherland, Ross-shire and part of Caithness. They were a 'Scout Regiment' with a role of observation and reconnaissance and an establishment which included one pony to every four men and bicycles for the remainder.

They were fortunate in having their former Commanding Officer, Lt. Colonel Duncan Baillie, C.M.G., D.S.O., in charge of them again, with Major Hon. Ian Campbell, D.S.O., as Second-in-command. Their Adjutant was Captain The Earl of Leven and Melville, formerly of The Royal Scots Greys, three of whose brothers had been in the Scouts. He had been 'wounded and missing' in August 1914 when the B.E.F. of which his mounted Regiment was the advance guard, had first met the invading German army. The Germans had left him badly wounded in a Belgian village as they swept on, but, with the help of some very brave Belgians, he had made an exciting escape through enemy-occupied territory with his broken leg still not properly set. He had eventually got home in mid-December 1914. He was succeeded as Adjutant later in 1922 and became a Regimental officer in the Scouts commanding first C Sqn. and then the Regiment from 1931 to 1935.

The first camp was at Beaufort in 1922. Most of the men and almost all the officers and N.C.O.s had seen war-time service with the Scouts. They were happy to meet again and the occasion was described by one W.O. as being, to start with, 'more of a re-union than a camp', but they soon got down to serious training and it was useful to have plenty of veterans.

Between 1922 and 1939 there were sixteen camps. They were held at

Beaufort (1), Beauly (1), Ardgay (1), Strathpeffer (4), Culloden (2), Forres (1), Boat of Garten (1), Nairn (2), Kinloss (1), Tain (1) and Penicuik (1). The latter was in 1938, the only occasion when they camped outside the Highland area, to allow as many men as possible to visit the Glasgow Exhibition and Tattoo, at which the Pipe Band played. Camp lasted for a fortnight or slightly more and usually began in the second week of June. Although camp was hard work with as much training and as many schemes as possible, it was also great fun. As in the old days, many men brought their own ponies to camp and got a good allowance for them, During the rest of the year, parades and instruction were carried out in the Drill Halls situated throughout the recruiting areas. Each Squadron had a good Regular Sergeant as P.S.1., living within the large district for which he was responsible, and the Adjutant himself had great distances to travel by road and sea.

Between 1922 and 1939, the Scouts had the following Territorial Commanding Officers and Regular Adjutants:

COMMANDING OFFICERS	ADJUTANTS
Lt Col D.G. Baillie, C.M.G., D.S.O.;	Capt J. Dennistoun (Seaforths);
Lt Col Hon. l.M. Campbell, D.S.O;	Capt A.P. Gordon-Cumming, M.C. (Camerons);
Lt Col J.P. Grant of Rothiemurchus, M.C;	Capt A.E. Grant (Seaforths);
Lt Col Earl of Leven & Melville, K.T.;	Capt P.H. Grant (Scots Guards);
Lt Col Hon. I. Leslie Melville.	Capt P.C. Drabble (K.D.G.)

During the same period, the Squadron Leaders were:

A Squadron
Maj. J.P. Grant, M.C.;
Maj Hon. I. Leslie Melville;
Maj. A.L. Grant.

B Squadron
Maj. D. Coles; Maj. John Stirling, M.B.E.; Maj. Hon. J. Pease; Maj.Allan Macdonald

C Squadron
Maj. Earl of Leven and Melville, K.T.;
Maj K. McCorquodale, M.C.;
Maj. James Stirling;
Maj W.H. Whitbread.

* * * * * * *

On 18th February 1933, Simon Joseph, 16th Lord Lovat, K.L, K.C.M.G., K.C.V.O., G.B., D.S.O., to whom the Scouts owed their existence and who had always, as Colonel Commandant, taken the greatest personal interest in them, despite the enormous amount of other important work he did for the nation, died suddenly. His death was a tragic loss to the country, to the Highlands and to the Scouts. Sir Francis Lindley wrote of his funeral:

> The countryside which had rejoiced so often with him was stricken at his death and bewildered at the loss of a leader on whom they relied for everything. They gathered in their hundreds and, weeping openly and unashamed, followed the simple coffin, wrapped in the Union Jack and lying on a farm waggon drawn by one horse, the four miles to the church. Snow was lying on the ground, but fitful gleams of sun lit up the long procession; and, as, led by Pipe Major Ross, it wound its way up the valley, the strains of Lovat's Lament filled all the woods and hills with wailing. The road was lined by Lovat Scouts and Archbishop Macdonald, brother to that Colonel William Macdonald who had so often stood by Lovat's side in danger, and the Abbots of Fort Augustus and Ampleforth, where Lovat's sons and nephews were educated, were waiting at Eskadale. And with all the rites due to a son of the true Catholic Church, Lovat was laid to rest in the quiet graveyard of the chapel which his grandfather had built within hearing of the waters of the Beauly... The general verdict of those who knew him can best be summed up in the words of Scripture: "Know ye not that there is a Prince and a Great Man fallen this day In Israel?"

* * * * * * *

Between 1935 and 1936, the War Office worked out a new role and establishment of the Regiment. On the recommendations of Major General Brownrigg (G.O.C. 51 Div.) and Major General Blakiston-Houston (Inspector General of Cavalry) the Scouts were to be fully mounted and were to have a special role as mobile scouts and observers. As an economy, they had so far had only one pony to every four men, the other three riding bicycles, although the War Office intention had been that the whole Regiment should learn to ride, look after ponies and do mounted work. This had been found difficult and unsatisfactory. The Scouts' new role was not to be that of Cavalry but 'to provide mobile troops for duties of reconnaissance and protection, probably in a minor theatre of war..' Each Troop was to have three Sections of eight men, all of whom will definitely be fighting men..' Each Troop was to have one L.M.G. 'of the new type known as the Bren (when available), carried by one man on his horse with pack-horse for ammo'. There were to be Austin cars for wirelesses, despatch riders on motor-cycles and all transport mechanised. The Scouts might sometimes be used as three independent Squadrons and the establishment was drawn with that possibility in mind. The total strength was to be about 580 with seven officers per Squadron. The Scottish Horse, who had also been a 'Scout Regiment' when re-formed after the war, were to become Yeomanry.

Before these proposals were accepted, the opinions were sought of previous Commanding Officers, who approved of them unanimously. The Colonel Commandant, Colonel Willie Macdonald, D.S.O., wrote enthusiastically to the Commanding Officer in December 1935 in reply to a letter setting forth the War Office proposals:

> My Dear Ian,
>   Seldom has a letter given me more satisfaction than yours of 11th inst. It is absolutely on the lines it ought to be, and if I

can help in any way in the negotiations I will be more than willing to do so, as I think you have made an admirable arrangement for the future.

This role is absolutely what we did in South Africa, and there we were offered a light gun on a Dundonald galloping carriage, and as Adjutant I took it on though much against my superiors' wishes; but I was right and it proved invaluable on several occasions.....

I congratulate you on the success of your negotiations, and please call upon me whenever you want.

With hindsight of forty-five years and from the comfort of a nuclear age armchair, it may seem strange that the War Office gave the Scouts this role and establishment, in which they trained for the next four camps and for the first seven months of the war. It was, however, in the days when Britain had a large Empire, in much of which mounted reconnaissance was still practicable, and when she still had several regular mounted Cavalry Regiments – there were three even at the outbreak of war – and a large number of Mounted Yeomanry Regiments, part of whose role and training was to charge the enemy with swords! At least the Scouts were spared that complication: their ponies were only intended to give them mobility. Although the mounted Yeoman ries had been mechanised or made into gunners before 1941, it is interesting that the Germans had a number of fully-horsed Cavalry Divisions throughout the war and still had two of them, from one of which the Scouts got some good horses, when the armistice came in 1945.

In 1936, S.S.M., Jessan Mackay from Strathnaver, who had served in the Scouts for twenty-five years and done an immense amount of work for them in Sutherland, was awarded the M.B.E. In 1937, the Commanding Officer and three S.S.M.s rode, as members of a Scout Regiment, at the head of the cavalry in the Coronation procession, and a very smart foot party under Lieut Beresford-Peirse helped to line the streets. During the practice parade, their fixing bayonets was momentarily delayed when the right hand man's spurs, through some extraordinary mischance, became locked together. Otherwise all went perfectly.

In accordance with Major Kenny Macdonald's advice, the Scouts took their peace-time soldiering seriously. There was training in the Drill Halls, there were courses for junior officers and N.C.O.s and there were training conferences and weekend Tactical Exercises Without Troops for senior officers. By the end of each camp, the Regiment had reached a surprisingly high standard in such a short time. It was demanding work and seemed quite 'up-to-date'; in some of the schemes Major Bill Whitbread, piloting his own aircraft, even represented the Luftwaffe, to the ponies' occasional alarm. One remembers Sports days with perpetual piping and sunshine, when the highlights were the V.C. race and inter-Squadron tug-of-war and when old Scouts, some of them very old, came great distances to see the fun. The officers were kindly invited to the annual Sergeants Mess Concert and Ceilidh at which the best musical talent in the Regiment was mustered – an evening of inspired fiddle music, piping, Gaelic songs and the 'mouth music', wth many good tales thrown in. But it is the strange and comic incidents which, for over forty-years, old Scouts have remembered best.

Stories of those happy days are legion. Some have doubtless been embellished, others needed no embellishment and many are unprintable. Like Norse sagas, they are best handed down by word of mouth, but the following account, apocryphal or otherwise, may be of interest. It records a rare visit by the Inspector General of Cavalry, a famous officer who was known almost affectionately in the Army as 'Bloody Mike', owing to his ruthless insistence upon the highest standards and his fiercely sarcastic way of expressing displeasure:

'For the Inspector General's visit, a special scheme had been laid on so that he could see the Scouts in action. Major Allan Macdonald ('Waternish') commanding the Island Squadron, had secretly decided to send some of his less experienced men and ponies, whom he did not wish the General to see, into a small wood about half a mile from the camp, under command of a reliable Lieutenant with orders to remain hidden there until the scheme and the inspection were over.

The General arrived early with his Staff and, as he motored slowly towards the camp, his eagle eye lit upon the tail end of Waternish's secret column disappearing into the wood. On his arrival in Camp, the General was greeted by the Commanding Officer, Lord Leven, the Second-in-command (his brother), the Adjutant and the R.S.M. The scheme was explained to him with the map and he was asked where he would like to go first. "That wood!", said the General, pointing. They were puzzled and told him there was nothing to see in that particular wood: it was not within the scheme. He insisted that he had seen men going into it and so they rode there, mounted on the best ponies available, an impressive cavalcade consisting of the General, his A.D.C. and Staff Officer, a splendid N.C.O. Orderly with lance and pennant and the Scouts' R.H.Q. party. On entering the wood, they came at once upon a scene which, at first glance, was more pastoral than military. The Lieutenant, an impecunious Highlander who worked for a London bank, was sitting against a tree, reading the Financial Times; the men were sitting about in groups, chatting in Gaelic and having a smoke, while the ponies grazed happily with their saddles off. The Lieutenant scrambled to his feet and saluted, the men sat up and gazed at what were obviously "English Officers", R.H.Q. were dumbfounded and the General was clearly in his element. "And what are you supposed to be doing?" he asked icily. The Lieutenant, always calm in moments of crisis, replied slowly, "We are in reserve, Sir: I am resting the ponies."

The General changed the subject. For his next trick he required an assistant. He looked carefully at the men and chose Trooper M., whose appearance was marred by a squint but who was, in fact, a wise and able recruit, though not very fluent in English. "You!" he said, "I want you to mount, ride back to camp alone with a message for the Quartermaster, and then return to your Troop Leader here." He dictated the message slowly and Trooper M. repeated it with difficulty.

The pony was soon saddled but when it came to mounting there was trouble. Hopping, with one foot in the stirrup and his rifle held out at arm's length behind him, Trooper M. tried to mount, but each time he brought his rifle near the pony, it shrank away. This dance macabre continued until the Trooper, fed up with it, impulsively handed his rifle to the General with the gruff command, "Hold you this till I'm on". The Staff closed their eyes and prayed, but when they looked again, they witnessed a miracle. For there was their Inspector General, terror of Lancers and Hussars, scourge of Dragoons and Carabiniers, meekly obeying an odd-looking but fearless Hebridean crofter. Trooper M. mounted quickly, took the rifle back from the General and plunged it into the "bucket". Then, with a charming smile, a kind of salute and a "Thank you awful much!", he trotted away out of the wood, shouting encouragement to his mare. The General suddenly laughed and everyone else thankfully joined in.

The scheme proved a great success. The General was particularly pleased with the reconnaissance he saw being carried out and by the spying and reporting from two observation posts. As the day wore on, he became more and more affable and complimentary. He gave the Scouts a good report and in it wrote, "This Regiment is a very fine body of men, all keen to carry out their new role. They are already specialists at their own job. All that is required is that their training shoud be directed on the right lines to enable them to make best use of their specialised knowledge... Their ponies, though on the small side for normal cavalry work, are just what are needed for the role for which the unit is trained".

Waternish's secret "reserve" spent the rest of the day peacefully in the wood. The Quartermaster later confirmed that during his busy morning he had received the most extraordinary message from a Trooper in B Squadron...'

* * * * * * * *

The Scouts had a very successful camp at Strathpeffer in June 1939 with the Regiment well up to strength, thanks to a good recruiting drive soon after the Munich crisis. They left in high spirits, looking forward to camp in 1940, for in spite of Hitler's invasion of Czechoslovakia in March 1939, most people still did not believe there would be a Second World War. But events moved swiftly. On 24th August, the Russians signed their despicable Pact with Nazi Germany and the next day Britain proclaimed her assurance of military help to Poland if she should be attacked by 'a European Power'. In the early hours of 1st September, Germany invaded Poland. The Territorial Army was mobilised and, on 3rd September, Britain declared war on Germany.

CHAPTER XII

SECOND WORLD WAR: MOBILISATION
(1st – 5th September 1939)

The Lovat Scouts' recruiting area – from the Drumochter Pass to Cape Wrath and from the Black Isle to the Outer Hebrides – was greater than that of any other Territorial Unit. Indeed, Brigadier Lord Stratheden recalls that when he was about to go to Africa as a Staff Officer in the mid-thirties to plan the raising and organisation of the Kenya Regiment, he first consulted the Scouts' Adjutant, Captain Patrick Grant, and received from him much useful advice on the running of a volunteer Regiment spread over a very wide area. A detailed mobilisation plan was of course in readiness to ensure that the Scouts were concentrated as quickly and efficiently as possible. The order 'MOBILISE' was received at 19.05 hrs. on 1st September 1939. By the next day, twenty-seven of the thirty-one officers had already reported for duty and the plan had swung into action. R.H.Q. was at the Phipps Institute, Beauly, A Sqn. at Bruiach Farm (later moving to billets in Muir-of-Ord), B Sqn. at the Beaufort Home Farm (billeted later in Beauly), and C Sqn. at Fanellan Farm, two miles west of Beaufort (before moving to billets in Strathpeffer).

Some detachments of A Sqn. and some of the Ross-shire Troop of C Sqn. – from places as near as Fairburn, Scatwell and Strathconon – were able to ride in to mobilise, as their forebears had done in two previous wars. The great majority of A and C Sqns. however, were collected in their Troop areas, concentrated at the nearest railway station and then brought by train to Beauly. Many difficulties had to be overcome but mobilisation went well and with great enthusiasm. B Sqn. from the Islands, had special geographical problems, but excitement and zeal in the Hebrides were just as great as on the mainland. 2nd Lieut. Simon F. Macdonald, from Largie in the Mull of Kintyre, wrote an amusing account of his experiences with B Sqn. in the first few days of September 1939. Because his story represents what was perhaps the most difficult part of the Scouts' mobilisation and because such events of a bygone age are now of historical interest, it is summarised for posterity.

By the evening of 1st September, Simon had reported to his Squadron Leader, Major Allan Macdonald, at Portree. He was given over 100 calling-up notices for the three Scout Troops in North Uist, Benbecula and South Uist and eleven bags of spare saddlery. His first task was to arrange for delivery of the notices to men in North Uist, who were being taken to Kyle of Lochalsh separately by their Troop Leader, Sir Simon Campbell-Orde. Then he was to deliver notices to the men in the two Troops of Benbecula and South Uist, collect all of them and their ponies together, take them to Lochboisdale pier and there embark them on a MacBrayne ship for Kyle of Lochalsh.

From Portree he was driven in a truck, which had dangerously loose steering to the small fishing village of Vaternish on the northwest coast of Skye. He was rowed out to a fishing boat which had been mysteriously arranged to take him across the Minch. At about midnight. as he sat in the stern on his bags of saddlery, "feeling rather like Prince Charles Edward", there came a shrill whistling from the shore. It was Sgt. Major Charles Halmshaw, B Squadron's English Cavalry P.S.I., who, remembering about the loose steering, had kindly come to see if Simon was all right. They shouted "Good Luck" and "Goodnight" to each other and the fishing boat, in pitch darkness and with no lights because of the black-out, set out for Lochmaddy. North Uist. Meanwhile, Halmshaw on his way back to Portree, was run into from behind by the truck.

In the small hours of 2nd September, Simon roused the hotel keeper in Lochmaddy – the bootboy was manning a Bren gun for defence of the pier – and borrowed a large car for himself and his saddlery. He handed over all the North Uist

106

notices to the Post Office, happened to meet Sir Simon who was also motoring through the night mustering the men of North Uist. and had many adventures as well as much hospitality and refreshment before dawn, when the tide was high enough for him to cross the ford by boat onto Benbecula. There he walked some distance to hire a lorry for his saddlery, delivered his notices. found the Benbecula Troop Sergeant, who was doing magnificently in blue patrol uniform (though he had temporarily mislaid his bonnet and was wearing a tweed cap,) and encouraged the road surveyor, whose job it was to requisition and purchase the necessary ponies. Crossing the next ford onto South Uist, where he was at last among the men of his own Troop, he made plans for the next two days with his Troop Sergeant. Archie McPhee. Simon wrote:

Next day we started to march to war; leaving from Benbecula we were to ride to Stoneypath school, where we were to stay the night and then on to Lochboisdale next day to get the boat for Kyle. It sounded simple but difficulties appeared from the start. The Troop assembly area was the back yard of the pub in Greogary – not a very good choice – and I spent what seemed like hours exhorting, pleading and eventually driving troopers out of the ever-open bar. One or two recalcitrant horse owners came and swore at me in Gaelic, but I quickly passed them on to the policeman. Then the minister had a word with each man and finally we got separated from the weeping female attachments, and rode forth bravely into the waters of the ford, followed by the less romantic figures of those who had no horses, in an exceedingly ancient lorry. The scene was not unmoving, the pipes playing, relatives waving from the shore and the horses splashing through the water".

They had a long, tiring ride with more farewells en route to Stoneypath where the people very kindly gave his seventy men a splendid evening meal. Farrier Sgt. McRury, a Scout of the 1914/18 war, cheered them repeatedly with his account of a telegram he had received that morning. It had read: TO FARRIER SGT. McRURY, LOVAT SCOUTS, BENBECULA. HOW MUCH TO REMAIN NEUTRAL? SIGNED HITLER. He had wired back immediately: NOTHING DOING. WE'LL FIGHT IT OUT SAME AS LAST TIME! SIGNED McRURY.

They tied the ponies to a substantial fence and settled down in the schoolhouse for the night in front of a cheerful fire. At 9.30 p.m. there was a terrific thunderstorm with sheets of rain. The ponies were frantic, many of them breaking loose and the Scouts "spent a couple of soggy hours catching them and re-wing them by the light of the lightning". When the storm passed, there was inky blackness. Simon sent the men into the schoolhouse to get dry and ordered a parade at dawn, when all the ponies were found to be present and correct except one which was dead. He remembered to rescue the surcingle, blanket and headcollar and gave the police instructions to dispose of the body which cost the Government 30/-. This episode ended in a Court of Enquiry, "To Enquire into the Cause of Death of a Horse Struck by Lightning"

A damp but cheerful band rode from Stoneypath to Lochboisdale. While Simon signed receipts for some eighty ponies on the pier, his warriors lost no time in making for the hotel for a last farewell dram, until the proprietor himself, Findlay Mackenzie, suggested that the bar should be closed till the ship sailed. Thanks to the storm, it was several hours late in arriving but eventually they and the ponies were all aboard and, with the pipes playing, they waved goodbye to Lochboisdale. It was already dark when their train from Kyle arrived at Beauly on 5th September. Operation Hebrides was over and the boys of Uist and Benbecula were now to become full-time soldiers in a very fine Squadron. For most of them it was to be six long years before they were civilians once more.

The Scouts were a family Regiment in more ways than one. In 1939 there were approximately 100, including eleven officers, who were sons of former Scouts. Each Squadron teemed with brothers, uncles, nephews and cousins. In A Sqn. for example there were four sons of Sgt. Duncan Fraser, head stalker at Braulen, and in the Ross-shire Troop there were four Ross brothers, all in the same Section. About a score of officers were to have served in the Scouts who were related by blood or by marriage to Colonel Archie Stirling, whose mother had been a Leslie Melville, and who had married Lord Lovat's sister. In some Troops a great many of the local men were of the same clan and surname, and so were called by their Christian names, nicknames or numbers. In another sense too the Scouts were like a family, in that there were lasting ties of friendship and understanding among them, regardless of where they came from.

In 1939 there was, for the first and only time, a feminine detachment within the Regiment. They were Highland members of the A.T.S. and were allocated to the Scouts – one for each Squadron and several for R.H.Q. – to help with the mountains of paper work with which every Regiment was burdened in the early part of the war. They wore their ordinary khaki uniform but with Hunting Fraser tartan skirts, were extremely efficient, took a great pride in the Regiment and were sadly missed when it went over-seas without them.

On the outbreak of war the Scouts were commanded by Lt. Colonel Hon. Ian Leslie Melville, who had joined the Regiment on the death of his eldest brother in 1912. He was forty-five and would normally have been ending his four years of command that year. Major Kenneth McCorquodale M.C., a year younger, was Second-in-command, and the Adjutant was Captain Peter Drabble of the 1st K.D.G., who would soon be returning to his own Regiment. The other Scout officers were as follows:

Maj. A.L. Grant (O.C. A Sqn)
Maj. W.H. Whitbread (O.C. C Sqn)
Maj. A.R. Macdonald (O.C. B Sqn)
Capt. C.l. Fraser (O.C. HQSqn)
Capt. D.H. Cameron (2 i/c B Sqn)
Capt. Lord Lovat (2 i/c A Sqn)
Capt. H. Beresford-Peirse (2 i/c C Sqn)
Lt J.W. Brooke (Transport)
Lt. R.E. Fleming (Asst: Adjt)
Lt. A.W. Haig (Signals)
Lt. A.I. Mackenzie (3 Tp C Sqn)
Lt. J.P. Grant (Gas Offr.)
Lt. Sir S. Campbell-Orde (2 Tp B Sqn)
Lt. Sir R. Levinge (1 Tp C Sqn)
Lt. J.H.G. Wyld (1 Tp B Sqn)
Lt. L. Balfour-Paul (2 Tp A Sqn)

Lt. Hon. F.A.H. Wills (3 Tp B Sqn)
Lt. Hon. H.C.P.J. Fraser (2 Tp C Sqn)
2/Lt M.I. Leslie Melville (4 Tp C Sqn)
2/Lt A.J. Macdonald (3 Tp A Sqn)
2/Lt S.F. Macdonald (4 Tp B Sqn)
2/Lt A.H. Fraser (4 Tp A Sqn)
2/Lt J.L. Macdonald (1 Tp B Sqn)
2/Lt A.I. Grant (1 Tp A Sqn)
2/Lt C.K. Murray (3 Tp C Sqn)

Lt. H. Thorpe (Quartermaster)

Lt. Col. W. Lornie M.C. (V.O.)
Capt. Rev R.A. Finlayson (Padre)
Capt. A.M. Campbell (M.O.)
Lt C.W. Gordon (Asst: M.O.)

The Scouts were in 9 Div., which was commanded by Major General G.M. Lindsay and was part of Scottish Command, the G.O.C. being General Sir Charles Grant. As a mounted unit, they also came within the authority of the Director General of Cavalry.

During the mobilisation there was one touching story of a C Sqn. Scout who, on being given his calling-up notice by an officer who had recruited him a year before said that he would prefer, after all, to join the Merchant Navy. When told that he must mobilise and apply for transfer later, he replied, "But don't you remember, Sir? I only joined up to frighten Hitler".

CHAPTER XIII

SECOND WORLD WAR: MOUNTED TRAINING IN THE NORTH
(September 1939 – April 1940)

The role which the Regiment had been given for war was that of 'Mounted Scouts, to provide mobile troops for reconnaissance and protection..'. There was great enthusiasm and the object of every Scout, from Commanding Officer to junior subaltern and from R.S.M. to the most newly-joined recruit, was to get the Regiment ready for active service in that role as quickly as possible.

Training was carried out in riding and horse-management, drill both mounted and on foot, weapon-training and shooting, spying and observation, map-reading and compass work, signalling and reporting, night training, anti-gas precautions and a host of other subjects. First at Troop and then at Squadron level, countless schemes were carried out to practise such essential operations as attack, defence, recce, patrols of all kinds, outposts, advance, rear-and-flank guards, night exercises, rounding up parachutists and long mounted marches. Originality in training included many exciting manoeuvres, one Squadron even attempting with partial success to swim its ponies and men across the River Beauly when it was nearly in spate. When C Sqn. rode through Dingwall wearing gas masks and tin helmets and looking to the inhabitants like something from 'Things to Come', it brought a letter from an animal lover to the Ross-shire Journal, asking rather sensibly why there were no masks for ponies.

By November, A Sqn. was at Muir-of-Ord, B Sqn. at Beauly and C Sqn. at Strathpeffer. This dispersal made training as a Regiment more difficult, but it had advantages too, for each Squadron gained an individual character of its own, Squadron Leaders had greater opportunities for initiative and there was keen inter-Squadron rivalry and competition. Officers and N.C.O.s were sent on as many relevant courses as possible and returned to train instructors for the Regiment. Anti-gas training was considered of the utmost importance, as that vile form of warfare might well have been used. Fortunately they had a brilliant and determined Gas Officer in Lieut. J.P. (Iain) Grant, who insisted on the highest standard of knowledge and gas discipline among all ranks. Woe betide anyone from Squadron Leader downwards found groping about in his gas mask, having forgotten to apply 'anti-dim' to his goggles! Physical training soon started for everyone when a Sgt. Instructor Sarjent came from Scottish Command to train a cadre of Scouts as instructors in these vital, if sometimes unpopular exercises. Excuses for escaping P.T. were at a premium and were crowned by one of the pipers who was said to have pleaded "cannot do the T.B.: the thumb of my foot, she is swollen".

There were many difficulties that had to be faced and overcome during that winter's training. There were inspections and visits by every conceivable army branch, miles of 'red tape' from a newly-strengthened khaki bureaucracy, administrative orders and counter-orders, shortages of rations and equipment and twice a complete stoppage of fodder for the ponies, which was with difficulty made good by local purchase. Most serious of all, and a dreadful reminder of the nation's unreadiness for war in 1939, was the shortage of small arms practice ammunition. With great effort, the Regiment only just got enough for everyone to fire his rifle on the Dingwall ranges and for Bren gun Sections to fire a few rounds with the Bren. However, there was much practice and keenly competitive shooting with army rifles tubed for .22 ammunition, of which there was an unlimited supply. No rounds were available at all for anti-tank rifles.

Infectious diseases, to which many of the men had not previously been exposed, were a great nuisance. German measles came first, then ordinary measles and, finally, mumps. By bad luck one bought-in pony in A Sqn. developed strangles, the highly-infectious equine disease which had been such a curse in both previous wars. There were twenty-four cases by the end of October and another twenty in B Sqn., but the fact that all except one soon recovered and that it did not spread more was a credit to the Scouts and to their efficient Veterinary Officer, Lt. Colonel Lornie M.C.

That winter was to become very cold after the New Year with five weeks of snow and frosts of up to twenty-seven degrees, but in mid-

November the trouble was continuous heavy rain, which made some of the horse lines knee-deep in mud and extremely unpleasant. A new and very successful way of managing the ponies was first tried at Strathpeffer. They were put into four fields, one for each Troop, and allowed to run loose, being fed alongside the fences with nose-bags morning and midday and with hay at night; and the back drive of Kinellan House nearby was converted into a hard standing for grooming and saddling. This method ruled out the misery of winter horse lines, gave extra time for training and greatly benefited the ponies. It was adopted by the other Squadrons too and was admired by visitors from the Cavalry Division, but was perhaps more suitable for the Scouts' hardy ponies than for cavalry horses.

The 'horse-management' was good and the ponies were kept very fit, but unfortunately three of them had to be put down as a result of an accident when, at early Stables on a dark and wild November morning with driving rain, some of the A Sqn. ponies took fright and broke loose. They were being led at exercise on the road while the lines were cleaned near Muir-of-Ord. They dashed forward, knocking down men and other ponies, became terrified and bolted. Several men, including Tpr. Tommy Macrae, who was badly injured, showed great courage and hung on for a considerable distance but, eventually, many of the ponies got away. They galloped two and a half miles to Beauly and some of them a mile or two further. Sgt. N. McLean (North Uist), Orderly Sergeant in Beauly, heard them galloping through and with a few men rushed out and stopped many of them. Lieutenants Andrew Haig and Iain Grant billeted at Teawig Farm, went out immediately with signallers in the wireless cars, located where the various other ponies were and wirelessed back, so that they could quickly be caught. Because some shooting had been heard near Beauly that early morning – a particularly good duck fight – the wildest civilian rumours spread to the effect that German parachutists had landed and that the Lovat Scouts were galloping back to previously prepared positions!

Recreation during those early months included football and shinty and much badminton in local halls. There were many concerts and ceilidhs. Sketches by a gifted group of H.Q. Sqn. actors and an officers' country dance band of eight mouth-organists, led and disciplined by Lieut. Iain Grant, caused amusement, and the great Harry Lauder sang his heart out to a packed audience in Dingwall, exhorting them to 'postcard' their mothers and to 'Keep Right On To The End Of The Road'.

Thanks to the kindness of many deer forest owners, who were also most generous in supplying the Scouts with extra telescopes for the war, there was plenty of stalking available. On one Saturday before the season ended seventeen stags were killed by Scouts. Later there was some hind stalking too, at which valuable experience was gained by some who had not been brought up to it. There was rough shooting and wild-fowling for some and, very occasionally, a little poaching for others. ('Och! What's a pheasant?', grumbled one Scout, caught red-handed on a Sunday afternoon, 'It's Germans I'll be shooting soon!') Six couple of the Oxford Drag Hounds, no longer needed there in war-time and described on their arrival at Beauly Station as 'pointers', were hunted once or twice a week over stiff obstacles which most of the ponies jumped well. Lieut. Hugh Fraser, riding as boldly as his father ever did, broke his collar bone, the Assistant Vet was stunned when he jumped a dyke and landed in a midden near Muir-of-Ord, and Tpr. Jimmy Clark, who fed the hounds, got badly bitten. Otherwise the drag-hunting was a success and the Scouts' horsemanship probably benefited.

Of the Scouts' riding ability a General commented before 1914, 'The men are rather hard on their horses, but the horses are very hard on the men; so they probably come out all square'. Since then however methods of instruction had improved and good, workmanlike equitation was ensured in a Regiment where a number of officers had done courses at Weedon or were used to hunting and point-to-pointing (Major Bill Whitbread had twice completed the Grand National course) and where there were several good ex-cavalry N.C.O.s. Some Scouts showed great ability and were natural horsemen. Two Urquhart brothers could do equitation at the canter, standing on their ponies' quarters and one Scout even taught himself to ride facing backwards – an ideal rearguardl

Soon there were some changes in the Regiment. At the first medical inspection fifteen Scouts were discharged as unfit and twenty-one were Grade C (Home Service only). Among these was Captain C.l. Fraser of Reelig, who was fortunately allowed to rejoin the Regiment in the Faroes as a Major, commanded H.Q. Squadron most successfully both there and in Scotland and in the post-war years became Colonel Commandant. A few Scouts, such as Major Macdonald (Waternish) were recalled to reserved occupations and some had sadly to leave on account of ill-health, including Major A.L. (Sandy) Grant, Lieut. Alick Mackenzie, who was Acting Adjutant and R.S.M. Audis. Captain Lord Lovat was given command of A Sqn., Captain Donald Cameron of B Sqn. and both were promoted to Major. When Captain Peter Drabble returned to his Regiment, Sir Simon Campbell-Orde became Adjutant and the new R.S.M. was J. Morgan of the l6th/Sth Lancers. There were various changes of officers between Squadrons and, with vacancies occuring, promotion came for some N.C.O.s and men. Several new officers were welcomed into the Scouts, including Second Lieutenants Joe Lawrence, Richard Rayer, Peter Scott and Pat Wootton; but the first to arrive was R.C. (Dick) Allhusen, the eldest son of Colonel Fred Allhusen D.S.O. who had played such a prominent part with the Scouts of old. Dick was posted to A. Sqn. where, until he was officially gazetted, he acted as a Troop Leader, smartly dressed in civilian clothes. The Regiment obtained permission to recruit in the Highlands and a letter from the Commanding Officer in the northern papers, asking particularly for stalkers and ghillies brought a good response. Some senior officers were sent to recruit from various centres of population in Scotland and some excellent men joined, especially from Glasgow, bringing the Regiment up to strength once more.

The Scouts' behaviour was again something on which they prided themselves. Shortly before they left the North, a newspaper article, headed 'A Pat on the Back for the Lovat Scouts', stated that a better behaved body of soldiers would be impossible to find. Local inhabitants were quoted as saying, 'Their behaviour is exemplary. When off-duty they are very quiet and act as good soldiers should...' . Excellent discipline was achieved as in the past tradition of the Scouts, by respect and mutual understanding between officers, N.C.O.s and men, rather than by harsher or more Prussian forms of militarism, which would have been both unnecessary and counter-productive. Naturally, a few Scouts were put on charges from time to time for minor offences and one of Major Ken McCorquodale's favourite stories was of a man who was said to have used insulting and obscene language in Gaelic to an N.C.O. It was a serious case and the accused was sent by his Squadron Leader to be dealt with by the Commanding Officer. The Colonel, who did not understand Gaelic, asked the N.C.O. if the language had really been very bad. 'It was terrible!', replied the N.C.O. "Indeed, Sir as YOU would say, 'Regular dog's piss!'"

In B Sqn. where more Gaelic was spoken than English, many N.C.O.s instructed most efficiently in their native tongue, interspersed occasionally with untranslatable words such as Bren gun, respirator or rifle bucket. This use of two languages caused endless good stories. On one night exercise with B Sqn. – a night so dark that their P.S.I. fell into the River Beauly and narrowly escaped drowning – the Colonel and the Assistant Adjutant were with one of the Troops, moving stealthily forward through the Beaufort Woods. The column stopped and waited for some time in silence. A man appeared out of the darkness, had a long, whispered conversation in Gaelic with an N.C.O., and then went away. "What did he say?", asked the Colonel. "Oh", came the reply, "he just passed the remark in Gaelic, 'ARE YOU THERE?'"

There is no doubt that by the early spring, each Squadron had reached a high standard of training in their role as mounted scouts. In addition to all the detailed training, countless schemes and numerous inter-Squadron battles, A Sqn. had done a long three day exercise, billeting at Dochgarroch and Drumnadrochit, B Sqn. had done the same in reverse order, and C Sqn. had done a similar trek into Easter Ross, travelling over sixty miles in the three days with schemes in addition each day and without any man or pony being any the worse. As a tribute to the ponies, it should be mentioned that most of them were only about 14 1/2 hands high and that some, when their riders were fully equipped, were carrying over 18 stone. The Regiment was ready to fight as mounted scouts, but where was the War Office thinking of using it?

First there was Finland. At the end of November 1939, the Russians attacked Finland for various strategic reasons, not least their fear of their own 'friends' at that time, the Germans. Unexpectedly and to the delight of the free world, including America, the Finns fought back under Marshall Mannerheim with astonishing success, although greatly outnumbered. There was a plan to send a Brigade of British troops to help the Finns and the Scouts were earmarked for it. They were ordered to train immediately for mobile operations with pack ponies in a sparsely populated country with very few roads and small scale maps'. They were naturally disappointed when this project was called off, but perhaps not many Scouts would have returned from fighting the Russians against overwhelming odds and in the coldest Scandinavian winter for 100 years. The Finns, after heroic resistance and little outside help, were forced to accede to Russian demands in March 1940.

Next, every effort was made during December 1939 and January 1940 to get the Regiment to France as front-line observers, the job which some of the Scouts had done so well from 1916 to 1918. The Commanding Officer wrote to the War Office on this subject and to Lt. General Sir W. Brownrigg at G.H.Q. in France. In reply, General Brownrigg wrote on 10th December:

> My dear Leslie Melville
>
> Thanks for yours of 1st, which has given me furiously to think, I have discussed the matter with the C.-in-C. out here and undoubtedly, trained observers will be very useful if and when we get into serious battle...
>
> We shall, in the near future, have three Corps out here and it seems to me possible that Lovat Scouts might be sent out

with a Squadron attached to each Corps for observation purposes, provided they will not mind being split up into very small packets...

you are at perfect liberty to use this letter in any way you like. I am not sure if it is very helpful but it is the best I can do at the moment.

The Commanding Officer replied by return, saying that they were already organised on a three Squadron basis and that 'provided we can retain our identity and make the best possible use of our men as observers, we have no objection to being split up into smaller parties. In 1918, we had a Troop attached to each Corps and were perfectly happy...'.

General Brownrigg answered on 24th December:

I have had a long talk with the C.-in-C. on this subject. He accepts my view..., that you will be most valuable as observers in certain types of country, but unfortunately the flat country of Flanders can hardly be considered the ideal terrain for the employment of the Lovat Scouts. On the other hand, Palestine would present great possibilities ... Please write again if you think I can be of any help...

In an immediate reply, the Commanding Officer wrote:

Many thanks for your letter. I am surprised that the C.-in-C. should think that useful observation would not be possible in the flat Flanders country, as it was in that very country that our men did good work in the last war... But we are equally ready to go to Palestine, or any other likely theatre of war, in any role which will give scope for our observers.

I still have no reply from the War Office either as to what sort of role they contemplate for us, or as to whether I may go and discuss the question with them.

The War Office eventually turned down the request for the Scouts to go to France as observers or to Palestine, but a warning order came to be ready to move in mid-February to Lincolnshire to become part of the mounted Cavalry Division. This was better news, as it was still thought that that Division might be going to the Middle East.

The destination was then changed and the move south postponed, but on 21st March 1940 the advance party set out for Sutton-on-Trent in Nottinghamshire to join the Cavalry Division. On 5th April, the Regiment left in three separate trains from Strathpeffer, Muir-of-Ord and Beauly. The War Diary records, 'In every case the civilian populations turned out in large numbers to see the departure and to pay tribute to the good behaviour of the men while in the area'.

CHAPTER XIV

ENGLAND: MOUNTED AND DISMOUNTED
(6th April – 21st May 1940)

R.H.Q., H.Q. Sqn. and two Troops of C Sqn. were billeted at Sutton-on-Trent. A, B and the remainder of C Sqn. were at Tuxford, Kelham and Ossington respectively with various Troops in the villages of East Warkham, Little Carlton, Carlton-on-Trent and North Muskham. Most of the billets were good but the War Diary mentions that the whole area was left by previous units in a disgraceful state. One Squadron found this an advantage. A regular Cavalry Regiment had left its yards so full of horse-dung that the ponies could hardly get in. It was promptly sold to market gardeners (to the great benefit of the Sqn. fund) and, while it was being removed, three complete army saddles and other useful equipment were disinterred! The Squadrons settled down quickly to training in this unknown countryside and the local inhabitants proved to be very friendly.

Soon after the Scouts' arrival, the Leicestershire Yeomanry held a point-to-point meeting with two races open to all Regiments of the Mounted Cavalry Division. Although most of these Regiments were about to be mechanised or made into Gunners, they still had some good horses. It was assumed at first that the Scouts would not be taking part as the course was quite unsuitable for Highland ponies. However, the Scouts had three or four possible point-to-pointers which had belonged to officers before the war. Captain Richard Fleming entered his charger (formerly well-known with the Heythrop) and startled the cavalry officers by winning the heavyweight race by about ten lengths. In the keenly contested lightweight race, it was good to see the Scottish Horse bonnets of Robin Lyle and Bobbie Campbell-Preston among the cavalry caps. The Commanding Officer's two chargers were entered. One, a grey cob, ridden by his son-in-law, Lieut. Tony Wills, made the early running and the other, a thoroughbred mare, ridden by his son, finished second, beaten half a length by a Northumberland Hussar with a Leicestershire Yeoman third.

Lady Lovat rode beautifully in the Ladies' Race and A Sqn. provided a magnificently turned out Troop of Scouts riding the best of dun garrons, which paraded on the course and was greatly admired.

The point-to-point was a success, but it also proved to be one of their last days as a mounted unit, for on 18th April they received orders to hand over all the ponies to Remounts and, four days later, loaded them onto cattle trucks for Melton Mowbray. The Regiment asked, as it had done in 1915, that when the ponies were no longer required for army service, they should be returned to the Highlands for sale, and this was agreed to. They were used mainly as pack ponies, although 'Dalesman' recalls that he much enjoyed hunting on an ex-Scout pony one winter of the war in the Welsh hills. Any Scouts who were sad to lose the ponies at that time certainly changed their minds when they saw pack-mules shelled in Italy later. The Regiment had done its best – and so had the ponies – in the role they had been given, but were keen now to tackle the next job, whatever it might be. The general feeling was perhaps well expressed by one Scout who said, 'We don't mind the ponies going, but we hate losing our spurs!'

The war, so far known as 'phoney', changed drastically with Hitler's sudden invasion of Denmark and Norway on 9th April 1940, an event for which both the Allies and the neutral Norwegians were totally unprepared. As the Scouts were to be somewhat involved with Scandinavian affairs for the next two years, a brief account of the German invasion of Norway is relevant.

Since the outbreak of war, Sweden had been exporting large quantities of iron ore to Germany via the port of Narvik in northern Norway. German ships carried this vital war material down the 'Norwegian Leads', the neutral sea passage within three miles of the Norwegian coast, which Britain had so far been reluctant to mine. British policy gradually hardened, but too late, and on the very day that British ships set out to mine that passage, German troops were already on their way north, many of them in the empty cargo ships. They were landed, including some well-trained 'Jaeger' ski troops, at the widely separated cities of Oslo, Kristiansand, Bergen, Trondheim and Narvik. In one of the most dramatic episodes of the war, President Carl Hambro of the Norwegian Storting (Parliament) arranged a last-minute escape at night from Oslo, just before the Germans landed, of the King and the Royal Family as well as 95% of the Storting. They went north and finally became Norway's exiled Government in Britain. To the fury of the Germans and of the traitor Quisling, the President also got Norway's entire gold reserve of £15 million out of Oslo, which eventually reached Britain intact.

The Germans had overwhelming early advantages: they had achieved surprise and had captured immediately most of Norway's important towns. They used paratroops to seize airfields and, as Denmark had fallen without resistance, the Luftwaffe could operate from Danish aerodromes as well. A small and extremely gallant Norwegian Army, though comparatively ill-armed and unprepared, showed great heroism; but – in the absence of a massive and well-supported invasion of Norway by the Allies – it had little hope of ultimate success or of providing more than delaying tactics and guerilla operations from the mountains. The short campaign that followed has been summarised thus in a history of the war:

> By 16th April virtually all of southern Norway had fallen under German control. After several changes in plans, Allied troops with the task of taking Trondheim had landed at Andalsnes and Namsos. This attempt was unsuccessful and by 3rd May the Allies had been pushed out of central Norway. More fighting took place in the Narvik area to the north, and the town was taken by the Allies. In early June, however, because of the critical situation in France, the Allied forces were evacuated, The King and his Government accompanied the withdrawing forces to England, where a Government in exile was established. General Ruge decided to stay in Norway with his men. Ruge negotiated an armistice and the campaign ended.

Both the Royal Navy and the R.A.F. gave the Norwegians all possible aid, but it was not easy for Britain to help with effective land forces at such short notice and for snow warfare. General Carton de Wiart was sent immediately with an Infantry Brigade, well trained for ordinary fighting, to land at Namsos on 13th April with orders to take Trondheim (about 100 miles south) 'in a flank attack'. Helpless in deep snow and without sufficient support, they got into grave difficulties and his badly mauled force had to be evacuated from Namsos on 3rd May.

If the British Army's early exploits in Norway had met with any success it seems probable that they would have been considerably reinforced (unless the Germans' Western front breakthrough on 10th May had caused a change of policy) and also that the Scouts would have been among many units to go there, after first being completely re-equipped with all necessary weapons and given a crash course of some weeks in a new Infantry role. The following summary from official records and from the Commanding Officer's diary, written daily in detail and confirmed in outline by the 1.O. of that time, throws light on some top secret conferences between 12th and 15th April:

TUES: 9th APRIL
    The Germans invaded Denmark and Norway.

FRI: 12th APRIL
    C.O. attended Conference at War Office with Lt. Colonel Holland, R.E. (M.l.R. Branch, dealing with "preparations for guerilla warfare" and two Staff Officers, one of whom was Capt. Peter Fleming, the well-known author explorer and brother of Capt. Richard Fleming. Object: to work out plans for forming a COMPOSITE BN. of 1000/1,200 men and about 60 officers, to include the whole of the 5th Bn. Scots Guards (a volunteer Bn. which had recently done some ski training at Chamonix) and about 400 Scouts. The Composite Bn. to be divided into ten or twelve mixed Companies, each

to land in Norway at a different place. 'Base' to be trawlers, working in and out of various fjords or wherever Norwegian Army H.Q. was on mainland. First contingent to depart in a week and others to follow daily thereafter. No supply arrangements but transport to be by sledges. Arctic equipment and clothing – originally for Finland – probably to be issued on embarkation. Other details to be worked out. Conference continued till 19.30 hours and adjourned till next day.

SAT: 13th APRIL

Conference continued with Maj. Gen. Beaumont-Nesbit (D.M.I.) in charge, it had been discovered overnight that the 5th Bn. Scots Guards were already disbanded. The Composite Bn. idea was therefore out and the General proposed a new plan by which the Scouts, as an INDEPENDENT UNIT, should be landed at a point fairly far north of Trondheim with the task of making their own way across country and cutting a railway said to be "about 150 miles inland". Captain P. Fleming left the conference to go that day to Norway as an A.D.C. to Gen. Carton de Wiart. A military adviser on Arctic conditions and two Norwegians explained that the west coast country is very steep with passes up to 3000 ft. and hills up to about 6000 ft. Snow would be deep and (depending on the year) lying nearly down to sea level. The Scouts' 2 i/c joined the Conference ("His accurate knowledge of Regimental strength and detail was particularly useful") and planning continued till late.

SUN: 14th APRIL

Planning continued all day working out details and establishment to include about fifty skiers and the necessary attached troops, etc. for the Independent Unit to carry out the tasks proposed.

MON: 15th APRIL

C.O. Instructed to attend a hastily summoned NEW CONFERENCE 'to investigate and recommend as to the composition, organisation, equipment etc. of an Expeditionary Force to Norway'. The President was Brig. A. Nye (later Vice-C.l.G.S.). Eighteen officers present, ranking from Major to Brigadier, representing all branches. e.g. recruiting, organisation, training, intelligence, operations, weapons etc.

Owing to nature of enterprise, the force to consist as far as possible of volunteers... No previously prepared scheme for Norwegian campaign existed but general policy was to form special companies and send them out as and when necessary with special arms and equipment to be decided on... As to how soon such Companies and the Scouts in particular would be ready to go, the C.O. stated that the Scouts were fit and trained to fight immediately in their present role, gave details of the training so far done and sought the opinion of experts present as to how long the necessary special training for the tasks proposed would take. No official view was given but unofficial estimates varied from one month to three months. The C.O. said the Scouts would be ready in the shortest time officially thought practicable. No definite plans made, but the C.Q. was told he would receive further orders shortly and meanwhile to continue training as at present.

On 17th April, secret orders were received for the Regiment to go overseas at an early date. ('Where to? What role? With ponies or without?') On 18th orders came to hand the ponies over on 22nd April. ('We go abroad dismounted. Where to?'). On 24th April Secret Information received by Commanding Officer as to their destination and task, i.e. to take over the Faroe Islands (in North Atlantic, between Norway and Iceland).

Although all the Conferences were TOP SECRET, there was a slight leak in security, but only on the first conference about the idea of a composite Battalion, with the disbanded 5th Scots Guards. An officer wrote:

> We were delighted to hear rumours that we might soon be fighting in Norway. None of us then, except a handful of First War veterans, had seen a shot fired in anger, but we were all longing to shoot Germans. It was therefore not surprising that we were disappointed when the rumours did not turn into reality. What is perhaps more surprising especially to those of us who were properly trained later as ski-mountaineers and knew the helplessness of even the toughest troops when first put on skis, is that the second and more definite scheme was seriously planned by senior officers for two days, until superseded by Brigadier Nye's Conference. After our subsequent Canadian training in snow-warfare, the mission proposed for us on 13th April would have been an ideal and challenging task for a patrol of our best long-distance skiers: without any such training one might as well have tried to reach the moon in a helicopter!

There was a comic sequel to the Top Security about their destination. Even the Intelligence Officer was not informed, but he recalls that the newly-arrived Dental Officer, Lieut. Young, happened to mention that in his joining instructions, which carried no security rating, a mysterious sentence read, 'There is a civilian dentist in Thorshavn'. H.Q. Sqn. officers quickly discovered from a World Gazetteer that Thorshavn was capital of the Faroe Islands; but they kept the dentist's secret.

From 22nd April when the ponies departed, all Squadrons concentrated on long route marches and 'tactical dismounted training'. There were infantry T.E.W.T.s for officers and N.C.O.s and A Sqn. had a very good night scheme against their old friends, the Scottish Horse. By 1st May the Regiment was under orders to move at forty-eight hours' notice and an advance party under Lieutenant S.F. Macdonald left with their transport for Greenock. When Germany invaded Holland and Belgium on 10th May, the move was postponed and they stood-to at dawn and dusk. Finally they left Nottinghamshire by train on 21st May, arrived at Glasgow docks next day and immediately embarked on the 'Ulster Prince'.

The Scouts' strength on board was 452 O.R.s and 28 officers, including Major R. Greig M.C. (M.O.) and 2 Padres, Captain Rev. R. Robertson (Presbyterian) and Captain Rev. C. Duffy (Roman Catholic). There were four attached officers, including Captain J. Findlay, the Paymaster, whose currency was to be the new war-time Kroner notes. Two officers and 101 O.R.s remained behind, consisting of those too young for overseas service and those unfit with injuries, measles or mumps. These Scouts, together with further recruits of officers and men, formed the basis of the Home Details. During the next few months they carried out rigorous training at Redford under command of Captain J.P. Grant, who in April was still recovering from a bad riding accident, and of Major Bache Hay (formerly 19th Hussars), and they provided excellent reinforcements for the Regiment later that year.

The 'Ulster Prince' sailed on 23rd May. With only one naval signaller on board, the Scouts took over all signalling duties from the bridge to the escort of two destroyers, which they did well. Tragically these two ships, the 'Ardent' and the 'Acastra', were both sunk by U-boats a fortnight later. A few survivors, suffering from exposure, were brought into Thorshavn by Norwegian trawlers.

In a very thick mist, which lasted all day, the 'Ulster Prince', dropped anchor off Thorshavn early on 25th May. The N.O.l.C. (Capt Crowther R.N.) and the officer commanding a Company of Royal Marines, who were temporarily in Thorshavn with one outlying detachment, came aboard. Plans were made, orders issued and the ship came in. The Commanding Officer went ashore to meet the British Consul and the Danish Governor and an unloading party under Captain Brooke started work immediately. A long entry in the War Diary for that day ended, 'As the ship came alongside the pier with the pipers playing, crowds of people including hundreds of children, came down from the town to look on and remained there all day'.

CHAPTER XV

THE FAROE ISLANDS
(May 1940 – June 1942)

The Faroes were of strategic importance in the North Atlantic. Some twenty small islands, of which seventeen are inhabited, rise from the vast space of ocean about halfway between Norway and Iceland and over 200 miles north-northwest of the Shetlands. Most of them have sheer cliffs of dark basalt rock, frequently battered by Atlantic storms, and above these rocky shores are steep green hills, often shrouded in mist, many of them over 2000 feet high and one, Slatteratindur, almost 3000 feet. The two largest islands are Stromo, thirty miles long by six miles wide, and Ostero twenty-two miles long and also narrow: they lie side by side in the centre of the northern group. Thirty-five miles south is Sudero, one of the larger islands. Although they are so far north, the Faroes are affected by the Gulf Stream and the climate is not arctic, but very wet, stormy and subject to constant change. Winter brings heavy snow but it seldom stays for more than a few weeks and intense frost is rare. In mid-summer the sun hardly seems to set; in mid-winter there are over eighteen hours of darkness. An entry in the War Diary on 16th December 1941 read: 'It is now completely dark till 10.00 hrs and dark again by 16.00 hrs. There have been a series of magnificent sunrises, which last until 11.00 hrs'.

In 1940, the total population was about 30,000 Faroese. a distinct and wholly Scandinavian people of Viking origin with their own ancient Norse language, used more commonly than Danish, their own national culture, history, and flag, but administered as an Amt or County of Denmark. The earliest known inhabitants were 'hermits of Celtic origin' in the 8th century A.D. There are early Celtic remains at Kirkebo and the name of the islands, Foroyar, is thought by some to come from the Gaelic for 'far away islands'. The hermits are said to have left because of the ravages of sea pirates and for a century the islands were occupied only by sheep, which had gone wild. The Vikings came next; and there is evidence of a Ting or parliament at Thorshavn – ancestor of the present Lagting – in the 10th century. In 1035 the Faroes were taken over by Norway, which became united with Denmark. In 1814, when Norway was ceded to Sweden, the islands remained under the Danish crown. In the latter half of the 19th century, the export of fine wool from their unique multi-coloured sheep, which was known as 'Faroe gold', helped to relieve the poverty of the islanders, who led an incredibly tough and precarious existence. In the 1880s, when for about twenty years the great whales – blue, hump-back and sperm – were caught in large numbers off the Faroes, there was employment. From 1900 onwards, there was fishing off Greenland and Iceland. Latterly, Denmark invested large sums of money in schools, hospitals, a few roads and some businesses, such as fish drying and small boat building with imported timber, for there are virtually no trees in the Faroes. Very little was spent on plumbing!

Mr. Kenneth Williamson, the distinguished naturalist and author, served in the Faroes from 1941 onwards. After the war he wrote an enchanting book called 'The Atlantic Islands – A Study of the Faroe Life and Scene', which was published by Collins in 1948. The book is a masterpiece of its kind and describes with great charm and scientific knowledge the islands, the people and their folk-lore, their fishing and their superbly designed small boats, their ferocious hunting of grind or caaing whales and the extraordinary variety of birds known in the Faroes. The oyster-catcher or tjaldur is their national emblem – when the tjaldur arrives back about the 12th March it is a day of joy – and nearly 2,000 gannets nest on Myggenes; but Mr Williamson lists over 200 species of bird known there from the tiny Faroe wren to the snowy-owl, the Iceland and Greenland falcons, the Arctic skua, the honey-buzzard and the white-tailed eagle. In his introduction to the book, Mr. Eric Linklater, who visited the Scouts in the Faroes in 1941, wrote:

> But what, you may ask, is the importance of the Faroes, that small and stormy archipelago, that justifies the expenditure of

THE FAROE ISLANDS
SCALE
0 5 10 MILES
FUGLÖ
VIDERÖ
KUNÖ
BORDÖ
SVINÖ
KLAKSVIG
EJDE
2746 FT
SLATTARTINDUR
FUGLEFJORD
GOTE
SAKSEN
KVALVIG
VESTMANHAVN
MYGGENÆS
BÖ
VAAGÖ
SÖRVAAG
MIDVAAG
STROMÖ
STRENDER
TOFTE
KALBAK
THORSHAVN
NOLSÖ
N
VELBASTAD
HESTÖ
KIRKEBÖ
SKOPEN
SANDÖ
SAND
SKAALEVIG
HUSEVIG
SKUÖ
STE DIMON
LE DIMON
SANDVIG
KVALBÖ
TVERAA
FAMIEN
SUDERÖ
VAAG
LOPRA
SUMBÖ
L. BALFOUR PAUL.

so much labour, love and talent on description of them? It is worth recalling, to begin with, that during the war the Faroe men brought to us most of the fish that we ate; the Iceland trawlers objected to being sunk by U-boats, but the Faroe men accepted the risks of bombs and torpedoes, and maintained a traffic of great value to us at heavy loss to themselves. That quality, moreover, of being undeterred by hardship and danger is typical of life in the islands: without it the people would not survive. Their agriculture is a miracle of hard, imaginative and continuous toil. Their seafaring is adept and bold as the voyaging of their Viking ancestors: in small wooden boats, bought from Britain sixty years ago, they regularly fish the far-off grounds of Greenland, and the navigation of their own island firths, that boil with the Atlantic tide, requires the liveliest strength and skill. They furnish their tables with seabirds caught on dizzy ledges of precipitous cliffs – taller by far than any in these islands that overhang the loud Atlantic. And in such circumstances of hardship and hard weather, their houses and social life are lively and clean and gay. Their housekeeping is characterised by a passion for cleanliness and a warm regard for conviviality. They like bright colours and are tireless dancers. They are imaginative cooks and highly !iterate. They are immensely patriotic, but no xenophobes. They have retained a primitive virtue, and added to it the graces of a native culture; they appear to have escaped the vulgarity and inertia of civilisation.

Their material assets are meagre, except for the vast, uncountable host of guillemots, kittiwakes and puffins that cover the cliffs in summer; and the fish that swim in the surrounding seas. The land they can till is only a flounce of green below the knees of their cloud-capped mountains, and a warm day is a day to remember. They cannot grow corn or wine, and their mineral wealth is small. But there are thirty thousand people in the islands, and every school is packed with hearty, fair-haired children. Native hardihood and energy have conquered a hostile environment, and given to it geniality and grace. Surely such a triumph of vitality and the spirit deserves its historian?

There were two towns: Thorshavn, the capital and main port with a population of about 3000, and Klaksvig to the northeast on the island of Bordo with 2000 inhabitants. There were also four large villages with populations of about 1000 each: Fuglefjord to the north of Thorshavn, Vestmanhavn to the west and, in the island of Sudero, Tveraa and Vaag. The rest of the Faroese dwelt in more than eighty small coastal communities, usually with a pier or landing place and sometimes with a few steep fields and hill grazing for sheep.

Ten miles north north-west of Thorshavn lay the long, narrow fjord of Skaalefjord, one of the finest deep water anchorages in the world. Until late in the war, there was no landing place for aircraft.

With only 450 soldiers, it was clearly impossible to occupy effectively the whole of the islands, but it was vital to control and defend both Thorshavn and Skaalefjord. Two Squadrons (A Sqn. commanded by Major Beresford-Peirse and B Sqn. commanded by Major Cameron), remained at Thorshavn, billeted in schools and other large buildings, until enough Nissen huts had been erected. They built defences, and one Squadron provided guards and fatigues, while the other trained and also carried out reconnaissance patrols to all the isolated communities and fjords in Stromo and the neighbouring islands. Meanwhile, C Sqn. under Major Whitbread, guarded Skaalefjord with, at first, three Troops at Tofte and one Troop on the west side of the fjord at Strendur. They too built defences, provided guards on each side of the fjord, reconnoitred every corner of Ostero with patrols, trained and made a rifle range. After a month, they were relieved at Skaalefjord by A Sqn. and returned to Thorshavn. From then on, each outlying Squadron was brought back to Thorshavn after a month or two as a matter of policy, in order to share the duties fairly and also to prevent anyone from going 'native' or even mad in isolated places!

The Scouts' duty in the event of an attack was to defend Thorshavn and Skaalefjord to the last man and last round, always hoping for ultimate help from the Royal Navy. In the case of a landing anywhere else, the plan was to send one Squadron by the quickest means possible to repel it. Reconnaissance of every fjord and remote place was important, but one of the most vital tasks was that of securing goodwill. The Faroese were foreign people: very few of them could speak any English at all, and Denmark, their parent nation with 3000 Faroese over there at the time, was occupied by Germany. The Scouts needed and gained the respect and friendly co-operation of the inhabitants – a proud people whose islands had never before (except very occasionally at Thorshavn) seen soldiers of any kind since the Vikings. There had been a German whaling station at Lopra in Sudero; and in 1938 a large party of the Hitler Youth Movement had toured most of the islands. An Intelligence Survey of the whole population was carried out under the Security Officer, Lieut. Hugh Fraser, and a number of aliens were deported.

Twenty-four-hour guard duties, especially in Thorshavn (four hours on and four hours off) and particularly in bad winter storms with driving rain and snow, were no fun, except occasionally when there was the opportunity of firing a Bren at a German plane; but even guard duty could produce amusing incidents. A Scout from Glasgow, posted to B Sqn. recalls one dark night when he was occupying a sand-bagged position on the Thorshavn pier. His neighbour, thirty yards away, normally spoke in Gaelic. There had been complaints from the Navy that some of the B Sqn. sentries were not 'challenging' strangers properly and were sometimes frightening them with shouts in Gaelic. The R.S.M. had therefore been ordered to give the Squadron a refresher course in the correct ritual of 'challenging', beginning with, 'Halt!... Who goes there?' The Glaswegian sentry heard the martial tread of the Orderly Officer, who that night was the R.S.M. himself, approaching with the Orderly Sergeant on his rounds. He heard a Hebridean voice cry 'Halt!' The

R.S.M. and the Sgt. stamped to attention. There was a long pause; and then the voice said, 'Who am I?' The R.S.M.'s reply could have been heard far out to sea, 'I don't know, but I'll damned soon find out!'

Patrols, constantly being sent out from one Squadron or another, were useful not only for the information they brought back, but also for training. They frequently meant long marches and steep climbs, sometimes with short sea voyages as well. As there were few roads, the best routes over the hills were often marked by ancient cairns. Sometimes, in thick mist, they marched by compass. There were many memorable patrols. Once Major Brooke led a Troop of C Sqn. in full marching order and steel helmets, on a very long march to Ejde and, on the last lap, climbed the steep, shingle face of Slatteratindur. Heroically reaching the summit, they came upon a terrified party of ladies, who had walked up there by the easier route from Ejde and were quietly enjoying a summer picnic! There was a wild winter's night when Sir Simon Campbell-Orde marched with the men of North Uist eighteen miles along the coast in such bad conditions that, on their return, they were issued with a rum ration. 'Well, boys, what shall we drink to?' asked Sir Simon, raising his tin mug. Silence... and then a voice said, 'Here's to we never have to do it again!'

Lieut. John Macdonald, who describes his memory of the Faroes as being of 'continual patrolling over high hills', recalls an occasion when the Colonel allegedly accused B Sqn. of not being fit enough. This resulted in Major Richard Fleming immediately ordering John Macdonald's Skye Troop to march from Thorshavn to Vestmanhavn and back in one day. The latter wrote, 'We covered a distance of 43 miles in 13 hours, carrying full equipment and crossing 3 hills each way in mist and rain. Nobody fell out and it was thought quite a feat. Sgt. MacLean carried 4 rifles the last three miles. There were no more accusations of being unfit!' Later, another officer ran and climbed from Vestmanhavn to Thorshavn in under four hours for a bet. Today there is a good motor road all the way, leading to the airport on Vaago.

They were determined to remain – even isolated in mid-Atlantic – a splendid and fit Regiment with high morale, and the fact that they did so says much for every Scout, and for the discipline that stems from enthusiastic leadership, comradeship, a sense of humour and pride in themselves, their Squadron and their individual Troops. But hard work was an important part of the recipe too. A tremendous amount of training was done in every possible subject – drill, fieldcraft and sniping, observation and spying, map-reading, signalling, infantry tactics and the use of explosives; but above all, weapon-training, shooting and field-firing. They built a good range behind Thorshavn for shooting at all distances up to 1000 yards; they had unlimited ammunition for rifles, Brens, Tommy guns and anti-tank rifles, and Lieutenant Pat Wootton trained a highly efficient Mortar Troop. Many N.C.O.s and a few officers went home on courses. They had two first class weapon training officers in Lieutenants Richard Rayer and Sandy Fraser; the Hon. F.A.H. Wills got a 'Distinction' on a Fieldcraft Course and Sgt. A. Ross proved a brilliant teacher of aircraft recognition. Several N.C.O.s came back from Drill Courses at the Guard's Depot wtih the coveted award of 'Excellent'. With all the panache and vocabulary they had learned there, they saw to it that their victims reached the same high standard. A Drill Sergeant from Uist was heard to shout at his squad, 100 yards away, 'And who do you think you are? Aldershot Town Band?' Even the attached officers and both Padres volunteered for drill in a special squad. Once, when they were learning to change step while marking time at the slow march, the Second-in-command who was watching, had to leave, feigning an attack of hay fever.

For recreation, they used every facility available and thought up every kind of sport possible in such steep, difficult surroundings. The hard grit football pitch in Thorshavn was in frequent use, and an inter-Squadron match there was as important as any game between Celtic and Rangers. There was some boxing, squash in a court built at Thorshavn, hill-running and even some archery. There was good, unspoilt trout fishing in several lochs and sea trout too at Sando and Saksen. They shot some puffins and guillemots for the pot ('bird shotting', the Faroese call it) as well as a few hares and some snipe. Both years they took part in the St. Olaf celebrations (28th/29th July), when the islanders meet at Thorshavn for sports, racing with Norwegian and Icelandic ponies and a two mile sea rowing race in ten oar Viking boats, for which the Regiment always had a crew and were not disgraced. Major Jock Brooke, a daring seaman who had been in the Fastnet Rock ocean race, had a speed boat with which, whenever possible, he helped the Faroe men with their 'grindebo' whale hunts and sped from island to island. As the Faroese dance frequently, and Mr. Restorff in Thorshavn had an excellent band, the girls soon learned to dance reels and Scottish country dances, even if it took the Scouts slightly longer to master the Faroe Dance. Hospitality and friendship are what they will always remember of the Faroe people.

After six months, there were changes in the Regiment, and from then on there was always one whole Squadron in Sudero. They received reinforcements from Home Details at Redford and volunteers from the Scottish Horse and five Highland Infantry Regiments, which brought the strength up to 757 O.R.s. Several new officers were also welcomed, including Second Lieutenants, Brian Wootton, Bob Ogg, Willie Gammell, Michael Dix-Hamilton, Geoffrey Forrest and Bill Budge. D Sqn. was formed, consisting of twenty-three O.R.s from each of the three old Squadrons, the remainder coming from the new draft. It was commanded by Major Whitbread and, later, when he was appointed Second-in-command of the 51st Recce Bn.,by Major Andrew Haig. A Sqn. was commanded by Major Cameron, B Sqn. by Major Fleming and C Sqn. by Major Brooke. Lt. Colonel Hon. I. Leslie Melville, who had joined in 1912, retired and was succeeded by Lt. Colonel Adam Fairrie, a regular Cameron Highlander, who had received the M.B.E. for his command on the Andaman Islands before the war, was a keen yachtsman and had boxed for the army. Captain R.C. Allhusen remained as Adjutant, a most exacting task in the Faroes, and Major Ken McCorquodale, M.C., continued as Second-in-command for another eighteen months before retiring. No Regiment can ever have had a finer or more devoted Second-in-command, an unselfish and modest hero of the First War, a friend of every man and officer in the Scouts and the embodiment of cheerful good humour. (His son, Alastair, was to become literally 'the fastest white man in the world', when he ran for Britain in the Olympic Games of 1948.)

The death of Lieut. Angus Grant was a tragic loss to his many friends. The younger son of a former Commanding Officer, Lt. Colonel J.P. Grant of Rothiemurchus, Angus was one of the finest and most popular Troop Leaders in the Regiment. Another tragedy was the sinking of the 'Arandora Star', when six Lovat Scouts were drowned, including Tpr. Colquhoun from Benbecula, whose body was washed ashore on Barra.

* * * * * * * *

Out at sea, the Battle of the Atlantic was being waged. Survivors, often in desperate plight and suffering from exposure and frostbite, were sometimes brought into Thorshavn, where the Scouts' medical officers and the civilian hospital did everything possible for them. They included British sailors, Finns, Norwegians and, on one occasion, twenty-two Greeks who had been in open boats for six days of February weather after their ship, the 'Isakhi', was torpedoed. Often small boats arrived, having escaped from Norway: one had on board the Norwegian Foreign Minister, General Fleischer, and an Admiral Diesen; another brought Colonel Dahl, a fine officer, who had commanded the Norwegian forces north of Narvik. One party of escaping Norwegian soldiers happened to include Lieutenant Tingulstad, who, much later, was to become a Scout officer; another party consisted of a Lieutenant and four men of the Sherwood Foresters who had got a boat south of Andalsnes.

The Scouts were in constant touch with the Royal Navy. When strange ships were escorted into Thorshavn, they provided boarding and search parties, sometimes an awkward job. When four Italian destroyers, flying the Swedish flag, sailed into Skaalefjord, C Sqn. stood to their Bren Guns, and, after the Navy had removed all the Italian sailors and two of the destroyers, the Squadron provided guards aboard the other two ships.

'AGRICULTURE' By L. BALFOUR-PAUL

From one Norwegian refugee ship, the Regiment obtained an Orlikon gun and 3,000 rounds of ammunition. Best of all, they were given by some Norwegians a small ship called the 'Jalso' which was renamed 'Poppy'. She did inestimable work carrying supplies and troops between islands, crewed by a Faroe skipper called Jakob Blabjorg and two Lovat Scouts who were former fishermen. The Scouts' closest friends in the Navy were the fearless and unorthodox R.N.V.R. sailors of the Northern Patrol, whose armed trawlers were usually called after English football teams, such as the 'Stoke City' and the 'Preston North End'. Several of their skippers were legendary figures, including one superb Australian, who even kept a cow on board when they were at sea.

Ships were only too often sunk by torpedoes, mines and bombs, but on

7th December 1941, it was a gigantic gale alone which sank their supply ship, the 'Sauternes', carrying 1000 tons of cargo, including 3,000 gallons of petrol, R.A.S.C. stores, much mail and all their Christmas supplies. She sank with all hands, including several soldiers returning from the U.K., off Svino. The huge sea made it impossible – even for Faroe men – to launch small boats: a few survivors, clinging to rafts, were glimpsed momentarily as they crashed against the cliffs.

Compared with such disasters, sea-sickness is just a joke. Nevertheless, to some Scouts who were 'bad sailors' it was one of the most distasteful features of their Faroe sojourn; worse even than the scarcity of leave through shortage of shipping, or the infrequency of mails – sometimes they took over a month to arrive. Sickness seemed only to accentuate the dreary diet of tinned 'McConnachie' stew and bully beef with whale liver was an occasional delicacy *('AGRICULTURE' by L. Balfour-Paul)* and ascorbic tablets to replace fresh vegetables and fruit, although twice the people of South Africa kindly sent gifts of 100 cases of oranges. Many Scouts experienced voyages in small boats ('Fart-botur') in winter storms, soaked, shivering and sick to the point of exhaustion and even despair! 'Smiril', the largest local boat, built for the summer run from Copenhagen, moved a whole Squadron at a time. Early one winter's morning, in a worsening storm, she set out from Thorshavn in darkness, to lessen the risk of air attack, taking C Sqn. to Sudero. By the time she arrived there, her small armed trawler escort had disappeared in the storm and struggled back to Thorshavn, and every Scout aboard had been desperately sick, except three ex-fishermen and Major Brooke, who was smoking a black cigar and directing operations from the bridge. The assistant M.O. was unconscious and had to be carried ashore.

Captain John Wyld, an Oxford Half-Blue but a deplorable sailor, recalls a long journey he once made in a small boat and a heavy sea, to inspect an A Sqn. detachment at Gjov, where the landing place was a rocky ledge, onto which one had to jump at the right moment. He was dreadfully sick the whole way. Having spent twenty minutes at Gjov, lying, almost unconscious, on the Sergeant's bed, he had to jump back onto the boat, as the tide was ebbing. His homeward trip was indescribable. Once an elderly Faroe skipper, member of a strict religious sect, was seen by his horrified passengers to let go of the helm altogether, as his ship negotiated a narrow channel in a terrific sea: he knelt down and prayed at the top of his voice. It worked.

The Navy laid many mines at sea, especially in the autumn of 1940, leaving channels for shipping; but they often broke loose after a few gales. Some caused disasters at sea and others exploded on the shore. This caused alarm and broken windows in villages nearby, and there were two instances of children being killed. Whenever mines were reported near the coast, patrols went to sink them with rifle, Bren or anti-tank rifle fire and it was good target practice in a rough sea. By February 1941, the Regiment had already sunk forty-eight of these mines and received formal congratulations from the Navy, but more continued to appear. While sinking a mine in a remote part of Sudero, one officer found a bottle with a message in it. It had been thrown into the Atlantic by an Edinburgh lady the day the war broke out, when she was halfway home on the Transylvania later sunk by a U-boat. A remarkably good job was done by Lieut. John Macdonald, Sgt. Iain MacLean and some other Skyemen, when a Sudero village was threatened by a mine drifting rapidly towards the shore. Repeated bursts from a Bren failed to sink it, so they hired a small boat and tried with rifle fire from 100 yards, again unsuccessfully, They then rowed up to the infernal machine, carefully tied ropes round it and towed it away out to sea, keeping watch over it till the Navy came and sank it with a large gun. John Macdonald's comment was, 'I never understood why it would not sink: we could see the bullets bouncing of it..' The record bag was probably scored by Lieut. Peter Scott and three men of H.Q. Sqn. who sank four mines from a boat in one expedition.

* * * * * * * *

In the first few months, only five German aircraft were seen but from early in 1941 they began to carry out attacks frequently and indiscriminately not only on installations in the Faroes and Naval ships but also on small fishing boats, villages and lighthouses. Only very rarely were British planes sighted. In all, the War Diaries record 164 occasions when German planes were seen and, in most cases, bombs were dropped or random targets machine-gunned. They were engaged, whenever possible, by the Scouts with Bren guns and tracer ammunition – a most satisfactory form of shooting – and, although the planes were undoubtedly hit on many occasions, the Scouts achieved only one definite 'kill'.

It happened on 21st February 1941, when two Heinkels attacked Thorshavn. One dropped bombs, narrowly missing the oil tanks, but received heavy Bren gun fire from A and D Sqns. and from a Vickers on the armed 'Lincoln City'. Obviously hit, it flew away towards Norway, dropping its remaining bombs in the sea. The other Heinkel then dropped a bomb beside the 'Lincoln City', which sank in about one minute, and flew on to Skaalefjord where it dropped three bombs close to a Finnish ship. But B Sqn. at Tofte and Strendur, were waiting and they punished it with every Bren they had. (The pilot later said in German, 'The flack was frightful!') The Heinkel flew low over the hill towards Gotefiord. Imagine the surprise of Tpr. J. Mackenzie (South Uist), who was at Gote on a routine motor-cycle patrol, when a Heinkel crashed into the fjord and sank, four Germans rowing ashore in a rubber dinghy. He captured and disarmed them, telephoned to Squadron H.Q. at Tofte and after giving the Germans coffee in a Faroe house, locked them up in the school. Major Fleming soon arrived to pick up B Sqn's well-deserved 'bag'. Lieut. John Macdonald and some of his Skye Troop came over from Fuglefiord to drag with a grappling iron, hooked the Heinkel and marked it with a buoy. He then persuaded the skipper of an Aberdeen trawler to try and pull it up, which they achieved with the aid of a Klaksvig diver. The skipper took the plane in triumph to Aberdeen, after the instruments had been removed for Intelligence and, thanks to B Sqn. a propeller thereafter adorned the Scouts' Officers' mess.

Attacks were usually by single German aircraft. Of those recorded in the War Diaries, many failed and were driven off, some caused damage and loss of life and some produced extraordinarily narrow escapes. In March 1941, a large Finnish ship, the 'Carolina', just outside Thorshavn, was hit by two bombs and set on fire, the final bomb, landing immediately west of the town and making a crater 40 feet wide and 20 feet deep. The crew were rescued, but she burned for a week, despite all efforts at fire-fighting in which the Scouts took part. She was bombed twice more in the next ten days and the Grimsby trawler, the 'Chandos', near her, was machine-gunned; her skipper and several of the crew were killed. A Junker 88 crashed into a 2,000 foothill on Bordo in a very inaccessible place and a party of Scouts under Sir Richard Levinge had to use ropes to get to the scene. Four sacks of human remains were collected for burial. In mid-September 1941 the 'Morning Star of Tofte', was bombed and sunk with all hands, bringing the total number of Faroese ships lost at that time to twenty-four and Faroe fishermen killed or drowned to sixty.

The 17th September 1941 was a lucky day for some of the Scouts. The 'Loch Garry' was taking forty-three Scouts on leave, including Sir Simon Campbell-Orde and Captain Thorpe. Also on board were twenty-two survivors from a bombed ship and five civilians. As she left Thorshavn, a German plane appeared from the south flying at 50 feet, which the 'Loch Garry' mistook for an R.A.F. escort plane. It dropped four bombs, two of which hit the ship, one bouncing off her into the sea and one lodging in a portside cabin. Neither exploded. Every gun on board opened up, the plane machine-gunned the ship, causing one casualty, and then flew off. The 'Loch Garry' hastened back to harbour, lop-sided with everyone on the starboard side, and disembarkation took place in record time. She then put to sea with a skeleton crew of volunteers and the unfortunate Bomb Disposal Sergeant, R.E. He managed to defuse the bomb and they hoisted it overboard. German bombs that did not explode were sometimes said to be the work of saboteurs in their factories. If so in this case, forty-three Scouts and twenty-five others probably owed their lives to some unknown Pole or Jew. The 'Loch Garry', after minor repairs, set off again with the leave party. Three months later, she landed some Scouts at Oban and sank within twenty-four hours off Northern Ireland. There was a grave shortage of shipping but eventually another leave boat, the Danish/Faroese 'Tialdur' was obtained.

Among other hostile acts, German planes demolished the Nolso W.T. station, made several attempts at bombing the oil tanks and attacked shipping in Thorshavn harbour with torpedoes, one of which exploded beside the Cable Hut guardroom without killing anyone. But they came close one day to causing a very big bang indeed. A large Swedish tanker was allowed to sail straight into Thorshavn harbour. As this was contrary to standing orders – foreign ships normally anchored well outside and were searched – the Scouts' Adjutant immediately telephoned Naval H.Q. While he was still speaking to the Naval Duty Officer, a Heinkel appeared and narrowly missed the tanker with several bombs. The Naval officer became speechless. No wonder, for the tanker had on board some 20,000 tons of nitro-glycerine destined for use in the Swedish iron-ore mines at Narvik. It was estimated that if one bomb had hit the tanker, the resultant explosion would probably have annihilated two Squadrons of Lovat Scouts and most of the 3,000 civilians in Thorshavn!

'Smiril', the Regiment's main means of transport between the islands, was attacked a number of times. One day eight bombs were dropped very near her, damaging her plates, and on 2nd December 1941 a Junkers narrowly missed her with two bombs, and then attacked with machine guns wounding two men, including Padre Robertson. He was invalided home, leaving the Roman Catholic Padre, Captain Duffy (a great jazz saxophonist and a brilliant left half in the Regimental Soccer Team) in sole charge of spiritual welfare till the arrival of another Presbyterian, Captain Rev. J. Macdonald.

Some A/A Gunners came to Thorshavn late in 1941 and, although they never shot down a plane, they certainly kept German aircraft much higher, and made their bombing even more erratic. Some Coastal Defence Gunners also came to Thorshavn and Tofte with 5.5 guns. A Scout Officer wrote of them:

In the event of an attack (and twice we stood-to for forty-eight hours, when a raid from Norway was said to be imminent) they would have been invaluable; but, as it was, they had a most depressing time, stationary beside their guns, with nothing to shoot at. They had more to put up with than we did but they had a good sense of humour and were always friendly and cheerful. One Christmas we visited them at Tofte: they had somehow managed to get a Christmas tree and had decorated the inside of their hut with over 100 very odd-shaped balloons.

The Lovat Scout Signallers did an outstanding job in the Faroes, under the leadership of Sir Richard Levinge, who was awarded the M.B.E. (as was Captain Harry Thorpe, the Quartermaster, for the exceptional efficiency with which he and his staff organised supplies under very difficult circumstances). The Signals Troop took on an entirely new and expanded role to provide a network of communications throughout the islands. It was greatly strengthened and was issued with an up-to-date establishment of signalling equipment, including the new 'Mark 9' WT/RT sets, which could transmit messages up to twenty miles and across hill country. The Scouts undertook all Naval Signal duties at Thorshavn and in Skaalefjord, which required very high-speed visual signalling with Aldis Lamps, not normally issued to the army. Sir Richard recalls that the signallers took this in their stride and without doubt earned the sincere (if grudging) appreciation of the Senior Service. The Signals Troop was also given the responsibility of establishing 'look-out and radio posts' to the north and east, facing Norway, and it was thanks to their efficiency that early warning was given on several occasions of the approach of German aircraft, including the Heinkel which B Sqn. shot down. The absolute reliability and initiative of all the Signallers' small detachments, including especially that of Cpl. George Mackay, who was at Nolso for eighteen months, is particularly remembered. Sir Richard writes of another aspect of the Signallers' duties:

The local telephone service, with R.T. connections to the smaller islands, was remarkably efficient but of course lacked security and could not be expanded to meet the widespread requirements of the Garrison both in Thorshavn and its various detachments in Skaalefjord and the outer islands. To meet this requirement was the major responsibility of Signals by field telephone networks within detachment areas and by Mk. 9 RT/WT between Islands. My Sgt. of Signals. Sgt. McCaskill, was a P.O. linesman in civilian life. I think we had an efficient telephone system and the credit for this lies with him alone.

Sir Richard was also Intelligence Officer. In that role, he was once told to complete an Intelligence form with largely irrelevant questions, including 'Nearest Railway Station and Distance?' He answered, 'Bergen – 250 miles'. Months later, a reply came from the War Office, 'Ref: your XY 3, I am directed to inform you that Bergen is in enemy occupation'. Sir Richard replied, 'Nevertheless, it is the nearest railway station to Thorshavn'.

* * * * * * * *

At long last, in May 1942, news came that they were to be relieved by the 12th Bn. of that fine Lowland Regiment, the Cameronians. The Scouts had repeatedly been told they had done a good job, but they were desperately anxious to get back to the U.K. to join the huge British force of twenty-two Infantry Divisions and six Armoured Divisions, which had already been training at home for nearly two years, in preparation for final victory. The Cameronians' advance party arrived on 28th May and the Scouts sent theirs by return. At 11.15 hrs on 10th June, the 'Lady of Mann', escorted by H.M.S. Chiddingfold, arrived at Thorshavn. To minimise the risk of air attack, a rapid change-over was required. The Cameronians disembarked and trans-shipped for seventeen different destinations with the right baggage, and the Scouts immediately

CABLE GUARD, THORSHAVN, 1941.

HOSPITALITY.
SKETCHES by J. Wattleworth 1941.

embarked with all their stores, the whole operation being successfully carried out in a few hours under direction of the recently-appointed new Adjutant, Captain W.S. Gammell and Lieut. Bob Ogg. At 22.45 hrs, on a beautiful summer's evening with thousands of Faroese waving goodbye and the Pipers playing 'Happy We Have Been Together', the troopship backed out into Nolso fjord with hoots from all ships, great and small, and set off at full speed for Invergordon.

Several Faroe girls, who had married Scouts, travelled bravely with them, but there were some broken hearts among those who waved farewell, whether from the shore or from the ship. However, some of them were happily reunited after the war. Any Scout who goes to the Faroes today sees many changes – a well-run fishing industry has brought great wealth – but he receives a kind welcome everywhere, for they still say in those far-off Atlantic islands that the Lovat Scouts were the best foreigners they have ever known.

CHAPTER XVI

SCOTLAND AND NORTH WALES
(June 1942 – December 1943)

Even the ocean seemed to bid the Scouts a kind farewell with a calm and uneventful voyage from Thorshavn to Invergordon. Captain Gammell, the Adjutant, recalls that after the Ship's Captain had inspected the empty ship and congratulated the Regiment on the ship's cleanliness, he commented, 'For the first time in my experience of troop carrying, never once during this voyage have I heard an officer or N.C.O. raise his voice!'

They arrived at Nairn by train on 12th June 1942 and became part of 157 Inf. Bde. in 52 Div., the other two Battalions in the Brigade being the Glasgow Highlanders and the 6th H.L.I. Over half the Regiment went on leave. They were then made into an Infantry Battalion; Squadrons became Companies, Troops became Platoons and Troopers were called Privates. The Mortar Platoon under Lieut. P. Wootton, was strengthened and given carriers; a Bren gun Carrier Platoon was formed under Captain Leslie Melville with a strength of sixty-one, including fifteen N.C.O.s, all drawn from the Rifle Companies, and, later, there was an anti-tank Platoon under Lieut. S.F. Macdonald and Lieut. C.K. Murray with a strength of thirty-eight, including thirteen N.C.O.s. These, together with Pioneers, Signallers and Transport, formed a very large H.Q. Company, commanded by Captain Allhusen. Battle School Courses were immediately arranged for as many officers and N.C.O.s as possible and Dunphail and the Carrier Platoon did a Battle Course at Coulmony. The Regiment was inspected by the Divisional Commander, Lt. General Sir John Laurie, Bt., C.B.E., D.S.O. There was some instruction for those who could not swim, much target practice on the Fort George ranges and a number of exercises with 52 Div.

In late July, word came that the Scouts were soon to move north to join 227 Bde. and a small advance party went to Halkirk, Caithness.

Meanwhile, the remainder were warned that they would shortly be going on secret manoeuvres, called 'Exercise X'. They moved from Nairn on 9th August and their mystery tour ended at Balmoral. There they were to guard the Royal Family during their six weeks' war-time holiday at their Highland home, it was a great privilege to have been chosen for this duty, especially at a time when there were so many other troops available in Britain, and the whole Regiment made a tremendous effort to show that in turnout, smartness and efficiency it was fully worthy of such a high honour.

Battalion H.Q. and three Companies at a time were billeted in and around Abergeldie Castle, while the 4th Coy. did continuous guard duty at Balmoral for a week at a time. Training, which included two route marches a week of over twenty miles, continued for those not on guard duty and, when there was grouse driving, they supplied beaters and flankers for this popular form of 'Special Training'. Some of the Scouts who had been keepers particularly enjoyed it and had strong views on how each day's shooting should have been run. The Royal Family showed the Scouts extreme kindness. All the officers were invited in pairs to dine at the Castle; those who were used to grouse driving were asked to shoot and the others to stalk in turn, and many Scouts attended and greatly enjoyed the annual Ghillies' Ball. Several Sergeants were kindly asked to stalk on Invercauld and shot with deadly accuracy. Extracts from the War Diary read:

> 25th AUGUST, 1942 HRH Princess Elizabeth and HRH Princess Margaret honoured the Regt. by coming to tea in the Officers' Mess today and listening to the Pipe Band playing Retreat.
>
> 6th SEPTEMBER, 1942. The whole Regt. was today inspected by HM the King....
>
> The CO has received the following message from the Master of the House-hold.
>
> "I am commanded by the King to inform you that His

Majesty was very pleased to have been present at the 1st Ceremonial Parade of The Lovat Scouts as an Infantry Battalion, which took place at Balmoral today. The King was much gratified by the smart turnout and bearing on parade of the Battalion and would be grateful if you would convey his congratulations to all ranks".

Further very favourable comments have been made by various spectators of the Parade, including the Queen and the Princesses. The setting on the lawn was of course very good indeed and the sight of the Battalion with the pipers at the head, marching up the drive with fixed bayonets was most impressive.

During his Inspection, the King spoke to a number of N.C.O.s and men. His first question was to a Sgt. Major, 'How tong have you been in the Regiment?' Instantly there came the reply, 'Sixteen years in the Royal Scots Greys: three and a half years in the Lovat Scouts, SIR' Next he asked the same question of a Gaelic-speaking piper. There was a long pause, for, like most of us, he could not remember off-hand; and then, with a charming smile, he said, 'Oh an awful long time!' an answer which the King enjoyed.

Major Andrew Haig recalls that when he first went to dine at the Castle his companion was Sir Simon Campbell-Orde. The King, whose eye for detail in uniforms was well known, noticed at once various minor differences in their Service Dress, which, as already explained, had always been permitted in the Scouts. The King asked how it was that two officers, who had both been in the Regiment for some years, came to be dressed so differently. While Andrew groped for some suitable explanation, Sir Simon, never at a loss, replied in his slow, deep voice, 'Your Majesty, it is a sort of tradition in the Regiment that no two officers are ever dressed alike'. At this the King was highly delighted and roared with laughter. The matter was never raised again.

On 30th September, the Scouts moved to Halkirk, eight miles south of

Thurso. A few days later, Lt. Colonel Adam Fairrie, the Commanding Officer, received the following message from the Queen:

> Will you please convey to the officers, N.C.O.s and men of the Lovat Scouts my congratulations and thanks for the very efficient way in which you have guarded us at Balmoral. I send heartfelt wishes that good fortune may attend them wherever they may be serving. ELIZABETH, R.

Throughout the winter, they trained hard as an Infantry Battalion, billeted in Nissen huts round Braal Castle, Halkirk. There were many exercises and night schemes; there were courses for officers and N.C.O.s in new weapons and at Battle Schools; Major McCorquodale retired after twenty-nine years' service and was succeeded as Second-in-command by Major T.C.J. Dickson, the second tallest officer in the British Army. In February 1943 they were re-organised again in common with other Infantry Battalions. There was H.Q. Coy. (Signals, Transport and Administration) commanded by Captain Allhusen, three Rifle Coys., A (Major Cameron) B (Major Sir S. Campbell-Orde), C (Major Sir J. Brooke) and D, a Support Coy., commanded by Major Haig with Carriers, Anti-tank, Mortars and Pioneers.

At first, permission was granted to the Scouts to fish for salmon on a stretch of the Thurso, but only with rod and fly. The previous Battalion there, observing this rule, had caught nothing, but within a fortnight some of the Scouts' best fishermen had caught so many that permission had to be withdrawn! The author collected and hunted a pack of beagles, kennelled at Braal. Anyone who beagled till 1 p.m. on a Saturday was excused P.T. The result was a huge 'field' till 1 p.m. and thereafter usually only a few 'whippers-in', including Captain Andrew Macdonald, Major Andrew Haig and Corporal Gillon, who all ran great distances in a wonderful beagling country. It had been hunted in 1939/40 by Captain Colin MacAndrew of the Ayrshire Yeomanry. There was good rough shooting, plenty of local dances and an occasional ENSA Show. It is recorded that Captain Pook, an Army Catering Adviser, inspected the camp, cookhouses and dining halls, and expressed himself pleased with all he saw 'except the officers' cooking arrangements'.

There was a comic ending to a very serious Brinade Security Week, during which each Battalion was to intensify its guards, raid other units and elicit 'BY ANY POSSIBLE MEANS', information useful to the enemy. The Scouts carried out a few minor raids but were furious when two men of the 10th H.L.I. at Watten crawled into the Braal camp one dark night and wrote 'BLOWN UP' in chalk on the Support Company's vehicles. Thanks to the iron nerve of Signaller J.E. ('Clunie') Vernon, a Scout from Yorkshire, revenge came soon and in the following strange manner.

Lieut. Richard Rayer (the Intelligence Officer) and Padre W.E. Caskie, a wonderful man whose brother was the famous 'Tartan Pimpernel', hatched an ingenious plot. (The Padre was a reluctant conspirator, his only excuse being his sense of humour!) Each Battalion had its own Presbyterian Padre, but for units with members of the Church of England an itinerant Padre was occasionally provided. Padre Caskie knew that this Church of England priest was on leave and also that the H.L.I. were due for their Padre's Hour next day. 'Clunie' Vernon was surprised when he was suddenly sent for by the Intelligence Officer and the Padre, and even more so when they asked if he were willing to be planted on the H.L.I. as a bogus Church of England Padre, in order to gain secret information. He accepted the task, went through the plan with them in outline and borrowed suitable clothing from the Padre for his mission. Vernon's story continues thus:

> Padre Caskie provided me with a sermon and I sat up late trying to commit it to memory... Next day, with Davie Peters driving a "tilly" with our Regimental markings painted out, we set off to Watten and when we were challenged at the gate we were passed without demur and told where we would find Padre Dunlop gathering his flock at the N.A.A.F.I. Ian Dunlop

was kindness itself, herded the Church of England chaps into the Sgt.s' Mess and left me to it... About four chaps awaited me, a wooden-faced lot, but they were my material and I had to make them talk... I knew I had them. I was different. I talked with the authority of my dog-collar but in their own language and, when I gave them my blessing, I hopefully suggested that if anyone had any problems to discuss, I'd be glad to help.

Half a dozen men remained behind. 'Clunie' invited them to come forward one at a time and gave the others some cigarettes while they waited. They each poured out to him their various personal woes and marital problems. He gave them comfort and sound, practical advice and had a friendly chat with each, during which he learned (1) that they were about to go on a four-day exercise in Ross-shire, (2) that they had just received new mortars and more portable signal sets, (3) that their carriers were obsolescent and constantly breaking down, (4) that the Battalion was about to be brought up to strength with intakes from North Africa and (5) that they were behindhand with leave and in an ugly mood about it. In the Mess afterwards he was introduced to the officers (... 'I drifted amongst them making small talk – nearly making a pig of myself with the variety of sandwiches and scones and tea out of a china cup – and made some gentle prods about training programmes, etc...'). Before leaving he thanked the Colonel, Sir John Collingwood, for his hospitality and complimented him on his Battalion. 'Oh, they'll be all right', said the Colonel, 'especially when I get my intake of seasoned troops later in the year'. Padre Dunlop asked how he was getting on with Brigade H.Q. 'Fine', said Vernon, 'Except that they have not given me much help about finding the various Units'. The Padre was surprised but said he would certainly help and, disappearing to his quarters, he returned with a list of every Unit in the Brigade and details of their location and strength. With that, Vernon summoned his driver and quickly departed. The story ends:

Back at R.H.Q. I gave a swift precis of events and, after a dram with Mr. Rayer and Col. Fairrie, I wrote my report. By noon next day, it and Padre Dunlop's list were at Bde. H.Q. and – wham! – the balloon went up. Col. Collingwood got the brunt of it, but I think he scalped a few of his officers and the Bn. was confined to barracks for a week.

While he was on his way back to his billet, still dressed as a Captain and Padre, 'Clunie' met a squad being marched to R.H.Q. by Roddie McPherson, the Provost Corporal, who called his men to attention and gave the strange Padre an enormous salute. If ever a salute were deserved, that was it!

In April, the Battalion moved to Thurso camp, adjacent to the Castle, in which the officers were made welcome by Sir Archibald and Lady Sinclair and their charming family. As a preliminary to each day's training, everyone ran to the ice-cold sea and swam before breakfast. In early May, in very bad weather, they took part in a six-day exercise in Sutherland and Easter Ross against the Norwegian Brigade. A few weeks later they were inspected by three Senior Generals and their Staff, who watched the three Rifle Companies training and saw demonstrations by each of the Support Platoons. The Scouts received an excellent report on their efficiency as an Infantry Battalion. That was all very well, but where and when would they be allowed to go and fight?

Sir Winston Churchill in his 'Hinge of Fate' refers to a Minute in which he wrote to the Secretary of State for War that because of the Lovat Scouts' 'origins, traditions and composition' they might well be sent to take the place of three Commandos which went to the Middle East in 1940 and were disbanded. He asked for proposals, but there is no record as to whether any were made. The Scouts however, were determined to keep their identity and, by June 1943 were proud of their efficiency as Infantry and anxious to get into a First Line Division as soon as possible. They then heard to their delight that they had been chosen to become the Mountain Recce Regiment for the famous 52nd Division which, although composed of Lowland Regiments, was the only Mountain Division at home. It seemed an ideal role and one in which all their previous training and aptitude in the hills would be of great value.

At first they trained in the Grampians and Cairngorms, based on a tented camp at Glen Clunie between Braemar and the Devil's Elbow. While there, they again had the high honour of being invited to guard the Royal Family at Balmoral. They knew their duties from the previous year and were once more shown the very greatest kindness. Scouts who were there recall many incidents of those six weeks. Some, like Sgt. Alec Leitch and Cpl. Willie Watson, who were fortunate enough to have a dance at the Ghillies' Ball with the present Queen Mother, still remember what a charming partner and beautiful dancer she was. Douglas Ramsay, then a Second Lieutenant, recalls that when he was asleep one morning, having just finished twenty-four hour guard duty, he was suddenly woken up by voices close at hand. Major Donald Cameron was evidently showing a visitor round the billets. Not knowing how to salute from the sleeping-bag position, Douglas pretended to be asleep, but then had a peep through one eye. He shut it very quickly when he observed that the visitor gazing down at him was the King! One N.C.O. formerly a keeper, who got a pellet in his cheek from the Royal gun (due entirely to a ricochet off a rock, for the King was one of the finest and safest shots in his Kingdom), came through the Italian campaign unscathed and would sometimes say with a broad grin that he was the proudest man in the British Army: he had served his King and Country for six years and the only scratch he ever got was from his King!

In early October, by which time the tented camp at Glen Clunie was a sea of mud, they moved to North Wales to learn rock-climbing from the Commando School of Mountain Warfare and their staff of skilled climbers under Major Rees Jones. Most of the Regiment was billeted at Bangor and Plas Llanfair, but they also had 120 'leaders' at Beddgelert, below Snowdon. There they quickly learned to climb up and down sheer rock faces, which they would never previously have dared to attempt, and were initiated into the mysterious techniques of roping, tying knots and abseiling. The 'leaders', had to be capable of instructing in all these subjects and of leading up (or down) a 'moderately difficult' climb. Those who thought they had a 'bad head for heights' soon overcame it: the unthinkable alternative was to be transferred to another unit. Every man in the Regiment had to learn rock-climbing. They must have tackled almost every hill in North Wales and some of them at night. There were a few casualties, including one officer with a fractured skull.

In the new role they had sixty-four snipers instead of eight, with telescopes and T/S rifles. Many of them were already well trained but Captain Leslie Melville took forty of them to Llanberis, where Major Hon. F.A.H. Wills had already set up the Army Sniping School with several Scout N.C.O.s, such as Sergeants A. Ross and J.M. MacLeod, as instructors. They did extremely well on a course of stalking and fieldcraft, shooting with telescopic sights and, above all, spying and observing. On the last day of the course, armed with climbing boots and telescopes, they followed the Ynysfor Fell Hounds, which hunt foxes in the high country round Snowdon. Never have the movements of those hounds been so closely observed, recorded and mapped as on that day.

An exceptionally high medical grade ('A1 plus') was required and unfortunately a number of good men and officers were graded out and transferred to other units or staff jobs at this stage. However, two drafts were received of selected volunteers, many being from other units in 52 Div.. They amounted to 165 O.R.s plus officers. The new Commanding Officer was Lt. Colonel J.S.H. Douglas (Seaforth Highlanders) and Major E.A.M. Wedderburn (Royal Scots), an experienced climber, came as Second-in-command. Among the new officers, mainly mountaineers, several of whom dropped a rank in order to join, were: Lieutenants T. Nicholson, D.W. Howe, J.N. Ledingham, W. Elliot, N.D. Walker, R. Urquhart, W.M. Mackenzie, W. Milne, W.S. Scroggie, D.C. Packer, A.R. Turnbull, T. Mowatt and G. Tingulstad (Norwegian Forces). Tommy Cumming (from Scatwell) who had already been an exceptionally good N.C.O. in the Scouts, rejoined as a Second Lieutenant. The Regiment was also lucky in getting a very fit and first-class M.O. in Captain John

Rowntree, and another fine Adjutant in Captain Geoffrey Forrest who had succeeded Captain Gammeli in September. The Quartermaster, Captain Harry Thorpe, M.B.E., now the only officer who had served in the 1914/18 war, passed the 'Al plus' test with flying colours and was a tower of strength right to the end of the war.

P.J. Dearden, in his *'Mountain Warfare Training 1943/44'* wrote:

> It was perceived that a Mountain Division. to be secure and to increase its striking power, needs light troops, moving far and fast who could protect the flanks, seize high ground in advance and penetrate as raiding parties and recce patrols to the enemy's rear... It was decided to earmark the Lovat Scouts, a Regiment of hardy Highianders, many of them accustomed to the hills as deer-stalkers and ghillies, for this purpose, and to train them as rock-climbers in Wales and as ski-mountaineers in the Canadian Rockies during the winter of 1943/44.

An advance party under Major Cameron left for Canada on 3rd December. A detachment of four officers and forty O.R.s under Captain Leslie Melville went aboard the 'Mauretania' at Liverpool to guard her over the Christmas period, and on 28th December, with the rest of the Regiment on board, as well as some American servicemen, British Honduras lumberjacks and several V.l.P.s bound for Washington, the 'Mauretania' sailed for New York.

THE OFFICERS AT TAIN CAMP, 1935

Standing:
Rev. R Finlayson, Lts: J. Brooke, H.B. Pierse, J.P. Grant, R. Fleming, C.I. Fraser, Ld. Elcho, I Sturit, A. Fraser, S. Campbell-Orde, H.B-Hawkes, Att. Off.

Seated:
Capts: W. Whitbread, T.W-Fiennes, A. Grant, Majors: J. Stirling, Hon. I. Leslie Melville, Lt.Col. Earl of Leven, Capt. P. Grant (Adjt), Majors K. McCorquodale, Hon. J. Pease, Capt. W. Robertson (Q.M.), Capt. A.R. macdonald.

Front:
2/Lts. A. Mackenzie, J. Wyld, A. Haig, L. Balfour-Paul, A. Cameron.

An A Squadron Troop arriving at Penicuik Camp; 1938.

*ELEVEN SONS OF OLD SCOUT OFFICERS, STRA THREFFER CAMP, 1939.
(L. to R.) – Maj. A.R. Macdonald, Capt. D.H. Cameron, Lt. Hon H. Fraser, 2/Lts. A.
Grant, C. Murray, J. Macdonald. M. Leslie Melville and Lt J.P. Grant
Absent: Capt Lord Lovat, 2/Lt A.J. Macdonald.*

Lt. Col. Hon. I. Leslie Melville with Colonel Dahl (Norwegian Army), Thorshavn, 1940.

Maj. K. McCorquodale, M.C., and Maj. D. H. Cameron, Thorshavn, 1940.

'GRINDEBO!' Whale hunt at Sando, 1941.

161

THE ROSS-SHIRE TROOP, C SQUADRON, FANELLAN, 1939.

THE EAST SUTHERLAND TROOP, C SQUADRON, APRIL 1940.
(Back Row)
    Tprs. Chisholm, S. MacLeod, D. W Munro, L. Bowran, A. Sutherland.
    J.J. Sutherland, I. Ross, R. Campbell, B. Gordon.
(2nd Row)
    Tprs. Gunn, Moir, A. Mackay, I. Graham, MacLean, D. Campbell,
    A . Sutherland, T. Campbell.
(Seated)
    L/Cpl F. Sutherland, Cpl D. Davidson, F/Sgt MacKay, Sgt D.G. MacKay,
    2/Lt C.K. Murray, Sgt W Sutherland, Cpl Macdonald, L/Cpl Mackay, F/Cpl Baxter.
(Front Row)
    Tprs. L. Murray, J. Muray, W.A. Murray. E. Campbell, J.F. Murray. J. Nicholson, J.
    Murray.

Captain R. C. Allhusen (Adjt.) with Faroese family and Norwegian ponies, 1940.

The Pipe Band. Thorshavn, 1941.

Summer Patrol above Kirkebo, 1940.

Winter Patrol in Sudero, 1941.

German airmen captured by B Squadron, Tofte, February, 1941.

Heinkel salvaged from Gotefjord by Lieutenant J. MacDonald and the Skye Troop. February, 1941.

The Pipe Band at Balmoral, 1942.

The Royal Family at Balmoral, 1943, with Senior N.C.O.s and Lt. Col. A. Fairrie, M.B.E., Major Dickson and Captain W. Gammell (Adjutant).

'ICE WORK' – Canada, 1944.

At the foot of the Athabaska Glacier, March, 1944.
(Right) Captain J. Rowntree (M.O.)

OFFICERS AT ABERDEEN BEFORE LEAVING FOR ITALY, JULY 1944.

(Back Row)
Lieuts. R. Ogg, W. Elliot, P. Scott, R. Milne, D. Ramsay, G. Tingulstad, D. Howe, T. Nicholson, T. Cumming, P. Wootton, P. Walker, W. Budge, B. Wootton, D. Packer.
(2nd Row)
Capt. Rev. W. Caskie, Lieuts. T. Oxley, R. Rayer, Capts. A. Macdonald, M. Leslie Melville, L. Balfour-Paul, J. Wyld, S. Macdonald, A. Fraser, Lieuts. C. Murray, N. Ledingham, Capt. J. Rountree (M.O.)
(Seated)
Majors Sir S. Campbell-Orde, A. Haig, Capt. G. Forrest, Lt. Col. J. Douglas, Col. Commandant D. Baillie, Majors E.A. Wedderburn, D. Cameron, Sir J. Brooke, Capt. H. Thorpe (Q.M.)
(Front Row)
Lieuts. S. Scroggie, R. Miller, R. Urquhart, P. Curtis and R. Turnbull.

CHAPTER XVII

CANADA
(January – May 1944)

At dawn on 6th January, the 'Mauretania' entered New York Harbour. There was no black-out and the Scouts were amazed at the sight of New York City with its colossal sky-scrapers all lit up. They seemed to be in a different world, an impression which was heightened when they arrived at Grand Central Station through a snow storm and were immediately offered delicious refreshments and lavish gifts of magazines, papers, chocolates and cigarettes by beautifully-dressed ladies of the American Red Cross. They were to travel over 2,500 miles by C.P.R. in two special trains to Jasper National Park, Alberta, 'in the heart of the Canadian Rockies'. An officer wrote of the journey:

> Just before departure, Douglas Ramsay noticed that one of the pipers from Uist was missing. He turned up at the last minute, every pocket bulging with bottles of whisky. In spite of all the Security about our movements, he seemed to have had a rendezvous with some Hebridean exiles at the barrier.
>
> The journey took over three days. There were three stops, where we exercised on the platforms. Throughout the journey snow lay everywhere. The scenery was monotonous and there were long silences in the officers' compartment. Once, after we had been travelling for over 100 miles through flat, snow-covered prairie with scrub, the Commanding Officer – a keen sportsman and a fine shot – suddenly said, "I wonder if there is anything tn shoot out there sir mon rubbed the window a nd looked very carefully at the desolate scene. "Yes", he said slowly, "I think one would get the odd bear".

Early on 10th January they saw the distant Rocky Mountains, an incredible horizon of countless snow-clad peaks, and an astonishing sight even for Highlanders used to their native hills and those of North Wales. By evening they were happily ensconced in the centrally-heated log cabins of Jasper Park with an outside temperature well below zero and with one Scout, who had rashly disobeyed orders and travelled on the step of a truck from the Station, already suffering from frost-bitten ears. They were soon to learn that an arctic climate and high mountains have swift and cruel punishment for any novice who believes in 'hardiness' alone.

The Scouts were reorganised yet again; this time into a Mountaineer Regiment with Squadrons and Troops and with each Private being addressed as 'Mountaineer' (e.g. Mtnr. Mackay A.). They were issued with superb arctic kit and ski-mountaineering equipment, mostly from the American Army. For the first two weeks the whole Regiment learnt the rudiments of ski-ing near Jasper, except for a small party of officer and N.C.O. 'leaders', who went off almost immediately to Lake Maligne and then to the Columbia Icefields for more advanced training.

The whole project was under the direction of Wing Commander Frank Smythe, of Everest fame, with Major Gibson, a Canadian, as Chief Instructor, assisted by a number of expert mountaineers, skiers and explorers, such as Major Pat Baird, Tom Peacock, Patsy Richardson, John Parnwell and several American officers. In all, there were some forty Instructors (officers and N.C.O.s), some of them French Canadians and one or two ex-trappers with Red Indian blood. The Canadian Army kindly provided a large administrative staff including cooks, so that every Lovat Scout could learn ski-mountaineering.

There were, however, certain key men in the Scouts, who were at first fully engaged in administration and the vital task of fitting and issuing kit and equipment. After a few days, Captain John Wyld, commanding H.Q. Sqn., ordered them all out to learn ski-ing. Every man had to be a mountaineer. He lined them up with their skis on and, before anyone had moved or the Instructor had spoken one word, Cpl. Crawford, the Q.M.'s chief storeman and of great importance to the Regiment, suddenly over-balanced and broke his leg very badly in two places. It could happen that way; but most of the early accidents occurred while the victim was moving and sometimes at very considerable speed. After three weeks, there were officially 'over thirty casualties with broken limbs or severe twists and sprains'. Those with lesser injuries struggled on, helped by Elastoplast bandages and sometimes by a strange, fierce liniment called 'King of Pain', sold with a flashing smile by Doreen of the Jasper Drug Store, which dealt in everything from milk shakes to ice-hockey sticks.

After nearly three weeks of relentless instruction and enthusiastic endeavour the Scouts began to feel at home on skis. On the Canadian word of command, 'Let's Go!', they went. Each Squadron departed for the second stage of its training, which was carried out from winter camps, mainly under canvas in virgin conifer forest at such isolated places as Tonquin Valley, Mount Edith Cavell, Watchtower, Snowbowl, Lake Maligne and Columbia Icefields. From those bases – some of them difficult to reach and to supply – they proceeded to have some really tough training. P.J. Dearden, in his Thesis, described it thus:

> During the first few weeks the Lovat Scouts needed intensive ski-training to enable them to move across high mountainous terrain efficiently in winter. Training thereafter included., glacier work, snow-craft, avalanche-craft, ice and winter rock-climbing, winter bush-craft and PATROLS OF OVER 60 MILES in difficult country without tents, bivouacking in snowholes and igloos at elevations exceeding 10,000 feet and temperatures ranging down to 30 degrees below zero (Fahrenheit). "Weasels" (small, tracked snow-vehicles), sledges and even some pack ponies were used at base camps. Aircraft was also employed to support training exercises and for parachuting supplies to distant patrols.
>
> The standard of training (aimed at and attained) was for all ranks to be capable of operating over any type of country, snow, ice or rock; of living under the severest conditions for several days on end (at least one third being trained as "rope

leaders"); of covering at least 30 miles per day on skis or snowshoes, carrying full equipment (60 lbs packs and weapons); for the Pioneer Troop to be trained to carry out hasty demolitions of bridges, railways, etc., behind enemy lines, and for the Signal Troop to maintain communications by pack wireless, visual or line, in all conditions over long distances.

Despite the excellent equipment and the experience of most of the Senior Instructors, there were, inevitably, further casualties including some fractures, many bad sprains and a few cases of frostbite and snow blindness. Considering, however, the intentional severity of this winter training and the risks that had to be taken in largely unknown, very high and sometimes unmapped country, it is remarkable that there was only one fatal casualty – the tragic death of CpI. A. Collie in an avalanche. Apart from that disaster, they were undoubtedly lucky; for on some occasions they could well have lost up to half a Squadron at a time in really bad avalanches. There were, of course, several individual close shaves, not least that of Major Sir John Brooke who was caught in an avalanche and swept down with it for over eight hundred feet ('swimming' with it in the approved style which probably saved him). Several people fell into crevasses on glaciers, but, thanks to being roped and to an efficient crevasse rescue drill, were hauled up. Some had more than their share of good luck. Two novice 'leaders', separated from the rest of their party in a bad blizzard at about 10,000 feet, decided to descend some 4,000 feet to the tree-line by the shortest route possible – the Saskatchewan glacier. Their pride at having done so without any trouble from avalanches evaporated when it was later explained to them that they had ignorantly crossed over forty dangerous crevasses without even being roped together!

The toughest training was done in the high mountains. Sleeping up there in snow-holes and eating pemmican warmed on solid fuel burners, was a hard existence; but camping below the tree-line was better, and with experience one could be comparatively comfortable in a well-sited shelter with a good camp fire. There are worse ways of falling asleep than under the bright, twinkling stars of a Canadian sky in fifty degrees of frost, with the smouldering scent of a dying camp fire, the faint murmur of Highland voices, and in the safe knowledge that one's boots, clutched within the sleeping bag, will not be frozen solid in the morning.

Two light aircraft with snow-skids gave the training an extra dimension; and anyone who witnessed from the air a sunrise over the immense grandeur of the Rockies will never forget it. For reconnaissance and for dropping supplies the aircraft were invaluable, but without wireless communication they could cause frustration. Lochiel remembers a four-day trek by A Squadron when rations were to be dropped in the late afternoon of the third day. Supplies were low and the Squadron was tired and hungry, but at last the plane came in sight. As it circled round, they could see Lieut. Bob Ogg and the pilot waving. On an orange parachute a container was dropped, but there was no food in it – only a message reading: 'How deep is the snow? – Bob'!

'Weasels' were comparatively new, lightweight tracked vehicles, which were ideal for transporting stores or a few passengers. They performed wonderfully in the snow and each could tow a Troop of men on skis across a frozen lake. An endurance test was carried out with two 'Weasels' by Lieut. Bob Ogg, Sgt. Bill MacIntyre, Cpl. E. Campbell and two American officers. In two days they drove successfully cross-country from Jasper to Banff, about 190 miles as the crow flies.

The Scouts were under strict orders not to shoot any wild animals and they certainly did not need to do so for food with a ration scale of 6000 calories a day. But they had the fun of living among wild life, including caribou (the reindeer of Canada), wapiti or 'elk', larger than red deer, the gigantic and hideous moose (a large 'bull' moose can weigh up to $3/4$ ton and measure $21\frac{1}{2}$ hands high at the withers and the speed at which it can trot through deep snow is phenomenal). They saw Big Horn sheep and occasionally the rare Rocky Mountain goat which could sometimes be spied 'grazing' at about 10,000 feet, surrounded by ice and snow with, apparently, nothing to eat within miles. Among the birds there was an odd creature called the fool hen. About the size of a grey hen, it sat on the lower branches of trees and allowed anybody to walk up and kill it with a stick – a tame sport, much frowned upon. One could almost always catch a rainbow trout by dropping a piece of tinned bacon on a hook through a hole in a frozen lake. As spring approached, beavers became active and bears began to wake up.

There were a few interesting back-woodsmen, who had spent most of their lives in the Rockies, including one whose father had driven a pair of bull moose in 'tandem' from Calgary to Edmonton. He claimed that if no horses had ever come to the Western Hemisphere, the moose would have become a beast of burden. In a wigwam near Jasper Station lived a Red Indian 'Chief' with several squaws and children. Whenever a train arrived he sold moccasins and gloves, beautifully made by his squaws, to the 'pale face' passengers. He was a man of few words and was said to be very fond of rum.

The following items of interest are taken from the War Diaries:

> 22 JAN. A 'Weasel'" went through the ice on Maligne Lake, but did not sink. Major Haig caught in avalanche but rescued unhurt.

> 23 JAN. Cpl. A. Collie's funeral held in Jasper. Service taken by Padre; burial followed at local Cemetery.

> 25 JAN. St. Andrew's Society of Jasper very kindly entertained 300 men of the Regiment at a Burns Supper in the Salvation Army Canteen (an example of the great and generous welcome we have received everywhere from Canadians).

> 26th JAN. In the interests of Security, the Postal Address of the unit has now been changed for the 5th time, which has caused much hard feeling and most of our mail to go astray.

28 JAN. E. Squadron move out to Tonquin Valley. Capt. S.F. Macdonald i/c. This is a difficult move, as all supplies have to be dragged by sledge over ten miles of very rough trail.

1st FEB. D Sqn. to Snowbowl. Difficult. Everything has to be man-handled up the creek (seven miles) or else carried by one "weasel" (hauled over Shovel Pass) along a very difficult six-mile trail.

10 FEB. Aeroplane successfully dropping supplies to Tonquin Camp. Pack horses now in use for supplies to Snowbowl and Tonquin.

12 FEB. Joe Weiss, a Swiss guide, has been successful in establishing a "weasel" trail to Tonquin after eight days work, including the cutting of much timber and the construction of twenty or more ice-bridges over Astoria Creek.

5th/6th MARCH. Regtal Ski Trials (two days) held at Mt. Edith Cavell. Slalom Race won by Mtnr. W. Watson (C Sqn.), Major Sir J. Brooke (C Sqn.) 2nd. Cross Country Race (twelve miles) won by Captain Leslie Melville, (A Sqn.). Overall Points Winner. Cpl. Hendry. Patrol Race won by D Sqn., A Sqn. 2nd, C Sqn. 3rd.

13th/14th MARCH. Forty men from Tonquin overdue on patrol. Found by search party. Six men to hospital with frost-bite.

30th MARCH. B. Sqn. party caught in avalanche on Coronet Glacier. Rescue party leaves under Sir Simon, 04.00 hrs. All rescued. No serious injuries except sprains and bruises.

17th APRIL. The Pipe Band departs to play in Vancouver by special invitation, with Major Haig, Captain Forrest (Adjutant) and Major Godby (Canadian Army).

21 APRIL. Pipe Band returns in triumph from Vancouver after excellent and very popular performances. The Baggage Room in Jasper (looked after by the Canadian Army) destroyed by fire last night. Much of the Regiment's equipment lost. A very serious matter: Court of Enquiry assembles.

22 APRIL. The Regiment leaves Jasper by two trains, for Halifax, Nova Scotia. Large crowd of Canadian friends gather to wave farewell and to cheer the Regiment on its way.

Throughout their visit the Scouts received the very greatest kindness and hospitality from Canadians everywhere, especially the people of Jasper, and many lasting friendships were made. Even from a purely mountaineering point of view, there had been a number of remarkable achievements. For example, Major Gibson wrote:

The first complete winter ascent of Columbia (12,294 feet, 2nd highest peak in the Rockies) took place on 14th March, 1944, during a three-day patrol on the Icefields, when the troops slept in snow holes dug down into the surface of the neve. Major D. Groff of Winnipeg was the leader, and about thirty men made the climb. On the same day I accompanied a troop of men from another snow hole camp at 10,500 feet with North Twin (12,085 feet) as our objective.

In the summary of his Thesis, Mr. Dearden states:

The training that the Lovat Scouts received in the Canadian

Rockies was as demanding as, and probably more so than, that of any other large Allied unit. Wing Commander Smythe's statement, "I believe that the Lovat Scouts are now the toughest and hardiest Battalion in the British Army" was no idle boast and was echoed by many. First-hand reports from officers who worked with them in Canada and from officers who fought alongside them in Italy reveal that they were indeed incredibly tough, rugged, and capable of remarkable feats of fighting and endurance. Although they never did use their hard-earned high altitude mountain experiences in Norway or the Alps, as the men themselves had hoped and expected, they fought in Italy's precipitous Apennines, where they acquitted themselves with great distinction.

On 22nd April they started on a four-day train journey from Jasper to catch a ship at Halifax, Nova Scotia, which would take them home. During the journey, however, two Scouts became seriously ill with very high temperatures. At the next stop, Riviere du Loup, they were removed to hospital with suspected scarlet fever. The Regiment was diverted to Number 1 Transit Camp, Windsor, Nova Scotia, and put in quarantine. There the Scouts were delayed for four weeks. They went for route marches through pretty country with apple blossom, shot on local ranges and practised Mountain Battle Drill, a training procedure invented by the Scouts. They had Regimental Sports and also competed against other units. On the last occasion, the War Diary records that the Scouts 'won every event in which they competed except the pole vault, in which they were second'!

Shortly before they left Nova Scotia, the Gaelic-speaking Sgt. Major of B Sqn. was waiting for a hair-cut in a local barber's shop. He heard two civilians talking to each other in rather an odd form of Gaelic. 'When were you last in the Highlands?' he asked, 'Three generations ago', answered one of the Nova Scotians, in Gaelic.

The voyage back to Liverpool on the Andes took a week. They landed there on 9th June, went by train to Aberdeen and marched to Haydon Camp. The 52nd Division was destined for the low country of Northwest Europe but the Scouts were to join the 8th Army in Italy. They were given embarkation leave, about half the Regiment at a time, and orders were received to be ready to go overseas by 9th July.

CHAPTER XVIII

ITALY
(July 1944 – May 1945)

Before the Regiment left for Italy it was again reorganised. Those not coming abroad were formed into 'Y' Sqn. (Home Details) under Lieut. R.A. Ogg. They included some who were still in Canada with injuries. The total strength of the Regiment going overseas was 832 (38 officers, 109 N.C.O.s and W.O.s and 685 O.R.s).

The officers were the following:

R.H.Q.   Lt. Col. J.S.H. Douglas (C.O.), Maj. E.A.M. Wedderburn (2i/c), Capt. G. Forrest (Adjt.), Capt. J. Rowntree (M.O.), Capt. Rev. W.E. Caskie (Padre).

A Sqn.   Maj. D.H. Cameron, Capt. A.H. Fraser, Lts. W. Howe, T. Cumming and T.G. Tinguistad (Norwegian Forces).

B Sqn.   Maj. Sir S.A. Campbell-Orde Bt, Capt. L. Balfour-Paul, Lts N.D. Walker, B.A. Wootton, and A. Urquhart.

C Sqn.   Maj. Sir J.W. Brooke Bt, Lts. R.J. Rayer, P.C. Scott, W. Milne, and A.R. Turnbull.

D Sqn.   Maj. A.W. Haig, Capt. S.F. Macdonald, Lts. W. Elliot and W.S. Scroggie.

'R' (Reserve)
     Sqn. Capt. M.l. Leslie Melville (Sniping Officer), Capt. A.J. Macdonald, Lts. P.A. Wootton and W.H. Budge.

H.Q. Sqn.   Capt. J.H.G. Wyld, Lts. C.K. Murray (Intelligence Officer), J.N. Ledingham (Signals Officer), D.H. Ramsay (Pioneer, Tpt Officer & Assistant Adjt) and Capt. H. Thorpe (Quartermaster).

On the 16th July 1944 the Regiment embarked at Glasgow on the 'Queen of Bermuda', which sailed on the 18th. The voyage was calm.

They changed into tropical kit on 23rd; by 25th it was insufferably hot in the troop decks; the coast of Africa was glimpsed on 27th, and at noon on 29th the ship arrived at Naples. The Scouts disembarked immediately and started, in blazing heat, to unload their stores which included white camouflaged skis and other ski-mountaineering equipment. They then marched nine miles to Afragola Staging Camp, where they had four days of route marches and re-packing. It was a malarial area and they were issued with white mosquito nets, suitable for Afragola but useless in the front line. Later, during their first few days in the line (also a malarial area) and before they received camouflaged nets, a number of Scouts were bitten by mosquitos and developed malaria, but most of them, with modern treatment, recovered very quickly.

At that stage of the war in Italy, the German Army, under an exceptionally able general, 'Smiling Albert' Kesselring, had withdrawn gradually northwards to strong positions roughly along the Arno Line. There had been fierce fighting and heavy casualties on both sides, particularly at the Battles of Salerno, San Pietro, Anzio and Cassino. Rome had fallen on 5th June and the front was now well to the north of it. The left of the Allied line was held by the U.S. 5th Army; the centre and the right of the line by the British 8th Army under General Sir Oliver Leese. Though mainly British, it included troops of various nationalities – Indians, Poles, Canadians, South Africans, some French and Italians and the Jewish Brigade. On the right was the Polish II Corps, on the left the British XIII Corps and in the centre – the most mountainous part of the line – the British X Corps under General Sir Richard McCreery, who later took over command of the 8th Army from General Leese. Within the British X Corps was the 10th Indian Division which the Lovat Scouts now joined. It was commanded by Major General D.W. Reid, C.B.E., D.S.O., M.C.

Kesselring's plan is described by Liddell Hart as being 'to slow down the Allied advance by a series of delaying actions throughout the summer and retreat to the Gothic Line for the winter'. He had some very tough and seasoned troops, almost as many Divisions (although they were

SKETCH MAP
OF
ITALY ~ 1944~45.

~~~~~~~~~~~ = GOTHIC LINE
—·—·—·—·— = ALBERT LINE (AUG. '44)

depleted) as the Allies had for much of the time and all the advantages of an Army withdrawing through difficult, mountainous country. The aim of the Allies was, broadly, to advance northwards, always fighting and harrassing the enemy, drawing off German forces from other theatres of war and, if a collapse occurred on the western front leading to German withdrawal in Italy, to exploit a breakthrough towards Trieste and Vienna.

From early August 1944, the Scouts were to be almost continuously in the line, first in the heat of summer and then in the cold, rain and snow of late autumn and winter. They were in hill country, in constant touch with the enemy and, whenever possible, moving forward. Their weapons were rifles, Tommy guns, a Bren to each Section and eventually some mortars. Rarely had the Scouts fought in such ideal country for the effective use of telescopes, which were carried by most officers and N.C.Ofs as well as by the sixty-four trained snipers. Binoculars were of course also used and were of the utmost importance on night patrols. A great deal of the Scouts' previous training proved invaluable and the equipment which they obtained in Canada – particularly the rucksacks and sleeping bags – was excellent.

It was a campaign of frequent action and patrolling, in which the ability of junior leaders was of crucial importance; and in this the Scouts excelled. The official War Diaries record that altogether 240 patrols, both fighting and recce, were carried out. They included over a dozen long-distance recce patrols behind the enemy lines of from two to five days' duration, ten of which were highly successful and brought back much useful information for Intelligence. One long-distance patrol and about half a fighting patrol were captured: otherwise no Scouts were taken prisoner. Although there were casualties on many patrols, these would undoubtedly have been considerably heavier and some of the patrols impracticable but for the Scouts' previous training and natural aptitude in fieldcraft and in hill country. Transport of ammunition and supplies was mainly by jeep but, in the steeper hills, mules were very often used with Indian or Italian muleteers. Occasionally, in bad, muddy conditions, oxen with sledges made ponderous progress.

The Regiment moved north from Naples on 4th August in lorries via Cassino and Rome and camped en route near Ferrinto, Spolleto and Citerna. After leaving winter stores at Anghiari, they joined 10th Indian Div. officially as 'mountain recce troops', on 7th August near Arezzo. Next day they took over two different parts of the line. C, D, and R Sqns. under the Commanding Officer, relieved a Battalion of Mahrattas in the area of Montaunto. They were shelled on their way into the line. Lieut. Peter Scott was wounded and Major Brooke had a piece of his shirt removed by shrapnel. Meanwhile, A and B Sqns. moved into the line near La Cesta and became part of Wheeler Force.

As well as holding their section of the line, all Squadrons carried out active patrolling from the start. The following abbreviated extracts from the War Diaries are but a framework within which those who served in Italy may recall some of the incidents of excitement, success and tragedy during engagements with the enemy, particularly during the first few months:

9 AUG.   Heavy enemy shelling on Casa di Montaunto.
11 AUG.   C Sqn. fighting patrol (Lt. Rayer) to Ponte alla Piera. Wirelessed has captured 8 prisoners and had one casualty. D Sqn. (14 Troop) ambushed on way into night position. Mtnr. Brown A. killed and 6 wounded.
12 AUG.   Lt. Rayer's patrol meeting opposion at P. alla Piera. D Sqn. (15 Troop) capture 5 prisoners on day patrol. Mtnr. MacLeod J. killed.
14 AUG.   No Germans now in P. alla Piera. M.O. attended woman there who had been shot (also her sister mutilated and now dead) by Germans as "informers". C Sqn. patrol (Lt. Turnbull) north of P. alla Piera surrounded by enemy and forced to withdraw.
15 AUG.   C Sqn. move forward of P. alla Piera. "H" Sqn. distributed among other Sqns. to replace sick and wounded.
16/18 AUG.   Night patrols by all Sqns. Among prisoners taken was an

enemy postman with all his Coy's mail. Heavy shelling of R.H.Q. (1 casualty).

19 AUG. C Sqn. patrol (Lt. Turnbull) took prisoner at Singerna and returned sniper's fire beyond it. D Sqn. patrol (Lt. Scroggie) found 8 Germans in house and threw in '36 grenades' Suffered one casualty. Recce patrol (Lt. Tinqulstad) fired on at Rancoci.

20 AUG. 68 Fd. Regt. R.A. now in support, engaging targets under Sqn. Ldrs. Recce patrol to Diciano engaged by several Spandaus (LMGs) and mortar, but got back without casualties. Recce patrol (Lt. Tingulstad) fired on and Sgt. Neil MacLeod wounded. C Sqn. patrol ambushed enemy near Papiano following interception of German message (one prisoner taken; remainder fled). Cpl. and 2 snipers sent to Garwhali Rifles for 3-day recce patrol behind lines.

21 AUG. D Sqn. fighting patrol (S.S.M. George) reached grid 58, North of Singerna river. C Sqn. patrol (U. Milne) had fire fight at Rocca. One killed and 2 casualties but took a prisoner.

23 AUG. D Sqn. fighting patrol (Lt. W. Elliot) contacted enemy beyond San Sepolchro. Surrounded while attacking house containing Germans. Several wounded. Only 8 Scouts got back (including Cpl. H. Gordon and A. Munro, also Cpl. H. Mackay and I. Gunn, both wounded, who got back next morning after hiding). Remainder missing.

On 24th August, C, D, and H.Q. Sqns. were withdrawn to the north bank of the river Arno ('A') bathed: first time we've been clean for weeks!') for three days, before relieving A and B Sqns. forward of Carda. The latter between 10th and 28th August had carried out patrols daily in the areas of La Cesta, Monte Lori, Massereci and Carda. 'A few casualties; some prisoners were taken.' On 13th, B Sqn. spied about fifty enemy troop carriers going north from San Martino. At dusk on 26th, two deep patrols

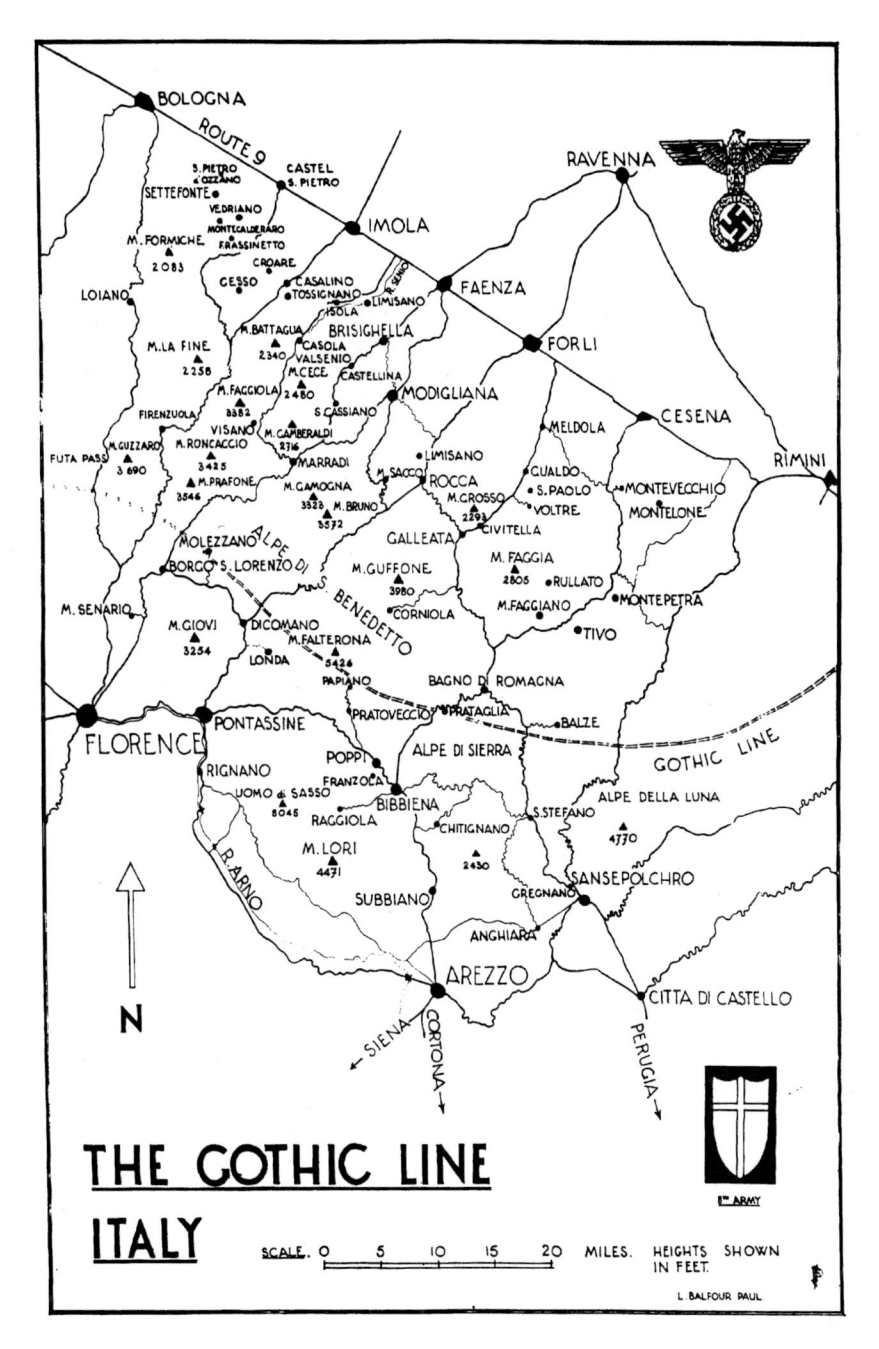

THE GOTHIC LINE
ITALY

(of five days) left under orders of the Div. Cmdr. to recce the Gothic Line. Lieut. Tingulstad led one (forward of Poppi) Lieut. Packer the other (north of Foresto). Each consisted of three snipers, a Sgt. interpreter and three Itajian partisans. Lieut. Tinguistad returned successfully on 1st September with much information for Division. Lieut. Parker got back with some useful information too, but was himself injured and his partisans all deserted when they came under fire.

On 2nd September the whole Regiment took over from 2nd/3rd Gurkhas forward of San Martino and Fronzola. Lieut. Oxley left at dusk on a three-day patrol behind the enemy lines to recce the Gothic Line beyond Soci with two snipers, a Sgt. interpreter and three partisans. During the next two days, each Sqn.'s fighting patrols were engaged in fights and inflicted some casualties. A prisoner, captured by D Sqn. reported to Brigade H.Q. that on the night of 2nd/3rd September, near Soci, a British officer and two soldiers were captured and an Italian Sgt. killed. The prisoners were presumed to be Lieut. Oxley and Mtnrs. Murray and Lewis.

6 SEPT.	Regt. congratulated by Bde. on its very good spying and observation of enemy shelling and mortaring. Combined patrol of A Sqn. Tp. and Indian Horse armoured cars. The latter were shelled and withdrew. D Sqn. patrol killed 2 enemy and captured one.
7 SEPT.	D Sqn. patrol found enemy in strength at Corsignano, had fire fight and killed or wounded 3 Germans. A Sqn. patrol attacked an occupied house in Agna at dawn. 2 prisoners; remainder escaped.
8 SEPT.	C Sqn. moved forward to Quorle. Torrential rain. Only one patrol (A Sqn.l managed to cross the Arno. 3 deep patrols (3 days) departed at dusk under Capt. Melville after his aerial recce of routes, to report to Bde. all enemy movements and positions behind line on Bde front. (Each patrol comprising Ldr. and 2 snipers; Sgt. Davidson and Cpl. R Ross led the

	other 2 patrols, forward of Pratagia, Serravalle and Camaidoli respectively).
9 SEPT.	O Sqn. patrol to Monte heavily mortared. Much burning and many explosions spied behind German lines.
10 SEPT.	Partisans looting in Poppi. Patrol sent to keep order captured 2 drunk enemy. A Sqn. took 3 prisoners at Poggiolo. B Sqn. patrol inflicted casualties at Mandrioli.
11 SEPT.	O Sqn. patrol again heavily mortared from Monte. A Sqn. spied 35 enemy at Bucena.
12 SEPT.	O Sqn. move forward. A Sqn. patrol mortared from Monte before daylight; listening post suspected. All 3 deep patrols under Capt. Melville returned tonight. Very full information obtained and reported to Bde. (1 enemy believed shot; 2 patrols mortared on way back).
13 SEPT.	A Sgn. recce patrol had running fight with enemy at Monte di Sopra. One man, badly wounded, had to be left behind. O Sqn. recce patrol fired on above Lonnano. C Sqn. patrol was attacked but drove enemy off.

From 14th to 16th September, each Squadron contacted the enemy nightly with recce patrols. On 17th the Regiment moved to relieve lst/2nd Punjabis on right of 10th Ind. Div. forward of Mignana, except C Sqn. which remained to hold part of the line at Fronzola with the Indian Horse. On 18th R.H.Q. was very heavily shelled at Gregnano soon after arrival while men were on their way to the cookhouse. Four O.R.s were killed outright and four wounded. The Regiment moved again next night and dug in forward of San Sepolchro. Recce patrols found the enemy had withdrawn and two-day patrols reported them now beyond Balze and Monte Laggio. On 28th September the Regiment moved forward to Alfero, and A Sqn. captured six prisoners at Sarsina. D Sqn. moved up to Tivo with a view to reaching Monte Petra on 1st October, but recce patrols found it very strongly held and the move was postponed. The other three Squadrons moved forward to Sapigno, Mescolino and Facciano.

2 OCT.	Torrential rains. Great difficulty in crossing streams.
3 OCT.	A Sqn. fighting patrol (Capt. Fraser) had successful fight with 15 enemy on Monte Petra. 11 enemy killed. Just as patrol was beginning to search for papers, heavy mortar fire came down, wounding 2. Patrol forced to withdraw. C Sqn. patrol to Bucchio cleared enemy from village, wounding one.
4 OCT.	A & C Sqns. relieved by the Rough Riders (11 L.A.A. Regt.), now infantry and A/A. They hold the Facciano ridge, while we patrol forward of them and step up. C Sqn. now controlling the shooting of 102 Medium Regt., R.A., from Civorio.
5 OCT.	B Sqn. night patrol of 1 Tp. under Capt. Melville reached position 300 yards from summit of Petra. (Sgt. I. MacLean & 2 men stalked and killed several Germans in trench). Intermittent fire fight throughout night. Patrol withdrew before light. D Sqn. moved to Monte Del.
6 OCT.	B Sqn. patrol finds M. Petra still strongly held. Harrassing fire on it all day by 457 Mtn. Bty. and 107 Medium Regt. Some enemy observed wounded.
7 OCT.	A Sqn. patrol (Lt. B. Wootton) inflicted casualties at Monte Bullato. B Sqn. patrol find M. Petra now clear and discover recent enemy graves.
8 OCT.	A Sqn. patrol capture 20 prisoners (including Russians) after surrounding house at Squarti. 5 Russians surrendered to T.A.C. H.Q. Enemy contacted on Monte Rulla and in Rullato.
9 OCT.	A Sqn. patrol (Lte Howe) ambushed enemy patrol near Detto. Killed 2 and captured 4 from 354 Fuse Regt. B Sqne Sections at Caresto withdrawn after further heavy mortaring. D Sqn. snipers report enemy at Civorio and Casetta.
10 OCT.	A Sqn. fighting patrol (Lt. B. Wootton) killed 3 enemy and

captured one (870 Regt.) at Rullato. D Sqn. 2eday patrol returned reporting enemy near Vallenetto who tried to intercept them. 2 deserters (Poles) surrendered.

11 OCT. 2 Tps. of A Sqn. attacked enemy holding Rullato. Heavy spandau fire. Withdrew, leaving one Section observing. Sgt. McMenemy killed by sniper. B Sqn. patrol (Capt. Melville) area Della Pietra, had 2 badly wounded (carried 2 miles to road). D Sqn. 2-day patrol found Borello river uncrossable.

12 OCT. B Sqn. patrol fired on near Donicilio. C Sqn. (11 Tp.) under Lt. Budge, advancing to Cornio, attacked enemy in house at Bisuntolo, killing 2 and capturing 19. Cpl. Je Gunn killed during attack. Heavy mortaring wounded 9 men (Sgt. Morrison.e Cpl. Thomson and 7 Mtnrs.). 11 Tp. withdrew to Catelaccio and another C Sqn. Tp. occupied Cornio.

During the next fortnight, day and night patrols continued and each Squadron moved forward and dug in three times, being eventually at Gualdo, Bindonna, Reveretto and Monticino. The Germans held a feature called Monte Corno very strongly. Patrols on 16th and 17th October met opposition and there with casualties on both sides. The Sniping Officer and Cpl. D. Mackenzie were sent on a two-day patrol to locate enemy positions in Monte Corno area.

These were then heavily shelled by 7th Mtn. Bty. on 18th and 19th. By 20th it was reported all clear. Lieut. Turnbull with C Sqn. patrol captured the summit of San Paolo on 24th and the same day one Troop of D Sqn. occupied Reveretto. On 26th October, Lt. Colonel Douglas took over command of 18 L.I.B. (an Italian mountain unit) and the Regiment was temporarily commanded by Major Wedderburn until mid-December. On 28th/29th there was 'extremely heavy rain making most rivers impassable and causing great difficulty in crossing Ronca river with men and mules'. On 31st October the Regiment was relieved for a week and moved to an area near Arezzo for re-fitting. As many men as possible were given two days' leave to Florence. The War Diaries for October end:

'During October the Regiment has inflicted the following casualties on the enemy: Killed 20. killed or wounded 5, captured 65. Total bag, 90.'

* * * * * * * *

On 8th November, the Regiment moved back into the line, taking over from 1 Bn. Polish Corps Bde. in the area Fornace – Acuto. The town of Modigliano lay ahead. Recce and fighting patrols had several fire-fights and some casualties. Lieut. Gunar Tingulstad, the courageous and very popular Norwegian officer who had led so many successful patrols, was killed near Modigliano on the 12th. On the 14th, A Sqn. moved along the ridge towards Modigliano and the War Diary records:

14 NOV. Recce patrol (Capt. Fraser) entered town during p.m. and found it clear. On withdrawing, patrol was fired on from house on outskirts; and part of it with Maj. Richards R.A. was unable to withdraw till after dark.

15 NOV. A Sqn. entered Modigliano at first light without incident before any other troops entered town. The 8th Army (and NOT the 5th Army, as announced by B.B.C.) captured the town. They ware at least 2 hours behind us! Small enemy counter-attack in p.m. driven off.

By this time, the Germans had been pushed back some twenty miles behind their Gothic Line, which Kesselring and his successor, Von Vietinghoff, had hoped to occupy for the winter. They held the next feature strongly and from it shelled Modigliano. Forceful patrolling continued for the next fortnight beyond Merle, Marchionni and San Casiano, some prisoners being captured and all four Squadrons moving forward. 7th Mtn. Bty. provided frequent support, shooting effectively at targets spied by the Scouts' O.P.s and an enemy H.Q. was bombed from the air. 'One plane crashed behind the lines but the pilot was rescued,

"As step I wi' my Cromach to the Po!"

M.I.L.M.
MONTE CORNO – OCT. '44.

With apologies to 'JON' of The Eighth Army

slightly wounded.' The enemy, shelling some of the Scouts' positions near Risano, had a direct hit on a slit trench and caused casualties, some fatal.

Lieut. T. Cumming led a good fighting patrol from A Sqn. on 22nd near La Fortuna. 'They surprised and over-ran an enemy position, inflicting about six casualties and withdrew under D.F. fire without loss.' A series of casualties from mines began on 23rd, when a recce patrol under Lieut. Packer had one man wounded by a Schu-mine. The next day, 'the enemy were seen withdrawing from Marchionni and D Sqn. moved there after dark. Captain S.F. Macdonald and three O.R.s were wounded by a mine explosion'. A number of mines and booby traps were cleared next day.

By the end of November, all four Squadrons were in the line between Marchionni and Lechia, but D Sqn. was then temporarily dispersed among the other Squadrons while a new draft was formed into 'T' Sqn., commanded and trained by Captain Rayer. Lieuts. Wardrop, Thomson and Drife joined the Scouts and Captain Rev. J. Gilmour came as temporary Padre. Eleven officers were in hospital, wounded or sick. An epidemic of jaundice had, with the cold weather, succeeded dysentery as the chief plague of the 8th Army.

In mid-December, Lt. Colonel Douglas returned from 18 L.I.B. to re-assume command. The Regiment then moved to Brisigella and took over part of the line between Monte Mauro, Castellina and Angogna, B Sqn. having casualties from mines (one killed and four wounded; two muleteers of the Cyprus Regiment with them being killed and one wounded). On 24th December, Major Sandy Wedderburn was killed in a tragic accident at Aquila.

For the next four weeks, until 20th January, the Scouts continued to carry out active patrolling and advanced to the river Senio, the Germans holding strong positions beyond it. An enemy fighting patrol celebrated the early hours of New Year's day by attacking B Sqn. at Bosche di Sopra, but had four wounded and captured and one killed. On 4th January, B Sqn. had some casualties when the Germans attacked again. The Regiment moved on 10th January to relieve the 2nd/3rd Gurkhas at

Crivillari, Redreto and Pridella, where they had four casualties. There was considerable artillery activity on both sides with patrolling and a slight advance.

* * * * * * * *

The whole Regiment moved about 200 miles south on 23rd January to Paganica and Terminillo where, for three weeks, they underwent a refresher course in ski-mountaineering on the Gran Sasso (9,560 ft.). This enabled all the new men and officers to learn the rudiments of ski-ing, so that the whole Regiment could still, if necessary, be employed in snow-warfare. Skis were, in fact, only very rarely used in the line.

Lt. Colonel D.H. Cameron, younger of Lochiel, took over command of the Scouts at the end of January (when Lt. Colonel Douglas was appointed G.S.O. 1 at Division) and he led them magnificently throughout the rest of the campaign as well as in Austria and Greece. He had commanded a fine Sqn. for five years and every man and officer was delighted at his appointment. Hesketh-Prichard, in his book on Sniping, had commented on the leadership and wisdom of the late Lochiel, when he was commanding the Scouts on the Western front in 1917. His son had certainly inherited those qualities, which had also been so evident in their illustrious ancestor of 'the '45'. Major A.H. Fraser M.C. then commanded A Sqn., D Sqn., was re-formed under command of Major Balfour-Paul and Major S.F. Macdonald took over command of B Sqn. Major l.P. Grant (Camerons) was appointed Second-in-command. In late March he left to command a Bn. of the London Scottish, with which he was sadly killed shortly before the war ended. Major Sir John Brooke, who had commanded C Sqn. with great dash for four years, handed it over to Major Andrew Macdonald (stalwart son of the Scouts' famous Colonel Willie) and became Second-in-command of the Regiment. In that capacity, Sir John's ability to obtain for the Scouts whatever supplies and equipment they needed proved far-reaching and almost magical. The Regiment continued to be blessed with an excellent R.H.Q. – Captain

Wyld (H.Q. Sqn.), Captain Forrest (Adjt.), Captain Thorpe (Quartermaster), R.S.M. MacSween from Uist and a small but highly efficient and mobile Orderly Room staff, including Sgt. Leitch and Cpls. Murray and Mitchell. Captain Murray, at T.A.C., H.Q., continued throughout the campaign to be an exceptionally able Intelligence Officer.

After their three weeks' ski training the Scouts moved north on 15th February to Saltino and thence into the line again in the Monte Grande sector under command of 25 lnf. Bde. (10 Ind. Div.) forward of Apollinare. Patrols were carried out in the areas of Settefonte, S. Pietro d'Ozzano and di Sotto. Some prisoners were taken, a few Scouts were wounded, including Lieut. Drife and there was a good deal of shelling. To the delight of both Regiments, the Scouts found themselves near their old friends, the Scottish Horse (80th Medium Regiment, R.A.), whom they had not seen since the days of the Cavalry Division in early 1940, and who were now an exceptionally fine Regiment of Artillery. At the beginning of April, the Scouts moved via Molezzano to relieve an Italian Army Bde. at Casola Valsenio and thence to C. Monte and Mongordino in 'Mac Force' with the Jewish Brigade, under XIII Corps. There were frequent recce patrols and there was heavy enemy shell-fire.

On the night of 11th/12th April there were serious casualties in mine fields during an advance on a three Squadron front to take the Gesso ridge:

> Advance to objectives took place during night. By first light A Sqn. close to objective but held up owing to mines. 1 Tp. of B Sqn. reached objective without incident but other Tps. had heavy casualties from mines... Total casualties 4 killed and 2 officers and 20 Q.R.s wounded (including Lts. Wardrop and Thomson, S.S.M. Ian MacLean, Sgts. Colin Macrae and Innes). Sqns. withdrew to old locations.

On 14th April, the Scouts relieved a Battalion of The King's Own on the Cerere-Monte Grande sector again under command of 25 Ind. lnf. Bde.

The entry for 17th April reads:

> All ridge towards Vedriano clear but area heavily mined and booby-trapped. Considerable enemy activiw on Monte Calderano, where Coy. attack by K.S.L.I., repulsed from Castellaro with casualties. D Sqn. moved forward to Sopra Sasso with 1 Tp. to Del Sarti. Lt. Scroggie and 1 OR wounded by mines.

The Scouts' sector of the line moved forward twice and finally dug in forward of Monte Calderano. At C Sqn.'s position there were twelve unburied corpses of American soldiers who had been killed there in an attack four weeks earlier. Many mines and booby traps had to be cleared. Much enemy transport was spied fleeing north along route 9. Rumours were rife that the war was almost over and, after concentrating near Brisigella, the Scouts heard on 5th May that there was a cease fire in Italy. This welcome news was duly celebrated.

* * * * * * * *

An unpleasant two-day iourney in cattle trucks began on 10th May, each Squadron travelling separately by rail from Faenza, escorting some 900 German prisoners to Taranto in the extreme south of Italy. The Scouts camped there in a very hot and unattractive place, but good news came on 25th May that they were to move north to Austria.

On 8th May 1945, Lt. General Sir Richard McCreery, K.G.B., K.C.B.E., D.S.O., M.C., G.O.C., 8th Army, wrote to the Scouts' Commanding Officer the following letter, a copy of which was given to all ranks:

> 'Dear Cameron,
> Now that the war with Germany has ended, I want to send my warmest congratulations to you and all Ranks of your

Regiment on the splendid part you have played in the Italian Campaign.

The Lovat Scouts have fought for nine months in Italy with great determination, enterprise and skill. Although you have had no real mountain fighting, you have carried out many difficult tasks in the Appenines with complete success.

I well remember the enthusiasm of the Regiment when you joined 10th Indian Division in X Corps last summer, and the immediate success that good patrolling gave you. From then onwards, with hardly a pause, you have all been hard at it, always in difficult country, probing the enemy with deep patrols, advancing through the hills, or holding a wide front.

Scotland may well be proud of the Lovat Scouts.

All good wishes and well done indeed.

Yours sincerely,
R.L. McCREERY.'

Among those who received awards for gallantry during the Campaign were the following: Military Crosses, Major A.H. Fraser, Lieut. W.H. Budge and Lieut. T. Cumming; George Medal, Sgt. Colin Macrae; Distinguished Conduct Medal, Sgt. Major T. Morrison; Military Medal, Sgt. Major J. George, Sgt. D. Davidson, Sgt. J. Sorley, Sgt. E. Cameron, Cp). J.W. Black, Mtnr. F. Scott and Mtnr. T. Gorrie; British Empire Medal, Sgt. D. Stewart, Cpl. A.Kennedy and Cpl. Hendry. The Commanding Officer and thirty-five other members of the Regiment were mentioned in Despatches. It may certainly be added that every Scout who came through those nine months of fighting in the Appenines had well and truly earned his Italian Star and could wear his blue bonnet with, if possible, even greater pride than before.

CHAPTER XIX

SOME MEMORIES OF ITALY
(1944 – 1945)

Every Scout who fought in the Italian campaign has his own personal memories of it – moments of intense excitement, of tragedy, of hardship and occasionally of comedy. The following are only a small cross-section of a vast number of personal experiences, but they may help to illustrate life in the Appenines at that time.

Sgt. Jock Urquhart, originally from Strathconon, has been head stalker at Lochluichart since the war. A good athlete and a fine shot, he was Troop Sgt. of a fighting patrol in late August 1944. Part of that patrol was captured but several members of it, some wounded, managed to escape. His experiences are described in the following letter:

> My first memory is of a fighting patrol we did on Woodpile Ridge on 12th Aug. I can mind thinking, 'Well, it's not grouse today – it's Germans!' Sgt. Jock Mackay (Monar) led the Tp. at night to within 400 yds. of the German position we had been spying. The attack went in at dawn. We surprised them and took 5 prisoners with the loss of one man (J. Mac Leod, Lochinver). We were shelled badly on the way back.
>
> The fighting patrol with Lt. Elliot, about 10 days later, was to find out where the enemy had withdrawn to. By dawn we were in the valley beyond San Sepolchro. We marched all morning in open formation with one Section well ahead – fairly open country with a few houses dotted about. At each house they said "The Germans left here 2 days ago".
>
> About mid-day we came to a house near the head of a small valley. Lt. Elliot took a Section forward while we covered the house. I saw a window open and was about to fire when a white flag appeared. It was the same story, "The Germans left

here 2 days ago". The next house was about 200 yards away. Cpl. Gunn's Section was going forward to it, with us lining out to give him cover, when they opened fire on us from the house with spandau, rifles and mortars. Bill Dunbar in front of me was hit through the face with a bullet. I left him with Roddy Mackay (Fairburn) and went forward to Lt. Elliot who was in a ditch trying to pinpoint the enemy positions. We put a Bren gun into the first house and got a signaller to call for our artillery support, but he was wounded. Another man took over the set and he was wounded too.

By this time we could see they were on 3 sides of us and would cut us off unless we acted quickly. We decided it was best to get out. 'Every man for himself' was the order. I went forward to help Cpl. Gunn's Section and saw him getting out with blood running down his back.

I got into a field of Indian corn, was hit by a ricochet in the back, but only a flesh wound, and was able to carry on.. I heard Lt. Elliot shouting on my right, so crawled over to find out what was wrong. He was leading 4 wounded men, crawling up a ditch, trying to get them out. He said, "Get in behind and keep them going. I'll lead". We crawled over an "Eye-tye", who was in the ditch. He never complained. The ditch peter-ed out and Lt. Elliot shouted "We'll have to cross this track quickly one at a time". He went first and it was sprayed by a spandau. This was too much for the wounded and they would not move, so he told them he and I would have to leave and try to get aid.

I crawled through the cornfield and into a field of tomatoes, under heavy fire. I looked behind and saw a line of Jerries approaching 100 yds. away. I fired a burst at them with the Tommy Gun and then heard something behind me. There was another line of Jerries right on top of me. They shouted "Hande Hoch I" and that was me in the bag. Lt. Elliot and the wounded also had their hands up.

They treated us quite well and got the wounded away quickly. I had very light-coloured K.D. shorts, so I had draped my camouflage net round my waist and let it hang down like a kilt. I think every German in that Bn. came to have a look at the "soldier in the kilt".

We were taken to a P.O.W. camp in Bologna, where I lost Lt. Elliot and the others, then through the Brenner Pass... While on the march in Bavaria, I managed to slip away with a Sgt. from 8th Manchesters. We were free for 4 days, raiding farms at night for food, but were caught by some Germans with tracker dogs, looking for deserters ... Donnie Mackenzie (Achnashellach) asks if you remember the patrol when you ate raw eggs and both got fleas!

* * * * * * * *

It was about 5 p.m. when R.H.Q. arrived at Gregnano on 18th September. As they were entering the buildings, Pipe Major Riddell, formerly a gamekeeper, noticed a carrier pigeon leaving through the roof of a shed and flying off northwards. He reported it. At about 5.30 p.m., he was coming out of the dilapidated farmhouse, when he suddenly saw a dud shell hit the ground just in front of him. A few seconds later another exploded right on the queue of men going to the cookhouse for their tea. There followed about five minutes of intensive shelling. From the first shot, the Germans had the range perfectly: four men were killed outright, one of them blown to pieces, and four were badly wounded. Several Scouts who were there remember Captain Rowntree and others attending the wounded while the heavy shelling was still in progress. Did the carrier pigeon fly a few miles north to a German Army loft, and was that the signal to shell Gregnano?

* * * * * * * *

Pat Wootton always had a highly efficient and accurate Troop of Mortars. Douglas Ramsay recalls that when he was in the line with Pat they used to 'watch for Germans every morning going to do their toilet. As soon as we saw them disappear into a certain small house, Pat would fire a number of mortar bombs and they would all come flying out with their trousers down!'

* * * * * * * *

Partisani were free-lance, semi-civilian Italians who wandered about in and around the front line, usually armed to the teeth with a variety of weapons, including grenades. Most of them were genuinely anti-German, some were useful and others a frightful nuisance. One of these characters arrived during the night at R.H.Q. wanting urgently to see an officer. The piper on guard shook one of the officers, who was asleep on the floor and who had not been with the Scouts for very long. 'Come quick', he said, 'There's a Faroe man to see you!'

* * * * * * * *

On 8th September, the Sniping Officer was flown in an artillery 'Spotter' aircraft, to reconnoitre routes for his own and two other three-day recce patrols behind the German lines. He wrote:

> The pilot was cheerful, looked about eighteen, spoke in the jargon of 'Flying Officer Kite" and wore more or less civilian clothes, including a spotted scarf which had formerly, he told me, been part of a girl's bathing dress. The run-way seemed very short with trees beyond it. I asked if we could clear them all right. "It depends on the wind", he said and took off.
> We flew slowly above the enemy lines and beyond. The recce, helped by aerial photographs, was extremely useful. We

saw enemy vehicles but no Germans: they were keeping their heads down. The pilot thought spying with a telescope was a great joke. When we had seen enough I foolishly asked him what he would do if a German fighter appeared. "I would dodge", he said, "I'll show you". With that he seemed to stop the plane, dipped his left wing and dropped like a stone. After several seconds I was certain the machine was out of control and that we would crash; but a few hundred feet from the ground it zoomed upwards again. "Why didn't they shoot at us?", I shouted. "Jerry doesn't want to be shelled", he laughed, "He's scared stiff!" The pilot's confidence, gained from air supremacy, was infectious. It was encouraging to start on a three-day patrol convinced that the Germans were "scared stiff".

* * * * * * *

Sgt. Jack Fraser recalls an occasion when a pig, 'liberated' by a patrol was being fattened on cookhouse scraps in a shed in the front line. One night with snow on the ground, a German patrol appeared, was shot up and had four casualties. Their three wounded were looked after and the body of the fourth, killed outright, was put into the shed for the night. By morning the pig had eaten most of his face. They were naturally squeamish about eating the pig after that, but managed to swap it for a crate of beer.

* * * * * * *

Major Sandy Fraser M.C., moved A Sqn. in darkness 13th/14th November with about thirty mules and six oxen to some farm buildings a mile west of Modigliano. By next morning the Germans had withdrawn from the town but kept up a desultory fire with two spandaus from a ridge about 500 yards away. That night A Sqn. moved into Mod igliano, guided through the mine fields by local Partigiari, two of whom were killed. The Squadron took up strong positions in the town and were warmly welcomed and fed by the citizens.

Meanwhile the W.T./Radio failed to work. Major Fraser knew that T.A.C., H.Q. urgently wanted information, so he decided to go back himself. He writes:

> This appeared at first sight to be rather dangerous, as it was a longish trip and in broad daylight. However, an ingenious Partigiaro produced Franciscan garb, dark brown and a foot short in length, complete with broad brimmed hat, which gave me confidence, despite Denis Howe's conviction that I was breaking various clauses of the Geneva Convention and would certainly be shot if caught. It worked a charm and I was unmolested on my journey...

His new instructions were to move out of Modigliano that night, because the official entry was to be made by another Bde. Group. Their route back involved climbing a precipitous hill in the dark. About half their unfortunate mules fell, broke their legs and had to be shot. The oxen were left behind as a reward for the Partigiari.

* * * * * * * *

Of various Russians captured, two may almost be said to have become temporary Scouts. One, called 'Mike', was an ex-merchant seaman from Murmansk and in his early forties; the other was a young chap called 'Nicky' from South Russia. It was decided not to hand them over with the other prisoners but to give them useful jobs in the Squadron cookhouse. They worked hard and became very popular. Nicky learnt English quickly and he was taken once on short leave, wearing a Scout bonnet. He was given a Pay Book with the name 'Nicholas MacBean', and was told to say that he came from Inverness. He was stopped by a Military Policeman, who quickly discovered that this Scout had a strange accent and knew nothing about Inverness, because, by bad luck, he happened to come from there himself. However, being a Highlander and knowing that the Scouts were an unusual Regiment, he very kindly decided to turn a blind eye to this irregularity.

* * * * * * *

For a short time we were in a formation called 'Mac Force'. It consisted of the Jewish Brigade and two Highland units – (the Lovat Scouts and the H.L.I.). An American Staff Officer, who had to do with supplies, found himself dealing with three Jewish and two Scottish Quartermasters. He once said he guessed our Brigade must be 'the meanest outfit in the British Army'!

* * * * * * *

The Gurkhas became great friends of ours. They were wonderful fighters and had a grand sense of humour. An article in the Inverness Courier of that time was headed, THE McGURKHAS IN ITALY and went on to say 'Due to an aptitude for operations in hill-country equivalent to that of the warriors from Nepal, a Highland Territorial Unit with the 10th Indian Division in Italy has earned for itself the nom-de-guerre of The McGurkhas...'. A popular, if doubtful, story of the Gurkhas was that one of their recce patrols had come on a trench with three snoring Germans fast asleep. With their dreadfully sharp kukris they had silently severed the heads of the two outside Germans, changed them over and then crept away in high glee, wondering what the German in the middle would say when he woke up!

* * * * * * *

The Pioneer Troop were all heroes, the greatest of them being their leader, Sgt. Colin Macrae G.M. Originally consisting of skilled tradesmen, they were then taught demolitions; and, in Aberdeen before leaving for Italy, they were instructed in defusing and lifting mines. Towards the end of the campaign the Germans, desperate to delay the Allied advance, continually laid mines and set booby traps. They used a variety of them – Schu-mines, Teller mines, S. mines (with a shrapnel burst six feet up) and many different types of wooden and other non-metal mines, which could not easily be detected. Certainly the Pioneers found and lifted hundreds of them, but there was always a grave risk. The greatest number of mine casualties occurred on the night of 11th/12th April 1945, when four Scouts were killed and twenty-two wounded, many of them severely. Sgt. Macrae was himself very seriously wounded that night. He was awarded the George Medal for great gallantry.

* * * * * * * *

Lieut. Sydney Scroggie joined the Scouts before we went to Canada. He was an enthusiastic skier – one of his treasured possessions is his medal for being fourth in the Regimental ski race – and a great man on the hill. He still is today for, despite being seriously wounded and blinded near the end of the war, he continues to walk the hills of his native Angus and has climbed countless 'Munros', Scottish hills over 3,000 feet high. He writes:

> Some fifty Scouts are not in a position to describe the last thing they saw in this life. Friends and comrades of ours, they fell in Tuscany and Romagna, carrying their secret with them to an Imperial war grave. My loss, in springing a schu-mine, was nothing but my eyesight and the lower part of a leg; the vivifying principle was unimpaired, and clearly I remember how at 19.10 hrs on 17th April '45, as seen from the lower slopes of Monte Grande, the planet Venus, big and serene, gleamed in an evening sky.
>
> Who else was with me on that patrol, aimed at advancing Sqn. H.Q. to a more convenient locality? Cpl. Sandy

McCaskill comes to mind, my batman Kirkpatrick, Bobby Vance, Wee Petrie, Alan Stoddart and others who had survived with 12 Tp. since the early days of Pante alla Piera and Woodpile Ridge and some reinforcements, such as Vic Ware and Happy Hopkinson.

There were shattered vineyards and rusty, knocked-out Sherman tanks around, 3 dead Jerries, mere skulls for faces, propped up in macabre charade against a bank, a good going battle samewhat to the left with shells exploding and grinning, steel-helmeted Gurkhas in slit trenches; and against this background, as gloaming faded into twilight, there was a crack like a .38, an acrid whiff, and CpI. Kennedy lay on the ground, an arm off at the elbow. A schu-mine he was defusing had gone off in his hand. "Kennedy's a joiner", someone said, "And that's his right arm".

I took one step, the amethyst sky was very beautiful, and instantly there was a ringing in my ears, dazzling lights before my eyes and a stunning shock that pervaded my body through and through. A schu-mine makes a little crater when it goes off and I was sitting in it when I came to, propped up against the rucksack on my back. The twilight had gone, Venus had switched herself off, and I was trying to peer, as it were, through a red mask when I heard the voice of Hopkinson. "Are you all right, Sir?", it said. From the outset I was certain of the facts. I said, "Yes, I'm all right, Happy, but I think I've lost the sight of both eyes".

Kirkpatrick, contemptuous of his own safety, rushed away for a Jeep, a probing squad was organised and Alan Stoddart carried me on his back. Then, as I awaited Capt. John Rowntree, I heard the soft Lochinver voice of Sandy McCaskiII. and I was grateful for his remark. "If I get it, Sir", he said, "I hope I take it like you."

Presently, the Scout's last casualty, together with CpI.

Kennedy, bumped and rattled away not only to the Field Surgical Unit, Naples, and to the U.K., but also to a different and quite unimaginable life.

* * * * * * * *

The following memories have been contributed by our Commanding Officer in Italy, Colonel Sir Donald Cameron of Lochiel, K.T., C.V.O.:

> My first impressions of Italy were of the dirt in the South, the dusty roads which left one covered in white dust when travelling in an open Jeep, and the friendliness of the inhabitants when we got further North. It was amazing how they uncovered in front of us all their precious belongings, which they had carefully hidden for years from the Germans and even from other Allied troops.
>
> Being Territorials and, in particular, Lovat Scouts, we were not hampered by any inhibitions or rigid rules. Some of us learned a little Italian and soon we were on excellent terms with the Italian peasantry. We had no hesitation in commandeering their oxen if we were short of mules, we became renowned for our long distance patrols behind the enemy likes and generally behaved as one would expect Lovat Scouts to behave.
>
> It was quite a revelation to us to encounter the magnificent Gurkhas and other Indian troops, whom most of us had never seen before, and we were very lucky to get initiated into the Italian campaign as part of an Indian Division. Another interesting unit we met in Italy was Popski's Private Army, an irregular unit that did a splendid job there. Popski (Colonel Peniakof) had as his personal driver and bodyguard a Lovat Scout, Sgt. Cameron, who had joined us from the Scottish Horse. I know that Popski found him excellent but, sadly, he was killed later in the campaign.

For a time we were on the left flank of the 8th Army and the connecting link between this Army and the Americans. We took over this position from an American unit and were astonished at the vast quantity of tinned foods that had reached them and grateful that so much had been left for us. Later, we operated under General Anders' fine Polish troops – a courageous body of men, but difficult to understand. We also formed part of the Jewish Bde. at the end of the war under a Brigadier Benjamin.

It was an interesting experience, though I fortunately managed to restrain him from sending the whole unit forward over mined country long after we knew the German Army had retreated from their postions.

During my period of command we were part of 13th Corps under General Harding, a most understanding and splendid commander. But we were basically an 8th Army unit and wore the 8th Army badge on our shoulders. We were very proud of this and when we went to Greece our new Brigadier was astonished and irritated by our not wishing to discard our 8th Army badge for the renowned badge of the 4th Indian Division.

The Lovat Scouts undoubtedly did a great job in Italy, and were always a very happy unit. It was a very proud moment for me when I was given the honour of commanding them.

CHAPTER XX

AUSTRIA (June – July 1945)
AND GREECE (July 1945 – October 1946)

In late May, the Regiment travelled by road up the east coast of Italy, the advance party visiting Venice en route, and thence to the Kiagenfurt area of Austria. R.H.Q. was at Radentheim with Squadrons dispersed in various villages, such as Patergassen and Ebene Reichnau below the high pass of Turracher Hohe, where a steep road goes through the mountains towards Judenburg and Vienna.

Their main duties were to intercept German soldiers escaping home through the hills, to comb the district for Nazi and S.S. officials – several high-ranking war criminals were caught – and to search for weapons, of which a great many were found.

It was heavenly country in the glory of early summer, with an abundance of trout fishing in the Gurk and other rivers. An occasional red deer was killed for the pot, and two officers shot a chamois in the high hills. Most of the Austrians in that highland district were obviously charming (indeed it was hard to realise they had been our enemies!) but there was a strictly enforced No fraternisation order, which was not lifted until later.

The 2nd German Cavalry Bde. (Mounted), disarmed except for its officers who had revolvers, was still in being nearby, and each British Regiment was allowed to choose about twenty of their horses for recreation. The Scouts got good ones and had minor successes in races and show jumping. But the star turn was a rough pony of incredible ability chosen by Sgt. Neil MacLeod from those belonging to a Regiment of unfortunate Cossacks, who had fought for the Germans, had surrendered to the British and Americans, and were later shamefully handed over to the Russians for execution or slavery. Riding this pony at Paternion on 30th June, Neil MacLeod won the Open Show Jumping against the cream of the German and Italian horses, which the British

Army had collected, some of them ridden by expert cavalrymen – a brilliant performance by a Highland shepherd.

This happy life in Austria was too good to last, and in mid-July the Scouts were flown in troop carriers to Salonika in northern Greece, where they joined the 11th Indian Infantry Bde. (4th Indian Div.), commanded by Brigadier John Hunt, who later led the first ascent of Mount Everest. R.H.Q. and A Sqn. were at Salonika with B Sqn. at Asprovalto and D Sqn. near Therma. C Sqn. was about eighty miles north in the Struma valley, camping at Sidhi Rokhastron, beyond Serres. It was near the famous Rupel Pass, where, across a small wooden bridge which represented the Iron Curtain, they sometimes glimpsed and waved to Bulgar and Russian soldiers. It was twenty-seven years since the Regiment had fought near Serres. They visited some of the war graves of Scouts who had been killed there.

Their chief task in that hot, war-weary and poverty-stricken country was to help in restoring law and order and, in particular, to keep the peace between the various rival factions. British soldiers were supposed to be impartial with, perhaps, a leaning towards the Communists, who had had the best record for resisting the Germans; but it was not always easy and they witnessed terrible bitterness. Once when a C Sqn. patrol raided a small village at dawn, after information that arms were hidden there, they discovered that the inhabitants were almost all widows or children. They were told (and shown the scene of massacre) that a few months before, as a reprisal, a Communist guerilla gang had tied down every male villager and, with 2 mules and a plough, had beheaded them. That was typical of the brutal acts carried out by both sides in the name of revenge. Peace and goodwill do not come easily after such events; nor do young men, used to the exciting, ruthless life of guerilla bands, readily give up their guns and return to peaceful poverty. During patrols in villages near the Bulgarian frontier, they saw rival factions shoot at each other, but only once were the Scouts deliberately fired upon. Sgt. Dick Gordon (C Sqn.), who had had an exciting escape when most of a fighting patrol was captured in Italy, describes the incident thus:

In late August, Major Melville told me to take a patrol with 3 Bren gun carriers along our side of the frontier, a certain distance west of the Rupel Pass. I chose eight or nine volunteers, mostly old Scouts, including Geordie MacLeod ("the farrier") and Sgt. "Oxo" Ross, who was leaving next day to be de-mobilised. The frontier was the watershed and we may, accidentally, have been a few yards over it when we saw below us about 40 Bulgars, apparently washing in a burn. We stopped and waved to them, but they ran off and 2 M.G.s opened fire on us. Two of the carriers were hit, "Oxo" had a narrow escape and one Scout got a bullet through his bonnet. We did not shoot back, of course, but withdrew flat out!l Next day the Communist papers reported that "a British tank attack had been driven off with casualties" and there was an Enquiry about it.

As the older age groups began to be de-mobilised, new drafts arrived of men from various Scottish Regiments and they were taught some mountaineering in the high hills beyond Serres. On a two-day expedition with Captain John Macdonald M.B.E. who had returned to the Regiment, one such party 'climbed Mount Ali Baba, capturing and disarming fourteen Bulgars'. Several wolves approached their camp one early morning. They had a few shots at them but missed.

In September, Lt. Colonel Donald Cameron went home for de-mobilisation. The Regiment was commanded for a short time by Sir John Brooke and then Major A.H. Fraser M.C. succeeded him as Commanding Officer. Promoted to Lt. Colonel, he commanded the Scouts for three months from Serres, in the country where his father had fought so well and won the D.S.O. Captain R.H. Thorp became Adjutant. The Scouts' duties, patrolling villages, keeping the peace and helping with the distribution of U.N.R.R.A. supplies continued. Vast numbers of wild geese came into the Struma valley for the winter: a few of them and many duck were shot. As the older men left and the

Regiment dwindled, A and C Sqns. were temporarily combined as 'X' Sqn. commanded by Major John Macdonald, and B and D Sqns. as 'Y' Sqn. commanded by Major Richard Rayer.

On Christmas Day, Lt. Colonel W.A. Stevenson, D.S.O. of the Cameron Highlanders (now Brigadier Mackenzie of Gairloch) took over command of the Scouts at Serres. There had been further drafts of new men and officers from other Regiments and by this time there had been many changes. As war-time Scouts departed homewards by age-groups, they rejoiced at the thought of seeing their families and the prospect of civilian life, but they had lasting memories too of friendship and great times in a unique Regiment. Soon there were few left who had known the wilds of the Rocky Mountains, fewer still who could recall the intricacies of the Faroe Dance, and only a venerable handful who had experienced the horrors of early stables in the winter of 1939.

One of those veterans was Major Charles Murray, whose father, Sir Kenneth, had been wounded near Serres serving with the Scouts in 1916. In early January 1946, he was sent with a reconstituted C Sqn. to Khalkis, over 200 miles south on the island of Euboea, where they took over from the 1st Northumberland Fusiliers. He was there for three months under direct command of a newly-formed Brigade whose H.Q. was a day's journey away near Pirans. He writes:

> Our prime task was to keep order and prevent the Greeks there from being more revolting than usual. They were about to have an election and there was some danger of a rebellion. One of our other functions was to look after the wife of a Labour Cabinet Minister. She owned a lovely Estate on the island where she seemed to rule the peasants with an iron and rather un-socialist rod! Another of my recollections is that the rate of exchange was then 20,000 Drachmas to the Pound and one more or less had to send a truck to collect the pay.

At the end of March the rest of the Regiment joined them at Khalkis. The majority of the men and officers were new to the Scouts, but the Regiment's traditions and high standards were maintained, smartness and efficiency being assured under the fine leadership first of Lt. Colonel Stevenson, and later of Lt. Colonel Digby-Hamilton, Scots Guards. They were proud of having an excellent and almost unbeaten football team.

At the Victory Parade in London, the Regiment was well represented by Major A.H. Fraser M.C. and six senior N.C.O.s.

Finally, in October 1946, as had happened at the end of each previous war, the Lovat Scouts were disbanded. The Regiment's possessions, temporarily in the care of the Colonel Commandant, Colonel Hon. Ian Campbell, D.S.O., were taken to the Cameron Barracks, Inverness, for safe keeping.

*Pack Batteiy Exercise near Aviemore, 1951
with (4th from left), Major General Viscount of Arbuthnott, C.B., C.B.E., D.S.O., M.C.
Commanding 51st Highland Division.*

The Pipe Band with Lt. Col. W. D. Johnston, O.B.E., at Weybourne Camp, 1955.

Infantry Section, Orkney, 1980

THE OPENING OF LOVAT HOUSE, GOLSPIE (HOME FOR THE ELDERLY) 1980.

H.R.H. The Prince of Wales with three former Scouts: (Left) Col. Allan Gilmour, OBE, MC, (1936-38), Major Norman Ledingham (1943-45) and John 'Corrie' Mackay, aged 92 (1905-1919).

CHAPTER XXI

POST WAR
(1947 – 1980)

Early in 1947, the Scouts were raised again, this time as one Squadron recruited from Inverness-shire. They were commanded by Major M.I. Leslie Melville with Captain W.H. Budge, M.C. as Second-in-command and Sgt. Major Jimmy George, M.M. as S.S.M. The great majority of the N.C.O.s and men had also served with the Scouts during the war. They were C Sqn. (Lovat Scouts) of the Scottish Horse, a tank Regiment in the Royal Armoured Corps, but had their own H.Q. in the Cameron Barracks, Inverness, with all the Scouts' Regimental belongings there. An assurance was given that in the event of a national emergency the Squadron would probably be expanded into a full Regiment, recruiting from all its traditional areas.

This arrangement worked well and the Scouts and the Scottish Horse got on excellently together, commanded by two regular officers, first Lt. Colonel T.G.G. Cooper, O.B.E. and then Lt. Colonel M.J. Lindsay, D.S.O. Two training camps were attended and in 1948 Major Leslie Melville and twelve senior N.C.O.s represented the Scouts and the Scottish Horse in a Parade of 3,000 T.A. troops in Hyde Park, London, King George VI taking the salute at the Cavalry Monument. Among the Scottish Horse Squadron Leaders were Major R. Barbour, M.C., who was to become (1979/80) Moderator of the General Assembly of the Church of Scotland, Major W.G. Gordon, D.F.C., who had directed their gunfire from the air in Italy, and Major A.M. Lyle, whose father had commanded the Regiment and who was himself later to be the last Commanding Officer of the Scottish Horse. In a beautiful building in Dunkeld the Scottish Horse now have an exceptionally interesting and well-run Museum, open to the public.

After India and Pakistan became independent, there was a shortage of Mountain Artillery and it was decided in 1949 that the Scouts should form two batteries, one with pack ponies, recruited from Uist and another from Inverness-shire, Ross-shire and Sutherland with Jeeps. They therefore bade farewell to the Scottish Horse and became 677 Mountain Regt. R.A. (Lovat Scouts) T.A. They learned gunnery and were commanded by a regular R.H.A. officer, Lt. Colonel D. Welsh, D.S.O. Camps were held at Bude (Cornwall) and at Otterburn (Northumberland). With ponies present again, it seemed like old times to some senior Scouts: Farrier Sgt. McRury, young as ever in heart, had rejoined and mounted sports were run by Michael Baillie of Dochfour, (formerly Scots Guards), another keen horseman.

Within a year, the Scouts had another change. They were merged, still under command of Lt. Colonel Welsh, with part of a Territorial Light Anti-Aircraft Unit. The new Regiment so formed was named 540 L.A.A. Regt. R.A. (Lovat Scouts) T.A. and consisted of three L.A.A. Batteries based on Inverness, Stornoway and Elgin, and also 850 Mountain Battery which was recruited in Inverness-shire, the Western Isles and Ross-shire. R.H.Q. was in Inverness.

540 L.A.A. Regt. (then called 40 L.A.A. Regt.) had had a splendid war record. Recruited originally from the Highlands it served in the U.K. till 1943, then became L.A.A. Regt. of 51st (Highland) Div., took part in every battle fought by the reconstructed Division throughout the war and was credited with over 100 enemy aircraft destroyed.

Almost unbelievably, in May 1950, there was yet another change both in the name and constitution of the Regiment. It amalgamated with parts of 532 L.A.A. Regt. in the Falkirk/Grangemouth area and was called 532 L.A.A. Regt. (Lovat Scouts) R.A., T.A. To be clear, it now had R.H.Q. at Inverness, Batteries at Inverness, Elgin and Falkirk, a Regimental L.A.D. in Glasgow and 850 Mountain Battery (Inverness-shire, Ross-shire, and the Western Isles, including Stornoway). Lt. Colonel W.D. Johnston quotes:

> 32 L.A.A. Regt, as it was then known, had a distinguished war record, having gone to Malta in 1941 as part of the famous

convoy reaching George Cross Island. It served there from July 1941 to March 1944, continuously in action during the siege period. It then returned to U.K. and went to N.W. Europe in August 1944 with the 1st Canadian Army.

1951 – 1955

The Regiment continued under command of Lt. Colonel Welsh until November 1951 when he was succeeded by his Second-in-command, Lt. Colonel W.D. Johnston O.B.E., from Elgin. He commanded it most successfully for four years and writes of that period as follows:

> In 1952 the Lovat Scouts consisted of a complete L.A.A. Regt. armed with Bofors guns with the additional Mountain Battery horsed and armed with 4.2 inch mortars – to say the least an unusual if not remarkable, establishment. Each year two separate practice camps had to be organised, one for Field Regiment and one for L.A.A. It was soon evident that one role should be discontinued and finally after pressure, higher authority decreed that the Mountain Battery should be disbanded and all ranks absorbed into the parent Regt., 532 L.A.A. Regt. This was done in 1953.
>
> In 1952, the town Pipe Band for Stornoway enlisted in the Lovat Scouts to form, overnight, the Regimental Pipe Band. The detachment from Stornoway, on being raised to Battery status, became the Ross Battery.
>
> Yet another reorganisation took place in 1954 and the Regiment was reconstructed to exclude the Falkirk/Grangemouth/Glasgow area of 532 Regt. and to restore 540 Regt. to its old recruiting area in the Highlands with Batteries in Inverness, Stornoway and Elgin.

1955 – 1959

During the first two years the Regiment was commanded by Lt. Colonel M. Reeves and then by Lt. Colonel D. Ainley. Both were regular

R.A. officers. Training continued successfully in the same role, the only change being when Coast Artillery was abolished in 1956, and 412 Coast Artillery Regt. became part of the Lovat Scouts. In 1958, the Ross Battery had the great honour of being presented with the Freedom of Stornoway.

1960 – 1963

Lt. Colonel J.A. Marchant R.A. commanded during this period. When he took over, R.H.Q. was in Inverness and there were three Batteries:

1. Inverness Bty. with outstations at Newtonmore, Kingussie, Wick and Thurso. 2.
2. Ross Bty. with H.Q. at Stornoway and outstations at Tain and Alness. 3.
3. Moray Bty. with H.Q. at Elgin and outstations at Forres and Nairn.

In 1961 there was an important reorganisation. The Orkney and Zetland Territorial Battery, called 861 (Independent) L.A.A. Bty. R.A. (O. and Z.) T.A. was brought into the Lovat Scouts; the Inverness Battery disappeared, its members becoming part of R.H.Q. and the outstations at Newtonmore, Kingussie, Tain and Alness were closed down. This was sad news for old Scouts, for those four places had been staunch supporters of the Regiment for sixty years and had supplied many fine soldiers in three wars; but it was the start of the Scouts' proud connection with the hardy Norsemen of Orkney and Shetland, which has become a great tradition over the last twenty years.

A popular link with the past came in 1960 when H.W. (Billy) Whitbread, son of Colonel Bill Whitbread, joined the Scouts. He served with the Stornoway Troop as a Lieutenant for six years.

In 1961 there was a particularly successful Firing Camp at Manor Bier in Pembrokeshire and in August that year the Scouts provided a Guard of Honour for the Queen Mother on her visit to Lerwick. In 1962, they camped at Millom in Lancashire and were trained in Civil Defence. At that time there were two Pipe Bands, the second being that of the original Orkney & Zetland Battery. In August they were invited to visit Norway on a National Trust cruise and this was a great success. Retreat was beaten

'BOS' IMPRESSIONS
540 Regt (The Lovat Scouts) RA (TA)
WILLOW 1962
JE SUIS PREST
LT JOHN MORTON
CAPTAIN EDWIN MORRIS
CAPTAIN DAVID DINGWALL R.E.M.E.
CAPTAIN 'BOBBY' BAIN
CAPT + ADJT ALAN RATTRAY
The PADRE MAJOR (REV) RODDY MACDONALD T.D.
MAJOR STUART MACDONALD
MAJOR DOUGLAS BROOKES TD
CAPTAIN (QM) FRED ROLLS
LIEUT. BILL BEATON HON. MESS SEC.
LIEUT DAVID WILKINSON
CAPTAIN SCOTT MURRAY ATTACHED
The 'DOC' CAPTAIN JOHN MACDONALD RAMC
B/MAJOR JIMMY MACKENZIE TD
CAPTAIN BOB HAMILTON
LIEUT 'RODDY' NEWALL
MAJOR JOHN MACKAY. TD PMC
The Commanding Officer LIEUT COLONEL JACK MARCHANT WITH THE 2ic MAJOR SIDNEY ROBERTSON. MBE
LIEUT WILLIE MACDONALD
LIEUT RUSSELL PRESTON
"THERE'S A CHIEL AMANG YE MAKING NOTES - - - AND BY ME SOWL HE'LL PRINT EM!"
LIEUT 'BOB' BRUNTON
LIEUT JOHN AIRD
2/LIEUT MURDO MACLEOD
2/LIEUT GRAHAM DIXON
2/LIEUT ERIC MARSHALL R.A.P.C.
2/LIEUT PETER HAMER
LIEUT PETER ATHAWES
O/Cdt BILLY WHITBREAD
2/LIEUT GARY GIBSON
LIEUT NORMAN THOMSON
LIEUT GRAHAM HUNTER
O/Cdt GEORGE BURGHER
O/Cdt. DICK SLATER
CAPTAIN GEORGE MARSHALL.

outside the Hakonshalle in Bergen, a thirteenth century Norse building, and again in front of St. Magnus Cathedral, Kirkwall, also built by Norsemen in the twelfth century. Through Major Alistair Munro, a telescope was presented to the Regiment by Donald MacMillan, who was one of the First Contingent of Lovat Scouts in South Africa. This telescope was thereafter always in front of the Commanding Officer on dinner nights. In the first six months of his command Lt. Colonel Marchmont travelled over 20,000 miles visiting his widely-spread troops.

1963 – 1965

The Regiment had three most successful years under command of Lt. Colonel S.P. Robertson, M.B.E., T.D. Living in Kirkwall, with R.H.Q. in Inverness and his three Batteries spread over some 50,000 square miles – Moray (Elgin and Lossiemouth), Ross (Stornoway, Wick and Thurso), and O. and Z. Battery (Orkney and Shetland) – he had a great deal of travelling. The 1963 camp at Manor Bier was described by the School of Artillery as 'a very successful camp indeed and one of which the Regiment can justly be proud'. The Brigade Commander's Report after his annual Inspection read as follows:

> I have been most impressed by the standard of efficiency of this Regiment. Because of its spread over so many counties and the Islands of Orkney, Shetland and Lewis it must be one of the most difficult to command and train to efficiency. Yet this is achieved with distinction. I congratulate the Commanding Officer and all those who contribute to this result.

In October, 1963, a detachment visited 16 Regt. R.A. (which provided all the Scouts' P.S.l.s) at Todendorf near the East German frontier. Later, four pipers were flown out as guests of Air France to the Mediterranean coast and, as a result of their excellent playing, the Lovat Scouts were presented with the Freedom of a town named Cassis.

There was an interesting mobile camp in 1964, near Thetford in

Norfolk. During these years in addition to normal training, many other activities were arranged, including week-end exercises, ski-ing and competing in the Ben Nevis Race. The Regiment co-operated frequently with the Royal Navy at Lossiemouth. There was a great feeling of unity in the Lovat Scouts, of which the Commanding Officer wrote:

> 'While the Batteries were indeed proud of their local traditions, there is no doubt that they were, to a man, predominantly Lovat Scouts.'

Colonel Robertson relinquished command in 1965 to become Deputy C.R.A. It was a great honour for him and for the Regiment when he later became C.R.A. of the 51st Highland Division Artillery and was made a Brigadier.

1965 – 1967

Colonel D.A. Swiney, R.A., a regular officer, commanded the Regiment during these two years, at the end of which there were again major changes in its organisation. Meanwhile there was another successful camp at Manor Bier when the Scouts were second in the Sunday Times Competition. The Pipes and Drums had several engagements, including one at Pembroke Castle.

In September 1965 news came that the Territorial Army was to be drastically cut. Colonel Swiney writes:

> There were two priorities: (1) to keep up interest and (2) to fight for the greatest possible representation in the future. The strength and normal training activities of the Regiment were maintained right to the end.

The Regiment's final camp was at Devizes in 1966, and both Battery and Regimental exercises were held. The Pipes and Drums played in the Horse Guards Parade as part of the Massed Scottish Territorial Bands, where the Scouts' Pipe Major, Neilan Macleod from Stornoway, was the senior piper present. At the Regiment's last parade in Devizes, the Salute was taken by Brigadier Somerville accompanied by Colonel Robertson. The Lovat Scouts marched past and off the parade ground to the Regimental March, Morair Sim.

1967 – 1968

On 1st April, the new organisation became effective. There were two separate Lovat Scouts units:
(1) The O and Z. (Lovat Scouts) Battery, recruited, as they had been since 1961 from Orkney and Shetland.
(2) The 3rd Coy. (Lovat Scouts) of the Queen's Own Highlanders (T.), which consisted of former Scouts from Inverness, Elgin nd Stornoway.

The enthusiasm of the O and Z. (Lovat Scouts) Battery may be judged by the fact that in 1967 they camped at Warcop voluntarily for infantry training with only a token bounty of £2 per man paid from Battery funds. The only uniform issued was the old army battle dress: combat suits were obtained from Surplus Army Stores and paid for privately by individuals with a small subsidy from the Territorial Association. In 1968 there was no camp, but otherwise normal training continued. When the Authorities decided to abolish T.A.V.H.III, it meant that the 3rd Coy. (Lovat Scouts) Q.O.H. (T.) became disbanded. This left the O and Z. Battery the only Lovat Scout unit in existence and they were converted into No. 1 (Lovat Scouts) Coy. of 51st Highland Volunteers. This same Company had its name changed finally in 1971 to: 'A' (LOVAT SCOUTS) COMPANY OF THE 2nd BATTALION 51st HIGHLAND VOLUNTEERS.

From 1968 to 1980, that Company, recruited from Orkney and Shetland, has been the only unit in the Army to bear the proud name and traditions of the Lovat Scouts, which greatly simplifies the end of this story. 1969 – 1980

The Lovat Scouts Company has its H.Q. in Kirkwall. The Battalion, of which it forms a part, has its H.Q. and H.Q. Coy, in Elgin with other

Companies based on Inverness and Aberdeen, and with Platoons in Stornoway and Wick. Lt. Colonel E.M. Gibson, T.D., writes of the Lovat Scouts Company during these years:

> The Lovat Scouts have now for over 10 years been trained as Infantry with special anti-tank skills ready to make up Britain's Regular B.A.O.R. forces in the event of hostilities in Europe... They are highly trained at all levels and retain pride in skills that have always been particularly remarkable in Lovat Scouts.
> Despite numerous attempts from "above" to get them into a T.O.S. (khaki bonnet) like everyone else, the Lovat Scout blue bonnet is worn as working dress and No. 1 headgear; the only alternative being cap comforter or steel helmet.
> Officers and Senior Ranks wear (as Mess Dress) blue patrol jacket with chainmail and Hunting Fraser trews or overalls... Working dress is combat kit with Lovat Scout bonnet. Since 1972 the No. 2 dress for all ranks in the Company has been khaki S.D. jacket, Hunting Fraser Kilt, black hair sporran with three short white tassles, red and white hose with blue garter flash, white spats and Lovat Scout bonnet...
> At present, the Second-in-command of the Battalion is a Lovat Scout and three of the four Company Commanders started T.A. life as Lovat Scouts.

In 1970, the rifle Platoons had their camp in Malta, while the anti-tank Section trained at Otterburn. During an exercise in Malta, the Scouts' assault boat landed in darkness from a coastguard vessel. The Platoon then scaled the cliffs of Pellegrin (over 300 ft.) and took the 'enemy', who were regular paratroops, by surprise in the best traditions of the Regiment. Subsequent camps have been at Shorncliffe (1972), Thetford (1973), Soltau, B.O.A.R. (1974), Ollerton (1975), Warcop (1976), and in 1977 the Scouts acted with their Battalion as 'enemy' in a large N.A.T.O. exercise involving armoured and helicopter-based operations in the area of Sennilagar, Germany. In 1978 they carried out ceremonial duties during three Royal visits – the Queen's visit to Kirkwall, the Prince of Wales' to Aberdeen and the Duke of Kent's to Lerwick. In 1979, camp was again at Thetford and in 1980 the Lovat Scout Company took part with distinction in a large-scale mobilisation exercise in Germany. Since 1967, the Officers Commanding the Lovat Scout Company have been: Lt. Colonel E.M. Gibson T.D. (1967-73), who is now County Commandant of the Orkney Army Cadet Force, Major I.J. Thain, T.D. (1973-79) and Major R. Marwick T.D. (1979 to the present).

What of the future? One can only hope that Scotland will always have a unit – even if it is only one Company – called The Lovat Scouts, and that they will always wear their famous blue bonnets. As long as they continue to be raised from the fine, proud folk of the North, the Lovat Scouts will always be true to their ancient motto of the Frasers, 'Je Suis Prest'. Whenever the nation needs them, they will be ready.

CHAPTER XXII

APPENDICES
1   THE PIPE BAND, 1900 – 1945
2   SERVICE OUTSIDE THE REGIMENT, 1939 – 1945
3   THE COMFORTS FUND, 1939 – 1946 4.
4   REMEMBRANCE, 1939 – 1945
5   COLONELS COMMANDANT
6   THE REGIMENTAL ASSOCIATION AND REUNIONS

APPENDIX 1: THE PIPE BAND, 1900 – 1945
The Pipe band was always the pride and glory of the Lovat Scouts. During the Boer War there were plenty of individual pipers in each Company and they wore the same uniform as the rest of the Regiment; but by 1907 there were officially four pipers on the strength of each Squadron, making thirty-two for the two Regiments. Henry Fraser was their first Pipe Major. 'They became an excellent Pipe Band with a full dress of blue doublets and with kilts and plaids of Hunting Fraser tartan' (Major C.I. Fraser). It is said that some experiments were made with pipers riding side-saddle, so that they could occasionally pipe ahead of a mounted column, but this was soon discontinued.

Owing to casualties and transfers during the First World War, the original Pipe Band became dispersed, but there were always some good pipers in each of the Scouts' Regiments and Squadrons.

From 1922 onwards, an exceptionally fine Pipe Band was gradually built up largely thanks to the late Lt. Colonel J.P. Grant of Rothiemurchus, himself a great authority on piping, who recruited for many years the very best of young pipers from the Islands, particularly South Uist. For twelve years the famous Pipe Major Willie Ross (formerly of the Scots Guards) was in charge of the Scouts' Band and he was succeeded by another outstanding Pipe Major, Angus MacAulay. Their playing, under him, at the Glasgow Tattoo in 1938 was widely acknowledged to be a great performance. His successor, Pipe Major Jimmy Johnston, died in 1939. At the beginning of the Second World War there were a number of brilliant individual pipers in the Band, who played for all parades and occasionally together but they also had other duties and a great deal of military training to do.

In 1940, when the pipers were concentrated at Thorshavn, the opportunity arose of re-organising and improving the Band. Lt. Colonel Fairrie was particularly keen on it and the Adjutant at that time, now Lt. Colonel Dick Allhusen, devoted himself to this task. Donald Riddell, who was then an N.C.O. in A Sqn. but had been a piper in the Camerons and also Pipe Major to the Wardlaw Pipe Band near Kitarlity, was made Pipe Major. He proved to be the ideal person for the job. He was a splendid leader, who insisted on the highest standard of smartness and military efficiency, as well as being a gifted musician and connoisseur of piping. Four more pipers were recruited from the Squadrons. Extra kilts were made by Sgt. Wilson, the Regimental tailor, and new aprons of Faroe sealskin were made for the drummers. The Band's dress was smart but simple: khaki jackets, kilts of Hunting Fraser, tartan hose, khaki ankle puttees and the original sealskin sporrans. Full dress was only once worn by three pipers, to play the reels at the Balmoral Ghillies' Ball.

When the Scouts returned to Scotland in 1942, the Pipe Major had moulded his team of talented individuals into a Pipe Band of the very highest quality. Most of them fortunately remained together, as a Band, throughout the rest of the war. The pipers (almost all Uistmen) and the drummers were as follows:

PIPERS:
>   CpI. Walker, L/Cpl. A. Scott and Pipers A. Beaton, P. MacLeod, J. MacIntyre, O. MacLean, R. Morrison, P. Lamont. O. Campbell, D. Macdonald, O. Westie and the 2 John Macdonalds.

DRUMMERS:
>   L/Cpl. J. Smith, and Tprs. J. Gauld, M. Mackenzie, J. Mackenzie, J. Duncan, W. MacLean and O. Campbell.

"MORAIR SIM"

THE REGIMENTAL MARCH

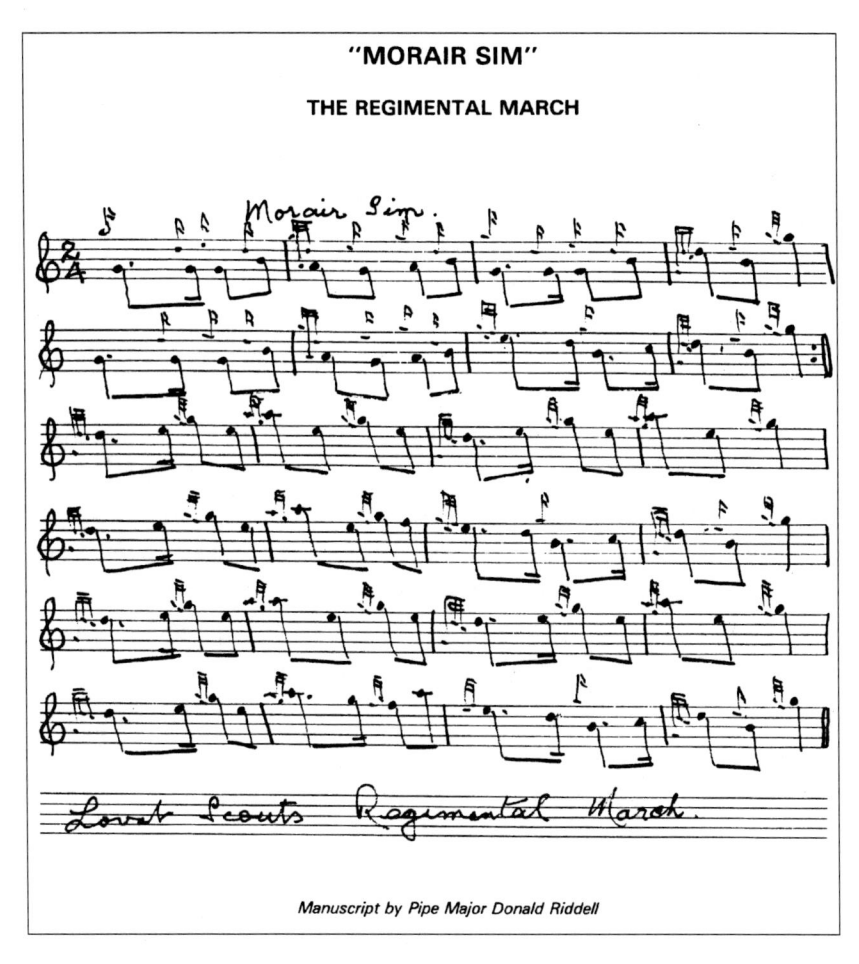

Manuscript by Pipe Major Donald Riddell

In the summer of 1942, the Scouts won the Scottish Command Pipe Band Competition by a very wide margin. At Balmoral they played superbly both years. In the spring of 1943, they broadcast from Glasgow, and Pipe Major Riddell recalls that it was the first occasion the public had heard an entire Pipe Band playing jigs together. It amazed even the City of Glasgow Police Pipers! In Vancouver they gave two performances which are remembered to this day; in Aquila they played to several thousand Italians and, after the war, they joined with the Scottish Horse Pipe Band to play to a huge crowd in Kiagenfurt, which received much publicity.

The Orderly Piper played 'Hey, Johnny Cope!' for Reveille, 'Brose and Butter' for each meal, and for On Parade, 'Inveresk House'. Each evening except in Italy, he played for the Officers' Mess – usually two 'Sets', some jigs and a piobaireachd. The Regimental March is, of course, Morair Sim (Lord Simon). This great tune is believed to date from about 1715, but was first published in 1874, then written as a Strathspey, by Captain Fraser of Knockie. 'The Lovat Scouts', never used as the Regimental March, was written by the famous Scott Skinner ('Talent does what it can: genius does what it must!') about 1900 as a fiddle tune, when he also wrote 'The Cameron Highlanders' and 'The Gay Gordons'. For ceremonial occasions each Squadron had its own slow march: 'Sons of Glencoe' (A Sqn.), 'The Mist Covered Mountains' (B Sqn.), 'The Hawk That Swoops On High' (C Sqn.) and 'Mo Dhachaidh' (D Sqn.).

In Italy the Pipe Band played an important role. As well as providing guards for R.H.Q. they were frequently used throughout the campaign as stretcher bearers, no light task, especially in hill country, and often a very dangerous one. Two of them were killed and one wounded in gallantly endeavouring to rescue the wounded from mine fields.

Lovat Scouts in the Second World War had good reason to be proud of their brilliant Pipe Band.

APPENDIX 2: SERVICE OUTSIDE THE REGIMENT, 1939 – 1945

Compared with many other Regiments, the Scouts were fortunate in having an exceptional number of officers, N.C.O.s and men who served continuously with them throughout the war, but a few also saw service outside the Regiment. The most distinguished of these was Lord Lovat. He was one of the only four Scouts ever to reach the rank of Brigadier, the others being his father, his uncle (A. Stirling of Keir), Hon. Ian Campbell and, in more recent times, Sidney Robertson, Kirkwall. Lord Lovat joined the Commandos in their early days and had a very fine career with them which included taking part in the Lofoten Expedition of 1940, commanding with great success his No 4 Commando at Dieppe in 1942 and leading the Commando Brigade which formed the spearhead of the Normandy invasion on D-Day. He was severely wounded a few days later in the ensuing battle. He was awarded the D.S.O., M.C., the Order of Suvarov, the Croix de Guerre, the Legion d'Honneur and the Norwegian Liberation Cross. Other Scouts with him in the Commandos were Captain Joe Lawrence (Despatches) and Cpl. G. Fraser, M.M., who was killed.

Colonel W.H. Whitbread, after being Squadron Leader of both C and D Sqns. commanded a Battalion in the Recce Corps and also became a parachutist; Major Richard Fleming, who commanded B Sqn. 1940-42, left to become Second-in-command of a Seaforth Bn. and won the M.C. in France, and Major Hon. Hugh Fraser, M.B.I.E., commanded a Squadron of the Phantoms (G.H.Q. Recce), was a parachutist and served with the S.A.S. Major J.L. Macdonald M.B.E. also had an exciting career in the Phantoms and returned to the Scouts in 1945. Several officers reached the rank of Lt. Colonel in important staff jobs, including Lt. Colonels J.P. Grant of Rothiemurchus, M.B.E., R.C. Allhusen and P.A. Wootton.

Major Hon. F.A.H. Wills (now Lord Dulverton C.B.E.) was appointed in 1943 to form the Army School of Fieldcraft, Observation and Sniping, which he ran most successfully at Lianberis, at Bisley and in Holland with a team of senior Sergeant Instructors from the Scouts. They instructed every unit in 21 Army Group and fully maintained the Lovat Scout Sharpshooters' reputation of the First War. Major Lord Elcho (now the Earl of Wemyss and March, K.T.) commanded the South Uist Troop before the war and served with distinction with the Basutoland troops in the Middle East (1941–44). Major Sir Richard Levinge M.B.E., Signals and Intelligence Officer in the Faroes, served with 7 Indian Div. in the Far East and was Mentioned in Despatches. Major Norman Ledingham, who was wounded while Signals Officer in the Scouts in 1944 (Despatches), became a Staff Major later; and Theo Nicholson, who taught many Scouts to climb in North Wales and served with A Sqn. in Italy, was Brigade Major to Brigadier Hunt (later of Everest) when the Regiment arrived in Greece.

These and others of all ranks who served elsewhere during part of the war remained primarily Lovat Scouts with great pride in the Regiment. They were sometimes found in unexpected places. Major John Macdonald of Tote remembers such an occasion in the autumn of 1943, when he was serving in Major Hugh Fraser's Squadron of the Phantoms in Italy, northwest of Bani. He was spying a village and suddenly saw a soldier wearing a Lovat Scout bonnet. He could hardly believe his eyes but, sure enough, it was a Scout – Sgt. Ewen Cameron, who was driver to Colonel Peniakov of 'Popski's Army' – and they greeted each other with delight, as Scouts always do.

APPENDIX 3: THE COMFORTS FUND, 1939 – 1946

Deep gratitude was due to the Lovat Scouts' Comforts Fund Committee – Laura Lady Lovat, Hon. Mrs. Ian Leslie Melville and Mrs. Donald Cameron of Lochiel – and to all those in the Highlands who worked so hard and generously for it throughout the war. They supplied the Scouts regularly with very many beautifully knitted socks, jerseys and other garments, as well as gifts of food annually at Christmas. Many a Scout often owed his warmth to their kind efforts and C Sqn. (mainly from Sutherland) were also deeply indebted to the Sutherland Comforts Fund, run by the Duchess of Sutherland.

After the war, the Committee, under the Chairmanship of Major Willie Gammell, undertook to find additional money for the Benevolent Fund of the Lovat Scouts Association and well over £2,000 was raised for this purpose.

APPENDIX 4: REMEMBRANCE, 1939 – 1945

In the Scottish National War Memorial, Edinburgh Castle, are written the honoured names of sixty-three Lovat Scouts of all ranks who died for their country during the Second World War. They did not give their lives in vain. They will always be remembered too with admiration and affection by their many old friends in the Regiment.

APPENDIX 5: COLONELS COMMANDANT OF THE LOVAT SCOUTS

1903 – 1933 Brigadier Lord Lovat, K.T., G.C.V.O., K.C.M.G.. C.B., D.S.O.
1933 – 1937 Colonel William A. Macdonald of Blarour, D.S.O., T.D.
1937 – 1945 Colonel Duncan G. Baillie, C.M.G., D.S.O., T.D.
1945 – 1953 Colonel Hon. Ian M. Campbell, D.S.O., T.D.
1953 – 1957 Major Charles Ian Fraser of Reeling, T.D.
1957 – 1962 Colonel Sir Donald Cameron of Lochiel, K.T., C.V.O., T.D.
1962 – 1967 Major the Right Hon. Sir Hugh Fraser, P.C., M.B.E., T.D., M.P.

The important honorary post of Colonel Commandant came to an end in 1967. Since 1968 the Lovat Scouts have been part of the 51st Highland Volunteers. Honorary Colonel from 1970 to 1975 was Colonel Sir Donald Cameron of Lochiel and is now Colonel R.A.A.S. Macrae M.B.E., Lord Lieutenant of Orkney.

APPENDIX 6: THE REGIMENTAL ASSOCIATION AND REUNIONS

The Lovat Scouts Regimental Association unites and cares for the interests of all Scouts, past and present, and has effectively administered the Regimental Benevolent Fund. Anyone who has even served in the Regiment is eligible for membership and made welcome. The Regimental Association tie is blue with blue and white dicing in diagonal stripes. Its President today (1980) is Major Sir John Brooke, Bt., Fearn Lodge, Ardgay, Ross-shire. The Honorary Secretary is Major John Aird, 20 Culduthel Street, Inverness.

After the Second World War, the Association became stronger than ever with a large influx of young men demobilised. For the next thirty years it was blessed with a most popular and enthusiastic Honorary Secretary in the late Captain Harry Thorpe, M.B.E. Local branches have flourished too, thanks largely to the great work of their Honorary

Secretaries, such as Andrew Kennedy in Glasgow and Alex Leitch in Edinburgh, and of their Chairmen, Majors Simon Macdonald-Lockhart and Charles Murray. Reunions have regularly been held in Inverness and those of the branches in Glasgow and Edinburgh. Lest any Scouts from the last war should begin to feel too old for reunions, they may look to the example of veterans like John Mackay (Connie) in Sutherland, who joined the Regiment in 1903, when he was only fifteen, can vividly recall every detail of the campaigns in Gallipoli, Macedonia and France and who, in May 1980, as upright as any Guardsman and as smart as when he first joined, was presented to Prince Charles at the opening of Lovat House, Golspie.

Friendship and loyalty have been at the heart of every reunion and it seems that old Scouts are renowned for having plenty to talk about. After the war, Leslie Bowran, Squadron clerk and later S.Q.M.S. of C Sqn., took to hill shepherding near Altnahanra. One evening his return home was long overdue. 'I wonder where Dad is', said Mrs. Bowran. 'He'll be a long time yet', replied their six-year old son, pointing far away up the glen, 'He's met an old Scout'.

CHAPTER XXII

UPDATE TO THE FIRST EDITION 1980 – 2002

The Lovat Scouts did not escape from the Territorial Army reorganisations of the late 1960s/70s. On the formation of 2/51 Highland in the early 1970s there was an opportunity for The Lovat Scouts to train, once again as a recognised Company formation.

A (Lovat Scouts) Company
Based in Orkney and Shetland. Lt. Col. Donald Grant writes:-

> I have the fondest memory of "The Scouts" both at home in the Islands and at annual camps. Their attitude was very positive and they were hard workers. As a company that had been trained as Gunners they were determined to show that they could adapt to their new infantry role and our perform everyone else. Major Gary Gibson was inspirational as the Company Commander and ran a very good company despite having his empire divided between Orkney and Shetland.
>
> One military feat that is graven forever in my mind is being driven from London to camp at Shorncliff by a driver from Shetland who had never experienced traffic, let alone a traffic roundabout! It did illustrate one of the problems of our outstations. Another was that as a Home Defence Battalion our equipment was limited. The only way that Captain Grenville Johnston, the Regimental Signals Officer, could maintain a radio link with them was by borrowing the wartime 19 sets from the Cadets.

Lt. Col. Neil Simpson wrote about the vulnerability of The Lovat Scouts in retaining their individuality. Their geographic situation had always made them under threat from successive reorganisations of the ORBAT by those who least understood the uniqueness of such units, but he recalls Sgt Wylie's epic journey from Kirkwall to Satlou training area in Germany with little or no instruction nor maps of how to get there; but get there he did!

Lt. Col. Gary Gibson, currently Honorary Colonel of the Orkney Army Cadet Force (Lovat Scouts), comments on the gradual "fading away" of The Lovat Scouts through the various reorganisations of the TA with even the uniform becoming less and less used and recognised. It is to be hoped that the Cadets are able to retain The Lovat Scout bonnet rather than moving into a Royal Artillery one.

Lt. Col. Ian Fraser writes:-

I suppose it was inevitable that a native of Keith, who spent most of his formative years in Dingwall, and the grandson of a 1916-18 Lovat Scout Sharpshooter I found nothing strange in meeting at the Soltau training area in August 1975 A (Lovat Scouts) Company 2nd Battalion 51st Highland Volunteers which was in summer camp at that well known training area.

The name of "Lovats" was a well-known diminutive in conversations in my grandparents' house particularly between 1940-45. What I did find a bit strange was that the company was recruited from Orkney and Shetland but thought no more about that until 1976 when to my surprise I was selected to command the aforementioned 2nd Battalion 51st Highland Volunteers.

And so in my new command I found A (Lovet Scouts) Company. I knew all about my Queen's Own Highlander & Gordon Companies but the "Lovats" were a bit of a mystery. An infantry company based on Beauly or even at a push Kiltarlity or Muir of Ord would have been instantly understandable, but the Northern Isles was another boat of herrings all together.

I eventually got hold of the tale from 1900 through the Boer War, WW1 and WW2 and the many hated and titled roles which culminated in the final and unlikely role as an infantry company in 2nd 51st Highland.

It was fascinating to get to know them all and to realise quite early on in my learning process that the Orkadians and Shetlanders were not the bosom buddies that the outside world might have expected.

However having said that anyone other than an islander trying to find division or dissension would find a solid wall of mutual loyalty raised against all comers.

I suppose the overriding attributes of A Company were strength and loyalty;

Strength – In choosing this word I just don't mean it in the physical sense although you only have to think of characters like Major Gary Gibson, WO2 (ORQMS) Neil Kirkness, WO2 (CSM) John Rendall and the formidable Sgt Wylie, who unaided after desertion by the Battalion convoy at the Hook of Holland and never before been on the continent arrived at Soltau with his 2 Wombat ATK guns 10 hours ahead of the convoy, to know that the Northern Isles produce some very hardy men, not just in legs and lungs, but all importantly also in the head and heart. I am talking about some indefinable inner self confidence that permeated the organisation and made a CO realise that if a particularly nasty job was to be done A Company were the boys to do it.

Loyalty – Again this is something which is in a way almost indefinable but in my estimation it manifested itself in:

a) The way in which A Company took everyone from outside the islands to its heart and made them into an honorary Lovat Scout. PSIs, Cos, Training Majors, Adjutants, RSMs and QMs in particular all got the treatment and without fail succumbed to the magic that was Weyland Park or Fort Charlotte.

b) The outward display of pride in themselves as a military force to be reckoned with inside and outside the Battalion and giving of their very best on every conceivable occasion."

In 1981 the organisation of the three Battalions of the 51st Highland Volunteers was rationalised to improve command and communications. The new organisation of the 2nd Battalion was:–

Battalion Headquarters	Elgin
A (Queen's Own Highlanders & Lovat Scouts) Company	Wick, Thurso, Brora, Kirkwall
B (Gordons) Company	Peterhead, Keith
C (Queen's Own Highlanders) Company	Inverness, Stornoway, Fort William, Dingwall
D (Gordons & Lovat Scouts) Company	Aberdeen, Laurenckirk, Lerwick
HQ Company	Elgin

Further detachments were opened at Nairn, Turriff and Inverurie.

This meant that The Lovat Scouts no longer had a single individual Company, but it did align Kirkwall and Lerwick more directly, for communication purposes, to Wick and Aberdeen respectively.

Lovat Scouts continued to feature in Battalion life. From 1982 – 1986 Lt Col. Grenville S Johnston OBE TD DL was the Commanding Officer of the Battalion. The son of a former Lovat Scouts Commanding Officer he had served in Moray Battery 540 Light Air Defence Regiment from 1963 to 1968. Lovat Scouts were well represented at the Presentation of Colours to the 2nd Battalion by HRH Prince Philip, Duke of Edinburgh at Elgin in 1986. 2nd Lieutenant Neil Thain from Orkney carried one of the new colours.

In 1985 the Territorial and Army Volunteer Reserve was reorganised, given a more active operational role, and reverted to the old name of the Territorial Army. To cover the defence of United Kingdom each Battalion raised Home Service Force (HSF) companies. Two companies were added to 2nd 51st Highland Volunteers.

Y (HSF) Company	Elgin, Inverness, Stornoway, Wick, Kirkwall, Fort William
X (HSF) Company	Aberdeen, Laurencekirk, Peterhead, Lerwick

In 1992, as part of reductions to the Territorial Army, the HSF companies were disbanded.

In September 1994, on the amalgamation of the Queen's Own Highlanders and the Gordon Highlanders to form The Highlanders, the 2nd Battalion 51st Highland Volunteers was redesignated as 3rd (Volunteer) Battalion The Highlanders (Seaforth, Gordons and Camerons). The Battalion wore the same uniform as the regular Battalion of the Regiment.

The organisation of the Battalion was:-

Battalion Headquarters	Elgin
Support Group	Wick, Thurso, Kirkwall
B Company	Peterhead, Keith
C Company	Inverness, Dingwall, Fort William, Stornoway
D Company	Aberdeen, Laurencekirk, Lerwick

Lovat Scouts still continued to serve and wear the uniform in Kirkwall and Lerwick as Platoons of the respective companies.

In 1999 A further reorganisation of the Territorial Army took place. It resulted in the disbanding of the three volunteer infantry Battalions and the formation of one Battalion, 51st Highland Regiment, with its Headquarters in Perth, The Platoons in Orkney and Shetland still continued to be called Lovat Scouts and wear the uniform.

Throughout this period there has been a particularly strong cadet representation in the Orkney Islands and this has ensured the continuation of the Regimental name and dress.

INDEX

A

Abassieh 64
Aberdeen 178, 224
Abyssinia 18
Acastra 127
Ada 86
Afragola Staging Camp 180
Agagiya 76
Ainsley, D. (Lt. Col.) 217
Aird, John (Maj.) 231
Alfero 187
Aliwal North 40, 44
Allhusen, F.H. (Maj. later Col.) 54, 66, 72, 90
Allhusen, R.C. (Dick) (Lieut. later Capt. then Lt. Col.) 115, 137, 149, 152, 226, 229
Amazone 88
America 30
Anderson (Cpl. of Horse) 26, 29, 31
Anderson (R.S.M.) 50
Andes 177
Anzac Cove 64, 71
Anzio, battle of 180
Appenines 197
Arabia 77
Arandora Star 138
Ardent 127
Army School of Observation and Scouting (S.O.S.) 91
Army Sniping School 157
Arno Line 180, 184
Atlantic, battle of 138
Atlantic Islands - A Study of the Faroe Life and Scene 130
A.T.S. Highland members 109
Audis (R.S.M.) 115
Austria 208-9
Azmac Dere barricade 65-6, 68

B

Baden-Powell (Gen.) 51
Baillie, Augustus C. (Maj. later Lt. Col.) 49, 54, 58
Baillie, Duncan (Maj. later Lt. Col.) 57, 78, 82, 85, 87, 94, 96
Baillie, Michael 216
Baird, Pat (Maj.) 170
Balfour-Paul, L. (Capt. later Maj.) 179, 193
Balmoral 150, 156
Banff 173
Barbour, R. (Maj.) 215
Barclay (Maj.) 50
Barret (Sgt.) 43
Basutoland 33
Beaton, A. 226
Beaufort 16, 29, 40, 45, 49, 52, 96
Beresford-Peirse, (Lieut. later Maj.) 100, 133
Binnie, Sgt. 26
Blabjorg, Jakob 139
Black, J.W. (Cpl.) 196
Black Watch 24, 77
Black Week 22, 31
Blakiston-Houston (Maj. Gen.) 99
Bloemfontein 31, 32
Bloody Mike 101
Boer armies 21-2
Boer War
   1st contingent 29-39
   2nd and 3rd contingents 40-5
   causes and opening phase 20-3
   raising of the Lovat Scouts 15, 23-4
   ultimatum to Britain 21
Boers 20, 31
Bowran, Leslie (S.Q.M.S.) 232
Braal Castle 152
Brander-Dunbar, James (Capt.) 44

Breadalbane, Marquis of 24
Brigade Security Week 153
Brisigella 195
British Army
   8th 180
   82nd Infantry Brigade 81
   Boer War
      inadequacy of 23
      sickness 31
   X Corps 180
   XIII, Corps 180
Brodie of Brodie, I. (Lieut. later Capt. then Maj.) 27, 32, 40, 43, 44, 50, 70, 72
Brodie, Ewen (Capt.) 49
Brooke, Sir John (Jock) (Capt. later Maj.) 127, 135, 137, 140, 152, 172, 175, 179, 193, 210, 231
Brown, A. (Mtnr.) 183
Brownrigg, W. (Maj. Gen.) 99, 117, 118-19
Budge, W.H. (Bill) (Lieut. later Capt.) 137, 179, 196, 215
Bulgars 80, 85, 86
Buller V.C., Sir Redvers 22, 23, 33
Burn Murdoch, C. (Lieut.) 40

C

Cairngorms 156
Cairo 74, 76, 77, 78
Calder (Lieut.) 85
Cameron (Maj.) 133, 137, 152, 231
Cameron, E. (Sgt.) 196
Cameron, J. (Tpr.) 43
Cameron, J.A. (Lieut.) 81, 86, 87
Cameron of Lochiel, Donald W. (Lieut.) 44
Cameron of Lochiel, Sir Donald H. (Lt. Col.) 91
Cameron of Lochiel, Sir Donald H. (younger) (Capt., later Maj. then Lt.

Col.) 115, 156, 158, 179, 193, 206, 210, 231
Cameron Barracks 44, 212, 215
Cameron Highlanders 24, 26, 40, 211
Cameronians 146
Campbell, A.H. (Capt.) 78
Campbell, E. (Cpl.) 173
Campbell, H. (L/Cpl.) 87
Campbell, Hon. Ian M. (Maj. later Col.) 57, 58, 59, 63, 65, 66, 68-70, 71-2, 77, 96, 212
Campbell, Sir J.A.C. (Capt.) 78
Campbell, O. (Drummer) 226
Campbell, O. (Piper) 226
Campbell, Hon. Ralph (Maj.) 49
Campbell-Orde, Sir A. (Lieut. later Maj.) 27, 50
Campbell-Orde, Sir Simon (Lieut.) 106, 115, 135, 143, 151, 152, 179
Campbell-Preston, Bobbie 120
Canada 169-78
Cape Colony 20
Cape Helles 64
Carolina 143
Carton de Wiart (Gen.) 123
Carver (Cpl.) 66
Caskie, W.E. (Rev.) 153, 179
Casolo Valsenio 194
Cassino, battle of 180
casualties
   British, Boer War 23
   Gallipoli 66
   Guadeberg 43
   Macedonia 83, 84
Chalmers, C.W. (Lieut.) 40, 43
Chandos 143
Charles, Prince of Wales 224
Chisholm, Angus (Cpl.) 29, 30
Chisholm, Rory 26
Churchill, Winston (later Sir) 33, 63, 155

240

Clark, Jimmy (Tpr.) 114
Clarke, A.C. (Lieut.) 44
Colenso 23
Collie, A. (Cpl.) 172, 174
Collingwood, Sir John 154, 155
Colquhoun (Tpr.) 138
Comfort Funds 230
Commando School of Mountain Warfare 156-8
Commandos 21
Connaught Rangers 39, 42, 43
Cooper, T.G.G. (Lt. Col.) 215
Corporalships 22
Craik, G.L. (Capt.) 78, 83, 84
Crawford (Cpl.) 170
Cronje (Gen.) 31
Crowther, R.N. (Capt.) 127
Cumming, Tommy (Lieut.) 157, 179, 192, 196

D
Dahl, Col. 138
Dardanelles 63
Davidson, D. (Sgt.) 186, 196
D.C.L.I. 84
de la Ray 45
de Wet (Gen.) 34, 35, 37, 45
de Wiart, Carton (Gen.) 123
Dearden, P.J. 158, 171-2, 176-7
Denmark 121, 122, 129, 130
Dewar, J. (Lieut.) 70
Dewar, John (Sgt.) 37, 44
Diamond Hill 33
Dickson, T.C.J. (Maj.) 152
Diesen, Admiral 138
Digby-Hamilton (Lt. Col.) 212
discipline 116
Dix-Hamilton, Michael (Lieut.) 137
Dorset Yeomanry 76
Douglas, J.S.H. (Lt. Col.) 157, 179, 189, 192, 193

Drabble, Peter (Capt.) 109, 115
Drife (Lieut.) 192, 194
Duffy, C. (Capt. Rev.) 127, 144
Duncan, D.H. (Pte) 84
Duncan, J. (Tpr.) 226
Dunlop (Rev.) 153-4, 155
dysentery 31, 66

E
Edward VII 45
Egypt 74-8
Ejde 135
Eland's Kloof 42, 43
Elcho, Lord (Maj.) 229
Elizabeth II 224
Elizabeth (Queen Mother) 152, 156, 218
Ellice, E.G. (Lieut.) 27, 35
Elliot, W. (Lieut.) 157, 179, 184
Emancipation Act (1834) 20
England, Second World War 120-8
Englishman 40
equitation 114
Exercise X 150

F
Fairrie, Adam (Lt. Col.) 137, 152, 155, 226
Faroe Islands 129-48
Fife and Forfar Yeomanry 56, 65, 66, 70, 74, 77
Findlay, J. (Capt.) 127
Finland 117
First Boer War 20
First World War
  Egypt 74-8
  Gallipoli 63-73
  Macedonia 80-8
  Sharpshooters 89-95
  training and home defence 56-62
fishing, at Thurso 152

Fleischer (Gen.) 138
Fleming, Richard (Capt. later Maj.) 120, 135, 137, 142, 229
Forrest, Geoffrey (Lieut. later Capt.) 137, 158, 176, 179, 194
Forsyth Grant (Lieut.) 66
Frankfort 33
Fraser (Sgt.) 92
Fraser, A. (Sgt.) 83
Fraser, A.H. (Capt. later Maj. then Lt. Col.) 179, 193, 196, 210, 212
Fraser, Hon. Alastair (Lieut. later Maj.) 40 18, 70, 78, 85, 86
Fraser (Capt.) 188
Fraser, C.I. (Capt.) 115
Fraser, Duncan (Sgt.) 109
Fraser of Glenburgie Distillery 28
Fraser, Hon. Hugh (Capt. then Maj.) 29, 229, 230
Fraser, Hugh (Lieut.) 114, 134
Fraser, Ian (Lt. Col.) 234-6
Fraser, Jack (Sgt.) 201
Fraser, Sandy (Lieut.) 136
Fraser, Sandy (Maj.) 201-2
Fraser-Tytler, E. (Lieut. later Maj. then Lt. Col.) 27, 35, 50, 54, 58, 87
Fraser-Tytler, W.T. (Lieut.) 27, 31
Fraser Lee, A. (Capt.) 84
Fronzola 187

G
Gaelic, use of 116
Gallipoli 63-73
Galloway, H. (Capt.) 44
Gammell, W.S. (Willie) (Lieut. later Capt. then Maj.) 137, 148, 149, 158, 230
Gatacre, Gen. 23
Gathorne-Hardy, Hon. F. (Capt.) 40, 43
Gauld, J. (Tpr.) 226
George, J. (Sgt. Maj.) 196, 215

George V 27, 50, 55, 58
George VI 151, 215
German Cavalry Bde. (Mounted) 208
Gesso ridge 194
Gibson, E.M. (Gary) (Maj. later Lt. Col.) 170, 176, 223, 224, 234
Gillies, J.A. (Pte.) 87
Gillies (Scouts described as) 33
Gillon (Cpl.) 152
Gilmour, Alan (Capt.) 84
Gilmour, J. (Capt. Rev.) 192
Glen Clunie 156
Glengyle 30
Gloucesters, 2nd bn. 81, 84, 86
Godby (Maj.) 176
Gordon, H. (Cpl.) 184
Gordon, R. (Dick) (Sgt.) 209-10
Gordon, W.G. (Maj.) 215
Gordon Highlanders 237
Gorrie, T. (Mtnr.) 196
Gothic Line 180, 186, 190
Grampians 156
Grant, A.L. (Sandy) (Maj.) 115
Grant, Angus (Lieut.) 138
Grant, Sir Charles (Gen) 110
Grant, Donald (Lt. Col.) 233
Grant, Ewen (Lieut. later Capt., Maj. then Lt. Col.) 27, 37, 51, 65, 89, 90
Grant, J.P. (Iain) (Lieut. later Capt. Maj. then Lt. Col.) 112, 113, 114, 127, 138, 193, 225, 229
Grant, J.P. (Maj. later Lt. Col.) 78, 85
Grant, Patrick (Capt.) 105
Gray, D. (Sgt.) 26
Greece 209-11
Gregnano 187, 199
Greig, R. (Maj.) 127
Guadeberg 42, 43
Gunn, I. 184
Gurkhas, 2nd/3rd 186, 192-3, 203

H

Haig, Andrew W. (Lieut. then Maj.) 113, 137, 151, 152, 174, 176, 179
Haig, Douglas (Maj. Gen.) 54, 88, 89
Halkirk 151-2
Halmshaw, Charles (Sgt. Maj.) 106
Hambro, President Carl 122
Hamilton, Sir Ian (Gen.) 32, 64, 66
Hampshires, 10th 81, 86
Harding (Gen.) 207
Hay, Bache (Maj.) 127
Haydon Camp 178
Heilbron 33, 34, 35
Henderson, G.F. (Capt.) 78
Hendry (Cpl.) 175, 196
Highland barricade 66
Highland Brigade 23, 33
Highland Division Artillery, 51st 221
Highland Mounted Brigade 56, 58, 63, 64, 68, 71, 74, 77
Highland Volunteers, 51st 236, 237
Hitler 121
HMS Chiddingfold 146
home defence, First World war 56-62
horse racing 120-1
horses
　management 113
　sickness among 30, 31, 34
Howe, D.W. (Lieut.) 157, 179, 188
Hunt, John (Brig.) 209, 229
Hunt, Rowland (Lieut.) 27
Hunter, Sir Archibald (Gen.) 36, 51-2
hunting, Thurso 152

I

Indian 10th Division 180
Indian Horse 187
infectious diseases 112
Inspector Gen. of Cavalry 101
Inverness Royal Horse Artillery 56
Isakhi 138

Italy 179-96
　memories of 197-207
　Pipe Band in 228

J

Ja'far 76
Jalso 139
Jameson, Dr 21
Jasper Drug Store 171
Jasper National Park 169-78
jaundice 66
Jewish Brigade 194
Johannesburg 20, 32
Johnston, Grenville S. (Lt. Col.) 236
Johnston, Jimmy (Pipe Maj.) 226
Johnston, W.D. (Lt. Col.) 216, 217

K

Kakarasaka 81
Kelham (Col.) 37
Kennedy, A. (Cpl.) 196
Kennedy, Andrew 232
Kent, Duke of 224
Kesselring, Gen. 'Smiling Albert' 180, 190
Kimberley 22, 23, 31
Kirkwall 224, 237
Kispeki 86
Kitchener, Lord 23, 38, 42, 66
Klaksvig 133
Kronstad 32, 34
Kruger, President 21
Kruitzinger's Commando 42

L

L.A.A. Regt. of 51st (Highland) Div. 216
L.A.A. Regt. (Lovat Scouts) T.A. 216
Lady of Mann 146
Ladysmith 22, 31
Lalla Baba 71

Lamb, C. (Lieut.) 40
Lamont, P. 226
Laurie, Sir John (Lt. Gen.) 149
Lawrence, Joe (Lieut.) 115
Leach (Surgeon Lieut.) 51-2
Ledingham, J.N. (Lieut.) 157, 179, 229
Leese, Sir Oliver (Gen.) 180
Leicestershire Yeomanry 120
Leitch (Sgt.) 26
Leitch, Alec (Sgt.) 156, 194
Leitch, Alex 232
Lemonfontein 41-2
Lerwick 224, 237
Leslie Melville (Capt.) 149, 157, 158, 175, 179, 186, 187, 188, 189
Leslie Melville, (Earl of Leven and Melville) (Capt.) 96
Leslie Melville, Hon. I. (Lt. Col.) 109, 137
Leslie Melville, M.I. (Maj.) 215
Levinge, Sir Richard (Maj.) 145, 146, 229
Lewis (Mtnr.) 186
Light Infantry, Duke of Cornwall's 2nd 81
Lincoln City 142
Lindley, Sir Francis 98
Lindsay, G.M. (Maj. Gen.) 110
Lindsay, M.J. (Lt. Col.) 215
Linklater, Eric 130-3
Loch Garry 143
Loch Ordie 53
Loch Ordie, battle of 54
Lofoten Expedition 228-9
Loos, battle of 91
Lornie, M.C. (Lt. Col.) 112
Lovat, Lady 121
Lovat, Lord (Capt.) 115
Lovat, Lord Simon Joseph
  1st contingent
    praise for 38
    sickness and recovery 34, 35
    volunteers to capture Vaal Krantz 37
    voyage to Cape Town 30
  2nd contingent
    concerns about 40-1
    Guadeberg disaster 43
    sport at Lemonfontein 42
    takes over command 43
  ancestry 15-16
  award of the C.B. 46
  Boer War, raising of the Lovat Scouts 23-4
  death 98
  early years
    adventure and sport 16
    Fort Augustus 16
    Life Guards 17
    Oxford University 16-17
    trip to South Africa 18
  First World War
    command of 2nd Cyclists' Division 89
    command of the Highland Mounted Bde. 56
    Director of Forestry 90-1
    Gallipoli 63, 72-3
    raising of two second line Regiments 58
    respect for 59-60
    Sharpshooters, organisation of 89
    sickness and recovery 65, 90
    visits Merlimont 94
  mounted scouts, command of 49, 53-4
Lovat Scouts
  Boer War
    first contingent 29-39, 47
    raising of 15, 23-4
    second contingent 39, 40-4, 48
    third contingent 44
    uniforms and equipment 27
  Colonels Commandant 231

Comfort Funds 230
First World War
  Egypt 74-8
  Gallipoli 63-73
  Macedonia 80-8
  reorganised as 10th Infantry Battalion 77
  Sharpshooters 88, 89-95
  training and home defence 56-62
mounted scouts (1903-14) 46-55
Pipe Band 225-8
post war
  (1947-80) 215-24
  (1980-2002) 233-7
remembrance 230
Second World War
  Austria and Greece 208-12
  Canada 169-78
  England 120-8
  Faroe Islands 129-48
  Italy 179-207
  mobilisation 105-10
  mounted training in the North 111-19
  Scotland and North Wales 149-58
  service outside the regiment 228-30
  territorial army training 96-104
Lovat Scouts Regimental Association 231-2
Lyle, A.M. (Maj.) 215
Lyle, Robin 120

M

Mac Force 194, 203
MacAndrew, Colin (Capt.) 152
MacAulay, Angus (Pipe Maj.) 225
MacBean, Nicholas 202-3
MacBean, Provost 43
McCorquodale, K. (Lieut.) 70, 83, 84
McCorquodale, K. (Maj.) 58, 64-5, 66, 76-7, 82-4, 86-7, 109, 116, 137, 152
McCreery, Sir Richard (Gen.) 180, 195-6
Macdonald, A.J. (Capt.) 179
Macdonald, Allan (Waternish) (Maj.) 101, 106, 115
Macdonald, Andrew (Capt. later Maj.) 152, 193
Macdonald, A.W. (Willie) (Capt. later Maj. then Lt. Col,) 27, 34, 37, 39, 44, 49, 50, 54, 58, 65, 78, 85, 89, 99-100
Macdonald, C.N. (Lieut.) 44
Macdonald, D. (Piper) 226
Macdonald, Duglald (Cpl.) 35, 37, 43
Macdonald, Flora 75
Macdonald, Sir Hector (Gen.) 33, 34, 37, 38
Macdonald, J. (Capt Rev.) 144
Macdonald, J.L. (Maj.) 229
Macdonald, John (Capt.) 210
Macdonald, John (Fort William) 37
Macdonald, John (Lieut.) 135, 141, 142
Macdonald, John (Maj.) 211, 230
Macdonald, John (Piper) 226, 226
Macdonald, John (Tpr.) 41
Macdonald, K.L. (Kenny) (Lieut. later Capt. then Maj.) 27, 30, 50, 65, 72, 75, 78, 101
Macdonald, Simon F. (Lieut. later Capt.) 105-9, 126, 149, 175, 179, 192, 193
Macdonald of Sleat, Godfrey 29
Macdonald-Lockhart, Simon (Maj.) 232
Macedonia 80-8
MacGregor, P. Pte. 84
MacIntyre, J. 226
MacIntyre, (W.) Bill (Sgt.) 173
Mackay, Angus (L/Cpl.) 66
Mackay, George (Cpl.) 145
Mackay, H. (Cpl.) 184
Mackay, H. (L/Sgt.) 83
Mackay, Jessan (S.S.M.) 100
Mackay, John 232
Mackenzie, Alick (Lieut.) 115

Mackenzie, D. (Cpl.) 189
Mackenzie, E.B. (Capt.) 44
Mackenzie of Gairloch, Brig. (formerly Lt. Col. W.A. Stevenson) 211, 212
Mackenzie, J. (Tpr.) 142, 226
Mackenzie, M. (Tpr.) 226
Mackenzie, W.M. (Lieut.) 157
Mackintosh, D.G. (Sgt.) 77
Mackintosh, George (Maj.) 37
Mackintosh of Kyllachey (Capt.) 40
Mackintosh of Mackintosh 46
MacLean (Sgt.) 135
Maclean, Ian (S.S.M.) 141, 194
McLean, N. (Sgt.) 113
MacLean, O. (Piper) 226
MacLean, Roderick 32-3
MacLean, W. (Tpr.) 226
MacLeod, J. (Mtnr.) 183
MacLeod, J.M. (Sgt.) 157
MacLeod, Neil (Sgt.) 184, 208
Macleod, Neilan (Pipe Maj.) 222
MacLeod, P. (Piper) 226
McMenemy (Sgt.) 189
MacMillan, Donald 220
McMullen (Cpl.) 84
MacMullen, N. (L/Cpl.) 84
McNeill, A.J. (Maj.) 65
MacNeill, J. (Sgt. Maj.) 26
Macpherson, C.B. (Lieut.) 90
MacPherson, John 35
McPherson, Roddie 155
Macrae, Colin (Sgt.) 194, 196, 203-4
Macrae, Tommy (Tpr.) 113
McRury (Farrier Sgt.) 216
MacSween (R.S.M.) 194
Mafeking 22, 31
Magersfontein 23, 24, 31
Mahrattas 183
Maitland 31
malaria 85, 180
Malta 77, 223

Manchester Merchant 44
Mannerheim, Marshall 117
Manor Bier 218, 220
Mansfield, Lord 26-7
Marchant, J.A. (Lt. Col.) 218
Marchionni 190
Marchmont (Lt. Col.) 220
Marwick, R. (Maj.) 224
Mauretania 158, 169
Melville *see* Leslie Melville
Mena House Camp 74
Menelek, Emperor 18
Merle 190
Merlimont 94
Methuen, Lord (Gen.) 23, 35, 45
Mignana 187
Miller, A. (Lieut.) 84
Milne, G.F. (Gen.) 80, 88
Milne, U. 184
Milne, W. (Lieut.) 157, 179
Milner, Sir Alfred 21
mines 141
Minnewaska 78
Mitchell (Cpl.) 194
Modigliano 190, 201
Monro, Sir Charles (Gen.) 66, 68
Monte Calderano 195
Monte Corno 189
Monte Petra 187
Morgan, J. (R.S.M.) 115
Morning Star of Tofte 143
Morrison, O. (Cpl.) 83
Morrison, R. 226
Morrison (Sgt.) 34, 189
Morrison, T. (Sgt. Maj.) 196
Mountain Battle Drill 177
Mountain Regiment (Lovat Scouts) 216
Mountain Warfare Training 158
Mountaineer Regiment, Canada 169-78
Mounted Yeomanry Regiments 100
Mowatt, T. (Lieut.) 57

Muir (Lieut.) 83
Munro, A. 184
Munro, Alistair (Maj.) 220
Munro, G. (Lieut.) 80
Munro-Ferguson (Capt.) 50
Murray (Capt.) 194
Murray (Cpl.) 194
Murray (Mtnr) 186
Murray, Hon. Andrew (Maj. later Lt. Col.) 26, 31, 37, 40, 42-3
Murray, Charles (Maj.) 211, 232
Murray, C.K. (Lieut.) 149, 179
Murray, Hon. E.O. 40, 43
Murray, K. (Lieut.) 84
Murray, Sir Kenneth 211
Myburg 42

N
Naples 180
Natal 20, 22
New York 169
Nicholson, T. (Lieut.) 157, 229
Nigoslav 85
Nigrita 81
Nominal Roll, volunteers 26
North Wales 156-8
Northern Somaliland 18
Northumberland Fusiliers 1st bn. 211
Norway 121, 122
Nova Scotia 177

O
Observer Groups 88, 89, 94
Ogg, Bob (Lieut.) 137, 148, 173, 179
Orange Free State 20, 31
Ostero 129, 133
Oxley (Lieut.) 186

P
Paardeberg 31
Packer, D.C. (Lieut.) 157, 186, 192

Paget (Gen.) 34
Parnwell, John 170
Partigiari 202
Partisani 200
Paterson, W.G. (Lieut.) 86, 87
patrols, Faroe Islands 135
Patterson, J. (Lieut.) 71
Peacock, Tom 170
Pease, Joe (Lieut. later Maj.) 70
Pelham Burn, A. (Lieut.) 44
Pellegrin 223
Percy (Turkish sniper) 66
Pipe Bands 218-20, 225-8
Pitgaveny, Laird of 44
Pocock, H. (Capt.) 49
point-to-point racing 121
Polish Corps Bde., 1 bn. 190
Polish II Corps 180
Pook (Capt.) 153
Poppy 139
Portland, Duke of 27
Post War 215-24
Precincts 21
Preston North End 139
Pretoria 31, 32
Pretoria, Treaty of 20
Prichard, H. (Maj.) 91, 93, 193
Prinsloo (Gen.) 37, 38
Punjabis, 1st/2nd 187

Q
Queen of Bermuda 179
Queen's Own Highlanders 17, 77, 237

R
Railston, G. (Lt. Col.) 85
Ramsay, Douglas 156, 169, 179, 200
Ravenshaw (Gen.) 81
Rayer, Richard (Lieut. later Capt. then Maj.) 115, 136, 153, 155, 179, 183, 192, 211

recreation and sport
   Faroe Islands 136-7
   Lemonfontein 41-2
   Thurso 152-3
recruiting centres 24
Rees Jones (Maj.) 156
Reeves, M. (Lt. Col.) 217
Reid, D. (Sgt.) 84
Reid, D.W. (Maj. Gen.) 180
Restorff, Mr. 137
Retief's Nek 37
reunions 231-2
Reveretto 189
Rhodes, Cecil 21
Richards, R.A. (Maj.) 190
Richardson, Patsy 170
Riddell (Pipe Maj.) 199, 227
Rimington (Gen.) 54
Roberts, Lord (Field Marshall) 23, 31, 32, 38
Robertson, R. (Capt. Rev.) 127
Robertson, S.P. (Lt. Col.) 220, 221, 222
rock-climbing 156-7
Rockies 169-78
Rome 180
Roodebergen mountains 36
Ross, A. (Sgt.) 136, 157
Ross, J. (Lieut.) 71, 94
Ross, R. (Cpl.) 186
Ross, Willie (Pipe Maj.) 98, 225
rough shooting 152
Rowntree, John (Capt.) 157-8, 179, 199
Royal Armoured Corps 215
Royal Family, guarding 150, 156
Royal Navy, Faroe Islands
   mine laying 141
   working with 138-9
Royal visits 224
Rupel Pass 209
Russians, captured 202-3

S

Salerno, battle of 180
Salmah affair 86-7
Salonika 78, 80, 209
Salt Lake reserve 64, 66
San Casiano 190
San Martino 184
San Paolo 189
San Pietro, battle of 180
San Sepolchro 187
Sarnia 64
Sarrail (Gen.) 80
Sauternes 140
School of Artillery 220
School of Observation 85
School of Observation and Scouting (S.O.S.) 91
scorched earth policy 38
Scotland 53-4, 149-56
Scots Greys 40, 96, 151
Scots Guards 212
Scott (Sgt.) 26
Scott, A. (L/Cpl.) 226
Scott, F. (Mtnr.) 196
Scott, Peter (Lieut.) 115, 141, 179, 183
Scottish Horse 52, 58, 63, 64, 66, 77, 85, 99, 120, 126, 137, 194, 215, 216
Scottish Horse Museum 215
Scout Regiment 96
Scroggie, W.S. (Lieut.) 157, 179, 184, 195, 204-6
sea-sickness 140
Second World War
   Austria and Greece 208-12
   Canada 169-78
   England, mounted and dismounted 120-8
   Faroe Islands 129-48
   Italy 179-207
   mobilisation 105-10
   mounted training in the North 111-19

Scotland and North Wales 149-58
Semphill, the Master of (Capt.) 40, 42, 43
Senussi 76
Sharpshooters 89-95
Sherwood Foresters 138
ships, sunk 139-40
sickness
   among horses 30, 31, 34
   British Army, Boer War 31, 34
   Faroe Islands 140
   Gallipoli 66
   Italy 180
   Macedonia 85
Signallers (Lovat Scout) 145
Simpson, Neil (Lt. Col.) 233-4
Sinclair, Sir Archibald and Lady 155
Skaalefjord 133, 134, 138, 142, 145
ski-ing 170, 175
Smiril 140, 144
Smith, J. (L/Cpl.) 226
Smuts 45
Smythe, Frank (Wing Cmdr) 170
sniping 157
Sniping in France 91-3
Sorley, J. (Sgt.) 196
Southwest Yeomanry Brigade 76
Spion Kop 31
sports *see* recreation and sports
Spry, B.C. (Sgt.) 87
Stein, President 21
Stevenson, W.A. (Lt. Col. later Brig.) 211, 212
Stewart, D. (Sgt.) 196
Stewart of Ensay, V. (Capt. later Maj.) 27, 30, 31, 32, 51
Stirling, Archie (Maj. later Lt. Col., Brig. Maj then Brig. Gen.) 50, 54, 65, 109
Stirling, Charles (Lieut.) 27, 44
Stirling, Hon. Mrs. 74

Stoke City 139
Stormberg 23
Stratheden, Lord (Brig.) 105
Stromo 129
Struma river 80
Struma valley 80, 81, 210
Sudero 133, 137
Sutherland, W. (Sgt.) 87
Suvla Bay 64, 68-72
Sweden 121
Swiney, D.A. (Col.) 21

T
Tahinos, Lake 80, 87
Territorial Army
   reorganisation 236-7
   training 96-104
Thain, I.J. (Maj.) 224
Thain, Neil (Lieut) 236
Thomson (Cpl.) 189
Thomson (Lieut.) 192, 194
Thorneycroft's Mounted Infantry 43
Thorpe, Harry (Capt.) 143, 145, 158, 194, 231
Thorpe, R.H. (Capt.) 179, 210
Thorshavn 126, 127, 130, 133, 134, 135, 136, 137, 138, 142, 143, 144, 145, 146, 226
Thurso 152, 155
Thurston, R. (Lieut.) 44
Tialdur 144
Tingulstad, G. (Lieut.) 138, 157, 179, 184, 186, 190
Tintagel Castle 31, 45
training
   Canada 170-8
   Faroe Islands 136
   First World War 56-62
   mounted troops 51, 111-19
   Scotland 150, 156
   territorial army 96-104

Transvaal Constabulary 38
Transvaal Republic 20, 31
Treaty of Pretoria 20
Treaty of Vereeniging 45
Trooper M. 102-3
Tullibardine, Marquis of 52, 53
Tumbitsa Farm 82, 84
Turnbull, A.R. (Lieut.) 157, 179, 183, 189
Tweebosch 45
Tweedmouth, Lord 27-8
Tyndale-Biscoe (Gen.) 54
typhoid 31, 66

U
Uitlanders 20-1
Ulster Prince 127
uniforms 27, 59
Urquhart, A. (Lieut.) 179
Urquhart, Jock (Sgt.) 197-9
Urquhart, R. (Lieut.) 157

V
Vaal Krantz 37
Vereeniging, Treaty of 45
Vernon, Sig. J.E. (Clunie) 153-5
Vestmanhavn 135
Virhanli 82
volunteers 24-6
Von Vietinghoff 190
Vredefort 35-6

W
Walker (Cpl.) 226
Walker, N.D. (Lieut.) 157, 179
War Diaries, Italy 182-90
Wardrop (Lieut.) 192, 194
Waternish's secret column 102-3
Watson, W. (Mtnr.) 175
Watson, Willie (Cpl.) 156
Wauchope, Gen. 23

weasels (vehicles) 173, 174
Wedderburn, E.A.M. (Maj.) 157, 179, 189
Wedderburn, Sandy (Maj.) 192
Weiss, Joe 174
Weld-Blundell, Herbert 18
Welsh, D. (Lt. Col.) 216, 217
Wessels (Boer Offr.) 42
Westie, O. 226
Whamond (Lieut.) 92
Wheeler Force 183
Whitbread, H.W. (Billy) (Lieut.) 218
Whitbread, W.H. (Maj. later Col.) 101, 114, 133, 137, 218, 229
Williamson, A. (Pte.) 87
Williamson, Kenneth 130
Wills, Hon. F.A.H. (Maj.) 136, 157, 229
Wills, Tony (Lieut.) 120
Wilson (Sgt.) 226
Wilson, W.B. (Cpl.) 83, 84
winter training, Canada 172
Wooton, Brian (Lieut.) 137, 179, 188
Wooton, Pat (Lieut.) 115, 136, 149, 179, 200, 229
Wyld, John (Lieut. later Capt.) 140, 170, 179, 193-4

Y
Ynsfor Fell Hounds 157
Young (Lieut.) 126